Praise for **Queer Devotion**

"This book is an absolute must for witches, pagans, polytheists, and other spiritual practitioners, regardless of their personal orientation. Burgess forges a path through pagan and Christian mythology, upending ideas and revealing deep and spiritual queer readings of popular figures and their stories. Each chapter ends with reflections and exercises to help the reader explore the themes in their life and reflect upon their values as they build a queer spiritual practice. There is a deep and rich magic in the pages of Queer Devotion, *and it is a marvel and a treasure that I recommend to anyone on a spiritual journey."*

— **Ariana Serpentine**, author of *Sacred Gender*

"Charlie Claire Burgess invites readers on a thought-provoking and heartfelt journey into the inherent queerness of the divine—so often overlooked or suppressed—in Queer Devotion. *With clever reflections on myths and sacred practices, Burgess reclaims spirituality in a way that is both intelligent and deeply inclusive.* Queer Devotion *is both engaging and deeply informative, offering fresh perspectives on spirituality and mythology that feels both timely and timeless. Through imaginative exercises and rituals, Burgess provides LGBTQIA+ readers meaningful ways to deepen their connection to the divine, making this book an empowering and illuminating resource for embracing a spirituality beyond the binary."*

— **Mat Auryn**, author of *Psychic Witch, Mastering Magick,* and *The Psychic Art of Tarot*

"Charlie Claire Burgess's Queer Devotion *is far more than a book about queer gods and heroes, or the queerness intrinsic to polytheistic worship. By turns thoughtful and passionate, measured and enthusiastic, academic and reverent, this book is itself a profound act of devotion before the gods themselves, and an exhortation to us all—queer and straight, trans and cis—to embrace that queerness, step into the mystic, and deepen our relationships with our gods, our communities, and ourselves. Read it, and be transformed. Hail, Holy Queer!"*

— **Misha Magdalene**, author of *Outside the Charmed Circle*

"A triumph for the queer heretics who are too often told we don't belong in sacred space. Charlie Claire Burgess has written a reclamation and a reckoning, essential for not only queer seekers but also anyone who has ever doubted their connection to the divine."

— **Jeanna Kadlec**, author of *Heretic: A Memoir*

T0370145

"Queer Devotion *grapples with the cross section of spirituality and queerness with so much heart and power. The emphasis on who we are as sacredly holy and where we go from there will not only inspire you, not only lift you up, but guide you on an explicitly healing journey. This is necessary for so many of us recovering from a lifetime of spiritual harm—and it will be beneficial to everyone trying to find or re-find a path forward."*

— **Cassandra Snow**, author of *Queering Your Craft* and *Queering the Tarot*, co-author of *Lessons from the Empress*, and editor of *Tarot in Other Words*

"Radical! Revelatory! Remarkable! Charlie's latest masterpiece not only rightfully reinvestigates a wide range of historical, theological, and mythological canons, but also reinvigorates them, inviting queer folks to see themselves reflected and recognized in the divine. Queer Devotion *is researched and educational, accessible, yet deeply personal, and also offers hands-on, interactive prompts and rituals to support anyone looking to build an authentic, engaged, and delightfully queer spiritual practice. A truly vital and healing offering, this is the book I, and so many, have been waiting for!"*

— **Rebecca Scolnick**, author of *The Witch's Book of Numbers*

"Charlie Claire Burgess expertly weaves together myth, queer theory, and contemporary queer life in a way that helps the reader connect with the divine. Reading this book was like processing my most recent spiritual discoveries with a dear friend at the queer coffee shop: breathless, open, and exciting."

— **Siri Vincent Plouff**, author of *Queering the Runes*, co-author of *Lessons from the Empress*, and host of *The Heathen's Journey* podcast

"Charlie Claire Burgess's latest book Queer Devotion *playfully and joyfully invites readers to find their true place within mythology, folklore, and spirituality—not one that must be carved out and claimed, but rather a place that has always been there. Burgess's clever, generous writing welcomes everyone into divinity, deftly offering pathways for curious seekers and scholars into religion, deity work, ancestry connections, and so much more. As someone who often gets lost in academic texts, who tends to prefer a more lyrical approach to myth and legend, I found myself hooked from the very first page, gobbling up stories and essays that serve as beautiful love letters to the queer community. If you've ever felt like you were too weird for conventional or popular spiritual practices, if you've ever wondered why mythology feels so straight or heteronormative, if you've ever craved a more vibrant connection to folklore,* Queer Devotion *is the gentle welcome you've been waiting for."*

— **Meg Jones Wall**, author of *Finding the Fool*

Queer Devotion

ALSO BY
Charlie Claire Burgess

Radical Tarot
Fifth Spirit Tarot

All of the above are available at your local bookstore,
or may be ordered by visiting:

Hay House USA: www.hayhouse.com*
Hay House Australia: www.hayhouse.com.au
Hay House UK: www.hayhouse.co.uk
Hay House India: www.hayhouse.co.in

***

Queer Devotion

Spirituality Beyond the Binary in Myth, Story, and Practice

Charlie Claire Burgess

HAY HOUSE LLC

Carlsbad, California • New York City
London • Sydney • New Delhi

Published in the United States by: Hay House LLC: www.hayhouse.com®
P.O. Box 5100, Carlsbad, CA, 92018-5100

Cover design: Charlie Claire Burgess • *Interior design:* Nick Welch
Interior illustrations: Charlie Claire Burgess

Cataloging-in-Publication Data is on file with the Library of Congress

Tradepaper ISBN: 978-1-4019-7852-5
E-book ISBN: 978-1-4019-7853-2
Audiobook ISBN: 978-1-4019-7854-9

10 9 8 7 6 5 4 3 2 1
1st edition, May 2025

Printed in the United States of America

This product uses responsibly sourced papers, including recycled materials and materials from other controlled sources.

The authorized representative in the EU for product safety and compliance is Penguin Random House Ireland, Morrison Chambers, 32 Nassau Street, Dublin D02 YH68, Ireland. https://eu-contact.penguin.ie

To Frank Erwin Body (1947–2022), unconventional thinker, theological inquirer, adversary of orthodoxy, man of faith. I bet you would have thought this book was cool.

Contents

An Introduction to Queer Historicity, Queer Evidence, and Queer Divinity

Flirting Across History with the Queer Divine

Our gods are queer, because they are what we want them to be.
— MARCELLA ALTHAUS-REID, *INDECENT THEOLOGY*

In the beginning, the Gods were queer.

Long before the monotheistic masculine gods warped the world in their totalizing image, long before the "sacred marriage" of the divine masculine and divine feminine deified binary gender, and even long before the gay gods romped over Mount Olympus, the Divine was undeniably, numinously, androgynously queer.

In pre-Christian societies, there were gods and goddesses, but sometimes they morphed between masculine and feminine, and other times they existed in some other, third-gender space. Frequently, the gods did not conform to our modern Western concepts of masculinity nor the goddesses to femininity. Take Inanna, for instance. The Babylonian creator-goddess held in her purview the realms of sex, love, and fertility, but she was anything but sweet and soft. Instead, Inanna was cutthroat, strategic, and power-hungry, all qualities that would most likely be lauded in a god and demonized in a goddess according to modern binary gender norms. Yet she was also the goddess of fertility and love. Now let's consider a god: Apollo, the lithe, beautiful, lyre-playing, man-loving Greek god of music, healing, light, knowledge, prophecy, and the arts. Renowned and beloved for his youthful beauty, Apollo is the honorary god of twinks. And he earns the role, having more gay love affairs than any other god in Greek mythology. Apollo's domains of music, dance, art, and healing might be considered more appropriate for a goddess by a modern, gender binary-bound Western audience. Meanwhile, Apollo's lesbian-coded twin sister, Artemis, the athletic goddess of hunting and wilderness who vowed never to marry or have sex (with a man, at least) and notoriously wrought vengeance on any man who male-gazed upon her, might seem too masculine for a "divine feminine" role.

The "divine" masculine/feminine binary is usually painted as essential and intrinsic in some biological or God-given way that is fabled to have existed since the dawn of humanity, but this is simply untrue. Masculinity and femininity are social constructs that change across cultures and time, and many cultures have more than two genders. If we stretch back to the earliest signs of human spirituality and devotional worship in cave paintings and figurines, what we find is not a binary but a *plurality* of divine forms, ones that are sometimes nonbinary or androgynous and, more often than that, not even human at all. Some of the earliest "earth goddess" figurines represent a rounded, feminine body with breasts and a long, phallic neck and head, combining human sex characteristics usually assigned to different genders into one divinely androgynous artifact. The earliest deities seem to have been personified features and forces of nature: goddexxes* of storm, mountain, river, sea, corn, deer, sun, moon, and star. Human fertility myths may have been applied to these natural forces—the sky impregnating the belly of the land with its fertile rain-semen, for instance—but this was at a time when humans lived in intimate closeness with the natural world, when humans were *part* of the natural world instead of artificially separate from it. Then, the rain also remained the rain. The land remained

* Goddexx is a queered portmanteau of *God* and *Goddess* that uses the letter *X* to connote queerness, gender neutrality, or gender inclusivity, a tradition used in the LGBTQ+ community since at least the 1990s *(Latinx, Mx., folx).*

the land. The sky remained the sky. They were divine and sometimes anthropomorphized, but they were also exactly what they are. Not divine masculine; not divine feminine. Rain. Land. Sky.

As humans formed societies and built cities, these nature deities began to look more like us. Or, rather, as human life became more human-centered, we began portraying the gods in increasingly anthropomorphic ways. Not so much "God" making humankind in "his" own image, but humans making the gods in ours. Still, for a very long time, the gods retained their wildness, straddling the line between human and nonhuman with slippery, queer ease. In Babylonian creation myth, the creator-goddexx is Tiamat, the primordial sea, who births the first generation of gods after mingling her salty waters with the god Apsu, the freshwater river. Referred to as a woman, Tiamat is given both human and dragon-like features, including a sea-serpentine tail, but remains synonymous with the sea. In the Burney Relief (c. 1800–1750 B.C.E.), Inanna is portrayed with a female human body and the wings and taloned feet of a bird, flanked by lions and owls.* In Egypt, numerous gods and goddesses have the bodies of humans and the heads of animals: Thoth has the head of an ibis, Anubis the head of a jackal, Bastet of a cat, Ra of a falcon. In Greek myth, the gods are masters of transformation, blurring the lines between human, animal, and divine. Dionysos morphs from human to bear to bull to goat. Zeus notoriously takes the form of swans, eagles, serpents, and even golden rain to seduce his conquests in some cases and rape them in too many others. Artemis turns Actaeon into a deer; Hera turns Callisto into a bear. With a flick of their divine fingers, the gods turn mortals into myrtle trees, flowers, grape vines, doves, snakes. Far to the north, in the Norse pantheon, the father-god Odin talks to his raven familiars who bring him news, and the trickster god Loki morphs into salmon, stinging flies, and, in one memorable case, a flirty mare that seduces a mighty stallion, becomes pregnant, and gives birth to an eight-legged horse.

The divine masculine and feminine are modern inventions, not ancient ones. But that doesn't mean there is no divinity in masculinity

---

* Some scholars have argued that it is Lilith or Sumerian Ereshkigal in the Burney Relief, but current consensus leans toward Inanna.

and femininity. For the countless individuals who have found healing, affirmation, empowerment, and spiritual connection through the mirrors of the divine masculine and feminine—including trans women and men, gay men, and lesbians—these gender expressions absolutely are divine. But the divine masculine and feminine are not the *only* divinity there is, and confining the Divine into two bifurcated poles does damage to individuals who don't fit into that polarity, not to mention a disservice to the vast, strange, ineffable, uncontainable Divine Everything, which is undoubtedly beyond human sex and gender.

The danger of the divine masculine/feminine duality comes from the gender essentialist assumption that the cis-heteronormative binary is the ultimate and only Divine, and that there's only one "right" way to be masculine or feminine. Under such a system, anyone who doesn't perform masculinity or femininity "correctly" is not only a social outcast but a spiritual outcast. When trans women are barred from divine feminine circles and festivals, when trans men feel sidelined at divine masculine events, when nonbinary, genderfluid, and other gender-nonconforming people aren't afforded a place in the divine gender binary whatsoever—that's not divinity; that's bigotry. When lesbians and gay men are either "doing it wrong" by eschewing the duality of heterosexual intercourse or are pressured to take on heteronormative roles within their relationships—as they sometimes are in strains of Wicca and Tantra, with one of the same-sex pair being the "woman" and one being the "man"—that's not divine duality, not the "sacred marriage," not a (whitewashed and Europeanized) yin and yang; that's homophobia and heteronormativity.

The divine masculine/feminine binary often functions as a deification of gender stereotypes, but masculinity and femininity are far, far more expansive than pink/blue, strong/soft, dominant/submissive, logical/emotional, or provider/caregiver. Likewise, sexual desire is far more expansive than "opposites attract" or an automated exercise of sticking things in holes. At the same time, I believe that gender and sexuality are two ways we can feel and connect to the Divine. If I didn't believe that, I wouldn't be writing this book. Gender may entwine with material bodies for some of us, but I believe that gender can also have a *spiritual* dimension. As Ariana Serpentine observes in her wonderful book, *Sacred Gender*, "[Gender] cannot be measured with tape measures or rulers; it has no weight or mass. Yet, like spiritual experiences, its effects on us are massive."[1] Gender is an expression of our deepest truth and authenticity, arising not necessarily from body morphology but from the soul and its unique seed of divine spirit. Gender is informed by culture but is not dictated by it. It's a dance among temporal culture, corporeal embodiment, and ethereal spirit, a weaving of above and below, inner and outer.

Queer sexuality can be divine as well. The divine masculine/feminine binary tends to locate the divinity of sex solely in its reproductive capacity or as a metaphorical meeting of complimentary opposites, but sexuality and desire do not have to be straight or binary to be divine. Sexual desire is a magnetism that tows us by the hips toward what lights us up, what sets us on fire—a phrase Sappho herself used over two thousand years ago. Desire is illogical in the best way, freed from the authoritative constraints of the conscious mind, coiling in the hips, catching in the breath, pounding in the blood. Sex can be a container for the meeting and mingling of souls. Sex can be a form of worship, an ecstatic release, a ritual of love. It can also be just sex—an erotic expression of enthusiasm for life, a shameless or vulnerable or playful liberation, a lusty embodiment of flesh that bridges connection between two (or more) bodies, even if just for a few moments—and is no less divine for it. According to Greek myth and Orphic cosmology, one of the first primordial deities created at the beginning of time was Eros, the queerly all-gendered force of love and desire that drives all beings toward connection. It is from Eros that we get the word *erotic*, and it is from Eros that all the gods and humans are born.

But sex doesn't have to be divine. Neither does gender. If sex and gender don't bring you into closer connection with the Divine, then those aren't the right spiritual avenues for you. There is nothing wrong with that, and there's nothing wrong with you. There is no shortage of ways to build spiritual connections with the Divine of your understanding. If one takes an animist view of the world, for instance, everything has a unique spirit—every rock, tree, worm, cloud, star, and speck of dirt. If one takes a pantheist approach, god is in everything and everything is a part of god. In this book, I will primarily examine the deities, spirits, and folkloric and historical figures of ages past through the lens of queer sexuality and queer gender, but my worldview is animist, and I revere deities and spirits as distinct beings who are in continual, interconnected relationship as part of the Divine Everything, which is life, death, energy, the land, the cosmos, the layered worlds—Everything.

My hope is to open pathways for LGBTQIA2S+* people to explore their unique connection to the Divine of their understanding through retelling and queering sacred stories—which include myth, folklore, and literature, as well as religious texts—and by offering reflection prompts, activities, rituals, and prayers for building a queer devotional practice.

In my exploration of these sacred stories, I will sometimes call a deity or figure queer, trans, gay, lesbian, nonbinary, etc., in order to name correlations and affinities I perceive in them. If you relate to them differently, I honor and celebrate that. My queer reads on these entities of myth and legend are *suggestions*, not definitive categorizations. The antithesis of queerness is orthodoxy, and the last thing I want to do with this book is attempt to codify any sort of religion or hegemonic belief system. With that in mind, the devotional prompts and exercises at the end of each chapter are designed to emphasize personal connection and exploration, rather than instructional doctrine, and to challenge existing worldviews and tease open emergent possibilities. While rituals and prayers are offered up for your use, you should scrap them or adapt them as you see fit. While this book does have an organizing ethos and a *perspective*, I have steered away from codifying a singular queer devotional mythos or practice, choosing instead to take the route of "organized queer chaos." I attempt to rupture and complicate my own readings at times to resist idealized narratives, which, for me, is part and parcel of a lived practice of queer devotion. The gods in these pages make mistakes and do bad things, and I believe these should be remembered and examined rather than

---

* LGBTQIA2S+ stands for lesbian, gay, bisexual, transgender or transsexual, queer or questioning, intersex, asexual or agender, and Two Spirit, with the "+" meant to acknowledge all the non-cisgender and non-heterosexual identities that are not listed or are yet to be named. This acronym is imperfect and frequently changes, and it is not my intention to leave anyone out. I often use the umbrella term "queer" instead, as it is broad enough to welcome all non-cis/non-het people.

swept under the rug in favor of a homogenous blanket of goodness or righteousness. One of the purposes of spirituality is to provide a mirror to reflect on ourselves and the nature of the human experience, and that includes *all* the human experience, good and bad and ugly.

While I do my best to be inclusive of a variety of queer identities and intersections of privilege and oppression, my perspective is subjective. I am a queer, pansexual, transgender, nonbinary person—or at least these are my identities today. I am also white, American, middle-class, able-bodied, and neurodivergent, with educational privilege. I was raised in the United Methodist Church in the Deep South, then I was Wiccan, then I oscillated between atheist and agnostic for a decade, and then I finally found my way to an eclectic, paganish, queer spirituality in my late twenties. My experience with institutional religion growing up has made me allergic to anything organized, so I've never sought initiation into any religious or spiritual tradition or coven, though that may change one day. If I've learned anything about the Divine over the years, it's that They'll surprise you.

In these pages, I delve quite a bit into ancient Greek and Roman mythologies because they are inordinately fruitful with homosexual pairings, shape-shifting and gender-shifting deities, and other myths that are ripe for queering. I also visit some older, Mesopotamian and Anatolian myths and deities that were the ancestors of the familiar Greco-Roman pantheon, and I swoop northward across Europe to consider gender-bending stories from Norse mythology as well. But our journey here isn't solely pagan: We'll also excavate queerness in the Bible and the Gnostic Gospels, as well as in the lives of transgender Catholic saints. Finally, we'll illuminate queer threads in Arthurian legend and European folklore and visit an ancient Lesbian poet and an underground Italian witch queen.

The mythologies and pantheons that I visit in these pages are not by any means a comprehensive account of all queer-aligned deities or spiritualities. There are queer shamans in Siberia and Mongolia, trans and genderfluid deities in Hinduism, spiritual leaders in Polynesia and the Indigenous nations of North America who exist outside of binary gender, and gay lovers in Japanese mythology—to reference just a handful. I focus on the so-called Western canon of spirituality and myth in this book, and I must acknowledge that the "West" has perpetrated grievous harms to Indigenous cultures and spiritualities across the globe through genocidal European and Christian colonization, including against the native pre-Christian spiritualities and cultures of Europe itself. I hope that by revealing queer streams running under the foundations of Western myth and religion, I might help to erode Western myth's totalizing facade and destabilize the sand beneath its hegemonic temples to colonialist patriarchy.

As to those who will cry *"Anachronism!"* to my application of modern ideas of queerness, gender identity, and sexuality to ancient and classical myths, I will say that I am well aware that dykes, twinks, enbies, drag queens and kings, and all our fellow queers did not exist *as such* in earlier eras. I am also aware that *we did exist*, albeit under different names or no names at all, seeing as we often aren't allowed a name that survives in the annals of history. We *did exist* in different forms, shapes, and expressions that flouted the normative ideals of dominant culture, which was already plenty misogynistic in ancient Rome. We *did exist* in the lives and spirits of every woman who loved other women, as the famous poet Sappho did, or every man who loved other men, as Socrates did, or every person who felt their spirit did not match the norms for their sex and who dreamed in secret of metamorphosis. We *did exist*, just as much as heterosexual and cisgender people did—which, by the way, are *also* recently constructed norms of white colonial society. We deserve to look back on the myths and stories that have shaped our world, art, deities, and beliefs for millennia and find ourselves reflected there just as much as heterosexual and cisgender people do.

When I first read Margot Adler's *Drawing Down the Moon* and Starhawk's *The Spiral Dance* many years ago, I experienced a feeling that I think must be similar to the feeling Christians have in church: connection. I felt myself connecting from afar to a world of people I never knew about, people who shared the same secret thoughts and feelings about the anti-patriarchal, naturalistic Divine that I'd always had but kept to myself. Not only that, but people were writing about these ideas in books *before I was born*, books that were not available to me growing up in institutionalized religion, so I had to search for them in adulthood. I had the same feeling when I read the essays of Audre Lorde—essays entirely left out of my primary and secondary education—the earth-moving feeling that the questions and struggles I'd had with society, that I'd labored over in silence, that I'd thought were *new* were in fact *old*. Older than me, older than Lorde, old, old, *old*. There is so much queer, revolutionary, liberatory knowledge out there. If only we knew about it.

One way that cis-heteronormative colonialist capitalist white supremacist patriarchy works is by repressing these voices, these questions and struggles, these realities of the queer, trans, Black, brown, disabled, disenfranchised, neurodivergent, heretic, contrary, revolutionary. Though the powers that be have not yet been successful enough to obliterate these "other" narratives entirely, they have succeeded in significantly slowing us down. They've made it harder to find one another, to share ideas and questions with one another, to find our gods. They tangle us in knots of self-doubt and self-hatred that we have to spend time and energy untying. They've conditioned us to question the unorthodox sacred and spiritual. *Was that an authentic spiritual experience, or was it all in our heads? Did we experience the Divine, or was it all brain chemicals, or are we losing our mind?*

In my research for the book, I came up against the cis-heteronormative blockade of "official" history and scholarship time and again. I became so despondent at one point that I was near depression. I felt like my task was Sisyphean and foolish. Who am I to go against those considered experts? Who am I to reread and retell the stories of gods worshiped in cultures long passed? Born and raised in the U.S. and trained in the academy of Western scholarship, I had to fight against the repressive voice in my head that told me I didn't know enough, that I was peddling falsehoods and reading queer phantoms where none existed in the grand cis-het monomyth of history.

But this is the lot of an underground people, the lot of a people continually erased from official history. Sometimes all we're left with are faint whispers, textual fragments, oral histories, and tenuous threads chased from hint to hint. Even when we have access to translations of ancient or medieval texts, the translations can be fraught with the pitfalls of the heteronormative worldview of their translators. Short of learning Coptic or Greek or Old English ourselves—which is hard to do, as many queers don't have extra time and money to spend on niche higher education due to systemic discrimination—there's not much we can do.

Or maybe there is. Queer theorist José Esteban Muñoz calls for reading the past through the lens of "queer evidence," which is "an evidence that has been queered in relation to the laws of what counts as proof."[2] When we look for queer evidence in the past, we're posed with a double difficulty: First, it has historically been disadvantageous to leave evidence of queerness, as it can be used to target and punish us. Second, as Muñoz observes, "when the historian of queer experience attempts to document a queer past, there is often a gatekeeper, representing a straight present, who will labor to invalidate the historical fact of queer lives—past, present, and future."[3] In other words, even when we find evidence of queerness in the past, the cis-heterosexist authorities of the present will do their best to delegitimize us and shut us down. So why should we play by their rules at all? Muñoz advocates for not only looking for queer evidence, but for *queering* evidence, "by suturing it to the concept of ephemera. Think of ephemera as trace, the remains, the things that are left, hanging in the air like a rumor."[4]

Thankfully, we queers are good at picking up on trace and rumor. We're fluent in subtle glances across the bar, eye contact that lasts a second too long, and body language, hairstyles, clothes, and accessories that signal—to those in the know—who we are and what we're looking for. We are experts at subtext and reading between the lines. So that's what we'll do in these pages: send a flirty glance across the nightclub of history and see who flirts back.

I may risk defining the indefinable by saying that the Divine is queer, but They are certainly not *not* queer. Queerness is indefinable in its vastness of wild and strange diversity, incapable of totalizing categorization. So is the Divine. If you believe in a celestial Creator/ix of the cosmos, a being unfathomable to the human mind, that's pretty queer. If you believe that God is *in* everyone, then God is all-gendered and all-sexed, attracted to every type of body and gender under the sun—ipso facto, queer. If you believe further that God/dess or Goddexx or the Divine is in every*thing*, in nature as well as in humans, then the Divine is human and nonhuman. The Divine is animal and vegetable and mineral, flame and liquid and gas and the void of outer space.

The Divine is so queer that They break down the divides between male and female, cis and trans, gay and straight, divine and mundane. The monotheistic world of "God the Father"—as well as the hierarchical and dichotomized world of male versus female, white versus black, human versus nature, body versus spirit, and us versus them—crumbles and dissolves in the gaze of the Divine.

So I'll say it: God, Goddess, Goddexx, Deity, the Gods by any name—the Divine is Queer.

QUEER DEVOTIONS

At the end of each chapter, you'll find a variety of prompts, exercises, ritual suggestions, and devotional practices for exploring your connection with the Queer Divine and building a queer devotional practice. Each chapter will be followed by "Queer Contemplations," questions designed to get you thinking about what you've read and coming up with your own thoughts about the Queer Divine. I recommend keeping a journal for recording your answers, questions, and ideas. There will also be an assortment of activities for spiritual exploration, as well as foundational elements for building a queer devotional tool-kit, such as prayer and altar-building.

As you explore these devotional activities, you may want to do them in a sacred space. At its core, a sacred space is simply an intentional space that you carve out for yourself. It doesn't have to be an elaborate altar or specially decorated separate location dedicated only for this purpose; it can be a multipurpose area like a kitchen table or a cozy reading chair. The important part is that you feel safe, comfortable, and supported. If you're performing a ritual, you may also want to make sure you're not interrupted or disturbed.

Queer Contemplations

- What does queerness mean to you?
- How is your queerness a reflection of the Divine?
- What does devotion mean to you?
- What or who are you devoted to?

CHAPTER 1

Queer Mysteries, Queer Initiations

Coming Out of the Closet with the Eleusinian and Orphic Mystery Traditions

In *The Myth of the Goddess*, Anne Baring and Jules Cashford imagine what the experience of initiation into the Eleusinian Mysteries, the Mystery religion of Demeter and Persephone, might have been like:

> Imagine the great hall of mysteries shrouded in darkness, thronged with people, waiting in stillness. Dim figures of priests move in the darkness, carrying flickering torches. In the centre of the darkness some secret drama is being performed. Suddenly a gong sounds like thunder, the underworld breaks open and out of the depths of the earth Kore [Persephone] appears. A radiant light fills the chamber, the huge fire blazes upward, and the hierophant chants: "The great goddess has borne a sacred child: Brimo has borne Brimos." Then, in the profound silence, he holds up a single ear of corn.[5]

The experience and exploration of queerness is, for many of us, mysterious. We fumble in the dark, wondering how to touch one another, feeling our way to revelations. Mysterious symbols are presented in blazes of light: the color purple, a pink triangle, a bandana in a back pocket, a pinkie ring, a single earring in the left ear—or was it the right? Sometimes we navigate this dimmed and thrilling territory by ourselves or with a partner who is equally clueless, eager, and awed. Sometimes we are guided by a more experienced queer lover or friend who reveals to us the secret words, signs, rituals of queerness. The blossoming awareness and exploration of queerness is a kind of initiation experience, to be sure. Perhaps one that brings us into contact with a Mystery.

Mystery religions abounded in ancient Mediterranean cultures. There were Mysteries of Persephone and Demeter, Isis and Osiris, Kybele, Dionysos, and more. Not much is known for certain about these rituals or the Mysteries they revealed because they were secret—initiates were forbidden to speak of them to non-initiates—and what recorded accounts do exist come from outside Christian sources that tend to be heavily prejudiced. The Mysteries were not puzzles to solve or codes to crack. They were not merely secrets or unknowns, though that was part of it. These were Mysteries with a capital *M*: ineffable truths, unspeakable because no words can describe them, incommunicable because they must be *lived* to be *known*.*

In the Mystery initiations, secret words and symbols were presented to initiates, such as the ear of corn mentioned by Baring and Cashford, but I do not believe their meaning was *explained*. While the revelation of the ear of corn may be read as somewhat anticlimactic, even comical, by a modern audience (I admit that I laughed the first time), ancient Greeks would not have been laughing. They would have had the *lived* knowledge of the importance of corn in their diet and survival, as well as the cultural understanding of its significance as a symbol of Demeter and of the fertility and rebirth of the land, not to mention other symbolic resonances that we can hardly guess at from two millennia away. Additionally, while 21st-century minds may conceive of myths and gods as merely symbols, in ancient Greece, the gods were *alive*. They were felt in every aspect of living. There was no distance between a material ear of corn and what it symbolized. The corn wasn't a symbol for the land's rebirth; it *was* the land's rebirth.

The Mysteries were revealed but not explained because a Mystery at its essence *cannot* be explained. One can try to demystify a Mystery, but one will lose the Mystery entirely in that pursuit. In Paul

---

* Try explaining the soul-deep certainty of being transgender to a cis-het person, especially one of an older generation, and you may hear the common refrain "I just don't get it. I don't understand."

Woodruff's introductory notes to his translation of *The Bacchae*, he shares his thoughts: "The point . . . is that clear understanding comes only by way of initiation, and not by active intellectual efforts. If a deity strikes you as mysterious, that is because you have not been initiated into his or her mysteries. The mystery will only deepen if you try to lead yourself to a solution."[6] That is, if you try to reason with a Mystery, you may end up with some nice-sounding rationalizations, but the Deity will have evaded you entirely. Or, as Baring and Cashford put it, "Only a mystic understands the Mysteries."[7]

In the Eleusinian Mysteries that Baring and Cashford described, initiation involved a reenactment of the story of Persephone's abduction into the underworld, her mother Demeter's search and retribution, and Persephone's joyful return. Initiates *experienced* Persephone's underworld descent with their own "descent" into fearful darkness and symbolic death, followed by the return of the light that symbolized Persephone's return to the land of the living and the initiate's own rebirth into the Mysteries. The symbolic death and rebirth of the initiates mirrored the mythic narrative of death/descent and rebirth/rise of the goddess—a theme that appears in different ways in the myth cycles of many cultures. Indeed, historians agree that symbolic death and rebirth was the central theme of ancient Mystery initiations at large.

Today, modern magical groups such as Wiccan covens and secret societies like Freemasonry also have initiations that involve a symbolic death and rebirth. In *The Spiral Dance*, Starhawk states that this is central to the initiation rite, which transforms the individual through "the experience of those inner secrets that cannot be told because they go beyond words" (note Starhawk's word choice: *experience*, not explanation) and "causes revelation and understanding and sparks further growth and change."[8]

The act of "coming out," whether just to ourselves or to our communities, as gay, lesbian, transgender, nonbinary, or any kind of queer is also a symbolic death and rebirth. We put our former identity (the gender or sexuality that was forced on us, the mask we've worn) to rest and are reborn as our true selves. Or tru*er* selves, as some of us have multiple coming-outs as we unveil successive layers of our own queer identities over time.* The experience can be very scary, as initiations typically are. It requires letting go of control and opening to the unknown on the other side of self-declaration. If we come out publicly, it often involves a commitment to a radically different path than the one prescribed for us by cis-heteronormativity. Every coming-out experience is different, but I think it's safe to say it is usually transformative. It is also a leap of faith, not necessarily faith in a god but faith in *oneself.*

The transformation of coming out begins when we come out to ourselves. That self-recognition takes strength. The revelation of our own queerness prompts a descent into our innermost selves with the hope of releasing any conditioned shame or fear around who we are, freeing ourselves of inhibitions, excavating our sublimated desires and mannerisms and feelings, and bringing our truth up into the light of day or into the light of our own private consciousness. We become initiated into an underworld consciousness, into the reality under reality and the history under history—into the manifest, living truth of queerness that pulses just beneath the skin of the world, that always has and always will.

Do I mean to suggest that queerness, especially our most powerful and transformative queer experiences, are Divine Mysteries? Divine initiations? Are akin to meeting God? No.

But also *not* no.

Judy Grahn writes of her experience of queer initiation via her first lesbian lover in *Another Mother Tongue*: "'Our color is purple, or lavender,' my first lover affirmed, intensely whispering to my avid and puzzled young ears the forbidden litany of who we were or might be. 'No one knows why this is, it just is,' handsome Vonnie said. . . . She taught me the words of Gay life; she could not tell me what they meant."[9] Queer Mysteries, sacred symbols, secret words. Grahn describes her entry into the gay underground culture of the late 1950s and early '60s as a metaphorical descent into the underworld, echoing the familiar myths of descent (death) and rise

---

* My spouse has just reminded me that those of us who choose to do so must come out repeatedly, even though our identities have not changed, with each new friend, co-worker, doctor, person who looks at our social media profile, and on and on. "It gets easier," he says, "but right before you say it, there's that split second of fear because it might change the way they treat you. That never goes away."

(rebirth). Grahn identifies the experience: "I can see now it was a necessary part of my initiation; going to my first Gay bar certainly felt as terrifying, mystifying, and life-altering as any ritual procedure could have felt."[10]

Here is the symbolic descent into the queer underground. Here is the gay bar as the reversed underworld, where after zombie-walking all day in the death of compulsory cis-heteronormativity, the queers finally come alive. Here are the sacred words—*dyke, bear, femme, queen*. Here are the secret symbols—a nose ring, a haircut, a particular way of holding eye contact, short fingernails. Here are the holy objects—lipstick, a binder, poppers, duct tape.

I remember the excitement, fear, and confusion of my first experiences in the gay bars and drag shows of Birmingham, Alabama, in the mid-to-late aughts, wide-eyed and reborn in the half-light of the disco ball lancing through cigarette smoke. I remember the numinous awe when I kissed a girl for the first time—the tremulous terror and excitement mingled with desire and something like peace. I remember hearing the word *transgender* for the first time, whispered in the high school hallway between classes, a word that stuck in my head, that I couldn't stop returning to, wondering if that was me, if that was who I was. (Still trapped in the binary of man/woman, I decided that I didn't feel like a man, so I must've been a woman.) I remember reading the word *nonbinary*, years and years later, in an author bio on the Internet. I googled the term, and the Mystery flashed before my eyes, all revealed in an instant.

That was the secret word, the *sacred* word, that initiated me into my Mysteries. Nothing more than a signifier, a symbol, a negation, and a creation, nine letters flickering on a computer screen. And also a lightning bolt, a Divine truth, an ear of corn, a world reborn. Death and rebirth in an instant. *Nonbinary.*

We cannot possibly replicate ancient Mystery religions in the modern day, and that's not my intent. The modern queer experience is not the same as the experience of initiation into ancient Mysteries. But I do believe that contemplating the experience of initiation and the nature of a Mystery can be a valuable and inspirational place to begin forging or deepening a queer devotional practice.

The thing that divided me from spiritual belief and devotion for so very long, aside from religious trauma, was *proof.* An insistence on explanation, legibility, empiricism, validation. Before I could *believe* in a thing, I had to *understand* it. This is also part of what kept me from embracing my own queer sexuality and nonbinary gender until I was 30 years old. I felt that I needed to check an appropriate number of queer and trans boxes, meet some burden of proof, know "for sure."* But this self-doubt, this burden of proof, did not come from inside me, but from outside. It was placed on me by a society, culture, and religion that didn't think I was "real." A society where a doctor is the one who can "decide" if you're trans. A culture that grooms children to be the "right" kind of masculine or feminine—no limp wrists for boys, no bossy attitudes for girls. When my spouse came out to his father as trans, his dad replied, "I don't believe in transgender." As if his transness were Santa Claus or the Easter Bunny. I was more fortunate. When I came out to my dad, he asked me to help him understand. When he still couldn't quite wrap his mind around it, he said he didn't have to understand it to believe me.

That's the secret right there: You don't have to understand in order to believe.

While I'm firm in my queerness at this point, I still struggle with my spirituality sometimes. I have days when I doubt all the insights, revelations, uncanny experiences, dreams, visions, synchronicities, signs, guidance, and assistance that I have received from my deities and spirits. Did Aphrodite *really* help resolve that relationship issue after I prayed to her for help, or did my partner and I just get over it? Did my accountant grandpa *really* intervene with the credit card processor after I asked his spirit for help, or did the issue resolve on its own? This, too, is a product of the cis-heterosexist, materialist Western culture of reason over emotion, fact over feeling, mind over body. This is the legacy of a culture that teaches us to question what we *know* in our queer bones and queer soul to be true about ourselves and our experience. Why does it have to be one or the other, after all? Why can't it be both? Maybe Aphrodite thawed my and my partner's

---

* Here's a hint, a magic incantation: If you're grappling with whether you're queer, if you're struggling with whether you're trans or nonbinary, *you probably are.* Cis-het folks aren't usually kept up at night stressing about their straightness and cis-ness.

hearts so we could work out that relationship issue together from a place of openness and love. Maybe Grandpa greased the wheels at the credit card processor, slipped my support ticket in front of the right eyes—or nudged me to change that one detail in that one setting in my account, the day after which all was resolved.

The big thing I had to learn in my spiritual path—the big, huge, *massive*, supremely challenging (for me) thing, the thing I'm always still working on—is letting go. Letting go of that control, that insistence on empirical proof and absolute understanding, that fear of being wrong or foolish.

Letting go is a kind of death.

Baring and Cashford describe the Mysteries of Kybele (Cybele) and Attis: "[The initiate's] old beliefs and way of life are sacrificed to his or her new understanding of the Mysteries, and [the initiate] is 'reborn' from the death-like state of his former level of understanding."[11] Initiation, whether queer or religious or Mysterious, always requires the death of understanding in order for *knowing* to be reborn. And I do believe that knowing is *re*born. I think the knowing of the Divine and the knowing of queerness are similar like that. Both are realities that were once alive within us, inseparable from us, knitted into our souls and cells as children—before the world got in the way. Before cis-heteronormative society taught us we were aberrant. Before trans- and homophobic institutionalized religion taught us we were going to hell. Before other kids on the playground learned this too and started the name-calling: *lesbo, sissy, faggot, dyke*. Before access to God was locked behind a pearly gate, a code of conduct and a clean report card required for entry. Before we learned to separate the mind from the body and forgot the spirit entirely.

We must forget what we've learned to remember what we know.

So much of the Divine has been lost in the empirical thrust of the scientific and industrial revolutions, in the violent hierarchical divisions of Cartesian dualism, in the dehumanizing labor extraction of capitalism and sexless Protestant productivity. Western intellectualism has parceled out the body of God into ordered taxonomies, hierarchies, and dichotomies, pinned and labeled like a butterfly specimen in a naturalist's display case. It has done the same to our souls. In one of Dionysos's two deaths in Orphic tradition, the infant Dionysos is abducted by jealous Titans and his body savagely torn apart and eaten. Only his heart remained, and it was from his heart that the "thrice-born" god was regrown.[12] Perhaps this story of Dionysos, the gender-bending god of transformation, can offer a remedy, a path to regrowing the spiritual body along with the queer soul: from the heart.

A feature of Dionysos's worship that was unique to the rest of the Greek pantheon was that his followers, through the paradoxical liberation (rebirth) of ecstatic surrender (death), experienced enthousiasmos, "having the god within."[13] The Divine was made manifest in the initiate, was one with them, after which they were reborn, changed, secure in the *knowing* of their god.[14] His heart, perhaps, beat with theirs. Apostolos N. Athanassakis and Benjamin M. Wolkow, in the notes to their translation of *The Orphic Hymns*, remark on the parallels between Dionysos's dismemberment by the Titans and the initiation ritual of the Orphic Mysteries: "As the god is ripped apart by the Titans and is born again, so, too, the initiates, blasted by the vagaries of life, are reborn through initiation into something pure and holy."[15]

I could not believe in the Divine until after I accepted and embraced my queerness. In remembering ourselves, in remembering the truths of our own heart, we re-member ourselves from dismemberment. We put ourselves back together. We are reborn into what we've always been: holy and whole.

The Gods, the Divine, have always been there, waiting for us to remember.

Queer Mysteries

In a world with "Women's Mysteries" and "Men's Mysteries" that tend to be cis-heteronormative at best and gender-essentialist, transphobic, and homophobic at worst, it is tempting to establish a tradition of "Queer Mysteries" for ourselves. In his book *Queerying Occultures*, Phil Hine cautions against organizing and codifying "Queer Pagan Mysteries" into any unified experience of queerness. To do so would only be another kind of essentialism, he notes, rooted in "the notion that 'all queer persons,' regardless of gender, race, culture, class, etc.—share similar experiences."[16]

Indeed, if we attempt to establish a set of Queer Mysteries that assumes a universality of queer experience—for instance, centering around common but far from universal experiences such as coming out—then we commit the same errors as the so-called Women's Mysteries and Men's Mysteries from which many of us have been excluded. Anyone who chooses not to come out publicly, for whatever reason, might be alienated from those Queer Mysteries. Those who have an easy experience of coming out rather than a fraught one, or those who never had a big, dramatic coming-out because they were raised by people who made room for gender and sexual diversity from their earliest memory, may also feel like they can't have a seat at the Queer Mystery altar because they haven't "suffered enough" for it.* Those not formally initiated into the Mysteries might feel additionally excluded, not queer enough, or shut out from their own people, or they might feel pressure to seek initiation in order to be a "good queer" and gain their proverbial "queer card." But the most dangerous hazard of a universalized Queer Mysteries is that it might serve to reinforce only one, privileged form of queerness, glossing over the infinite diversity within queerness and ignoring the ways queerness is experienced differently based on culture, race, class, gender, age, and more.

Queer people deserve a spirituality that not only includes but centers and celebrates them. Nonbinary folks deserve experiences of the divine that are unfettered by the binary gendered trap of polarity, trans myths in which we might hear the echo of our own souls, and queer devotional praxis that grows out of our own life rhythms and lifeways (a term I picked up from Phil Hine as an alternative to life*styles*, which, to my ear, implies a frivolous decorative choice rather than a sacred, lived reality). At the same time, we must not fall into the barbed, enclosing pit of categorization, taxonomy, orthodoxy, and essentialism.

The good news is that queerness is particularly suited to our task. Queerness is not only an identity; it is a *praxis*, or practice, of engaging with the world that dissolves binaries and categorization, questions the rules and prods the cracks, troubles seemingly stable notions of reality, and opens spaces for what else *is* and *might be*. Hine writes

---

* I was hesitant to claim the title "queer" for myself for some years because I felt that I had never experienced anti-queer oppression. Of course, that was far from the truth, as I had been forcing myself to wear the stifling mask of cis-heteronormativity for the better part of 30 years out of fear, which is one of the insidious ways oppression works.

that, for him, queer is "less about a certain mode of being, and more an ethical position with which to engage the world."[17] This "ethical position" for Hine includes intersectionality, a commitment to difference and complexity, a resistance to dichotomous oppositions that provide the foundation for systems of domination and oppression, and an attention to everyday experience and people's actual lives and stories without reducing them to identity labels.[18] This resonates with my own approach to queerness as praxis, and we would do well to intentionally infuse this ethic of queerness into our devotional practice.

When I talk about not only being devoted to queerness but being devoted *queerly*, this is what I mean. I mean staying open to curiosity, possibility, wonder, and change. I mean questioning the rules and "official" narratives, resisting orthodoxy and codification. I mean seeking a sideways perspective, a marginal mentality, an underworld consciousness that teases and troubles the normative. I mean courting sensuality, connection, complexity, strangeness, wildness, freedom, and Mystery. I mean putting queerness into practice.

Is it possible to cultivate a queer devotional practice, a queer ethic of questioning and disruption, and not constantly undermine our own belief in ourselves and in our Gods? I think so. Belief is not the same as understanding. Knowledge is not the same as knowing. There is a difference between a hermeneutics of curiosity and desire, an expansive consciousness that desires to understand while knowing absolute understanding is impossible, and a hermeneutics of suspicion that seeks only to disprove. One cannot prove God, but one cannot disprove Them either. I think a queer ethic *is* devotional. In my experience, integrating a queer ethic into one's devotional practice does not undermine its integrity. Just the opposite. It *builds* integrity, along with confidence and trust in oneself and the Divine.

There are certainly mysteries—and Mysteries—to queerness, but they are not fixed or universal. Such a thing would be contrary to the subjective, experiential nature of Mysteries. There are certainly experiences that function like initiations, but these are not regulated nor hierarchical, and they are certainly not required.

The Mysteries are the threads of purpled smoke that drift from you to Divine, the baffling but undeniable connection from us to one another, from us to the more-than-human Earth, from us to Spirit or Source. They are the symbols and stories that vibrate with significance but elude explanation. The untranslatable truth dancing on the tip of your tongue, the breathing unknown, the peace of paradox. They are whatever whispers to you of your own truths, whatever signifies your essential belonging. And they do not need to be translatable, legible, explainable—that's the wonder of a Mystery.

And initiation? Initiation is whatever gets you there, to the Mystery. It can be a long course of study followed by a formal ritual initiation into a group. It can be a ceremony welcoming you into a community in which you are loved and belong. It can be a heartfelt self-initiation in the privacy of your bedroom.

But I think most initiations are more frequent and mundane than that. A personal epiphany, a horrible loss, a life-changing experience. A drag mother, a lesbian lover, a butch haircut, a testosterone shot. There are many ways to cross the veil, enter the underground, remember, and rise again, transformed. And most of them don't involve a formal, choreographed ritual—they just happen. An initiation is whatever turns you inside out, whatever shakes your world to pieces, whatever changes you completely, whatever introduces you to Divine.

The Gods are many, and there are many ways to meet Them.

On Self-Initiations

I have never been initiated into any organized Mystery tradition, nor any spiritual, magical, or religious tradition aside from Protestant Christianity—and I didn't really have a choice about that. So there's no way for me to know what truly goes on behind the initiation veil in any secret or closed tradition or group. Maybe that makes me the wrong person to write this chapter. Or maybe it makes me the right person, or *a* right person. My hope is to be another voice—an *Other* voice—speaking to those like me who have a solitary spiritual path, whether by choice or necessity, or who are initiated into a tradition in which the Queer Divine is unacknowledged or sidelined.

In *Sacred Gender*, Ariana Serpentine, an initiate into various traditions who has performed initiations herself, makes the distinction between "lineage initiations" and "spirit initiations."[19] The former is the more traditional initiation into a group, which comes with built-in spiritual community and lineage. The latter is solitary and personal, carried out between the individual and the Divine. Although self-initiations tend to be looked down upon as "lesser" by some initiates of formal traditions, both are equally valid and sacred, just different. In her book on Inclusive Wicca, *All Acts of Love and Pleasure*, Yvonne Aburrow identifies six aspects of initiation: inner transformation, making contact with the Divine, experiencing the Mysteries that cannot be spoken, being given the coven secrets that must not be spoken,* joining the coven's group mind, and joining the lineage or tradition of the coven.[20] The first three aspects can be achieved in self-initiation, but the last three cannot due to their group-specific nature.

Importantly, Aburrow also points out that these aspects of initiation *do not have to happen at the same time.* The timing of making contact with the Divine, which Aburrow calls "initiation by the gods and goddesses," is possibly more accurately phrased as the Divine making contact with *you.* It does not happen according to our human timetables but whenever the Divine wills it, possibly during an initiation ritual or possibly before or after. Likewise, experiencing the Mysteries and the process of inner transformation will be ongoing. As Aburrow points out, "To initiate means to begin something."[21] This is only the beginning.

There are also some practical elements of group or "lineage" initiations that cannot be easily replicated in solitary or "spirit" ones—the elements of surprise and the unknown, for instance, are hard to replicate when you're the one organizing your own initiation ritual. In my experience, these can be reached in a solitary setting via meditation, divination, vision, or spontaneous activities like ecstatic dance. The tarot, for instance, surprises me *all the time.* The community element of lineage initiations is also missing in self-initiations. I have found that after self-initiation, I tend to find my people and my people find me. It can just take some time. This is not the same as being part of

---

* The distinction between what *cannot* be spoken and *must* not be spoken is important and elucidative. The Mysteries cannot be spoken because they are beyond language and can only be experienced. The secrets of the group are forbidden to be spoken to non-initiates for reasons particular to the closed lineage or tradition.

a coven or other initiated group, but I have found uncanny linkages and synchronicities occur with other individuals who are working with the same deities or in similar pathways as me. With any initiation, we enter into a relationship with the Divine and things tend to fall into place from there.*

QUEER DEVOTIONS

Queer Contemplations

- What is the nature of mystery? Is mystery sacred and why?

- What are the benefits of being part of a spiritual community or tradition? What are the drawbacks of being part of a spiritual community or tradition?

- What is the purpose of initiation?

- What is the purpose of ritual, and how can ritual help connect you to the Divine?

Devotional Tool-Kit: Rites of Passage

What are some rites of passage you've been through in life? How did they change you? Did you acknowledge them in any ritual way (a party, funeral, ceremony, etc.)? If you didn't, do you think acknowledging them through ritual would have been helpful?

If it feels right, consider incorporating ritual, big or small, into future rites of passage. You might also choose to remember some of your most meaningful rites of passage as personal holidays. In our household, for instance, we celebrate my partner's T-day (the anniversary of the day he started testosterone) by going out to get a nice cup of tea.

---

* To be clear, things "falling into place" do not necessitate any assurance of ease, bliss, and privilege in life. Often, devoting oneself to a deity initiates challenges, lessons, steep growth curves, and transformations. At the same time, in relationship with Divine, they are easier than they would be otherwise.

Creative Mythology: Personal Queer Mysteries

Make a list of your personal Queer Mysteries. What would be your sacred symbols, words, objects, truths? What Mystery would you reveal to your younger self at the start of your queer journey, if you could? How would you represent this as a symbol, object, performance, or incantation?

Next, write an imaginary initiation into your Queer Mysteries. You might choose to model it off the symbolic death/descent and rise/rebirth pattern of the ancient Mystery religions, or you might come up with something entirely different. You might write it like a theater production, perhaps using Baring and Cashford's imagined scene from the Eleusinian Mysteries at the beginning of this chapter as inspiration. I can see that scene translating stunningly well into a drag performance, for example. Be creative. Think big!

When you're done, imagine what an initiation experience would feel like. Visualize yourself going through the initiation from beginning to end. Feel all the emotions. Reveal your Queer Mysteries to yourself. Write down any insights, impressions, messages, or surprises that come.

See Appendix 2 for a ritual for Queer Self-Initiation.

CHAPTER 2

The Birth of Transgender Venus

Self-Love Through Transition with the Queens of Heaven

Like all of us, Aphrodite, goddess of love and beauty, was born of blood. However, in Aphrodite's case, this blood did not spill from a womb, but from a castration.

Let me back up.

There are two primary versions of the birth of Aphrodite, or Venus, as she's known from Roman mythology. The first, given by the Greek epic poet Homer, tells us that Aphrodite is the daughter of Zeus and Dione, begat and borne, one assumes, the usual way. (Though you never can tell with Olympians, who have been known to gestate inside their father's thigh or leap whole-formed from foreheads.) The far more interesting version of Aphrodite's birth comes from Hesiod, the 8th century B.C.E. Greek poet and mythographer of *Theogony*, who places the naissance of our goddess of love near the dawn of creation—before Zeus, the supreme patriarchal king of the gods, before Hera and Athena and Ares and the rest of the Olympians, possibly even before living things grew on the Earth and roamed its lands and waters.

In the beginning, so the story goes, Heaven and Earth were inseparable and were lovers. Hesiod tells us that Ouranos (Heaven) laid himself over Gaia (Earth) each night, and they had many children together. Their first children were the powerful godlike beings known as the Titans, but after a while, Gaia began birthing a new and diverse range of children: the one-eyed, lightning-forging Cyclopes and the Hecatoncheires, mighty giants with fifty heads and one hundred arms each. Hesiod tells us that Ouranos was not a fan of his new progeny, so as soon as each was born, he would hide it in a "secret place" inside the earth, which was Gaia, causing her great suffering, all the while taking glee in his wicked work.[22] Ouranos continued to have sex with Gaia, at this point nonconsensually, so let's call it what it is: rape. And he continued hiding their children back inside Gaia's body as soon as they were born, essentially keeping her forever pregnant and in great physical and emotional pain.

If one thing can be said for the ancient Greeks, it is that they did not shy from exposing the horrific sides of gods and humans.

But our story does not end there. To get free of her abuser and liberate her children trapped inside her body, Gaia came up with a plan. She asked her free children, the Titans, to aid her, and her youngest Titan son, Kronos, stepped up. She fashioned a sickle using iron from the earth that was her body and gave it to Kronos. The next night, when Ouranos came to rape Gaia, Kronos took his mother's sickle and castrated his father, throwing the offending appendage into the sea.

The sky god's severed testicles plunged into the waves with a mighty crash, perhaps like the lightning bolt that scientists have proposed catalyzed the first unicellular organisms into life in the ocean's salty belly. Hesiod tells us that "a white foam spread around them from the immortal flesh, and in it there grew a maiden."[23] This nursery of blood and salt, flesh and foam, gestated the maiden and carried her in its gory waves to the shores of Cyprus, where she emerged "an awful and lovely goddess."[24] Aphrodite, goddess of love, was born.

A Goddess of Life and Death

On the Cyprian shore, Aphrodite was greeted by the Horae, the goddesses of the seasons, and accompanied by Eros (Love) and Desire. Where she stepped, grass grew around her feet. A surviving fragment of the lost epic poem *Cypria* describes her landfall: "She clothed herself with garments which the Graces and Hours [Horae] had made for her and dyed in flowers of spring—such flowers as the Seasons wear—in crocus and hyacinth and flourishing violet and the rose's lovely bloom."[25] Accompanied by the Seasons, clothed by them in their own garments of spring flowers, with grass springing up wherever she steps, Aphrodite is situated as a goddess of something much wilder, much greener, and much more vital than what she has become relegated to in the 21st century. This is no goddess for selling Valentine's cards and leg-hair removal products, no goddess for coyly pornographic paintings that codify unattainable female beauty standards and celebrate the male gaze. As historian Bettany Hughes observes, "Born from abuse and suffering, this sublime force [Aphrodite] is being described to us not just as the goddess of mortal love, but as the deity of both the cycle of life and life itself."[26]

The birth of Aphrodite is more than a creation myth for a singular goddess; it's a cosmic creation myth for life itself. Many scholars have observed that the tale of Ouranos's castration serves as an explanation for why the sky arches in a dome above the Earth but does not collapse upon it—after the castration, Ouranos and Gaia broke up, as it were. But it also does something much more interesting by placing love at the genesis of life—similar to Orphic cosmology, which places Eros (love) as the force that hatched from the cosmic egg and created the world. Hesiod's placement of love via Aphrodite at the genesis of creation is perhaps an acknowledgment that what Aphrodite represents—the generative force of love and desire—is far older than any of the gods of men. Indeed, the goddess can be traced back through various forms, through Phoenician Astarte and Sumerian Inanna, through nameless goddesses of agrarian societies before Indo-European invaders brought their conquering patriarchal gods to the Mediterranean and to Mesopotamia's fertile river valley, all the way even to the oldest hints of deity in the human record. Baring and Cashford observe "that love belongs to the original nature of things, for Aphrodite is born of the moment when Heaven is separated from Earth, and creation, arrested till then by the weight of Heaven, is suddenly set free."[27] Aphrodite is born of a separation and a liberation; she is destruction and also creation.

The castration of Ouranos was more than just a desperate act of violence, after all; it was an act of liberation and, one could argue, love. Though he describes her plot as "crafty" and "evil," Hesiod also relates Gaia's immense pain, distress, and grief at her continual rape and abuse at the hands of Ouranos:

> But vast Earth groaned within, being straitened, and she thought a crafty and an evil wile. Forthwith she made the element of grey flint and shaped a great sickle, and told her plan to her dear sons. And she spoke, cheering them, while she was vexed in her dear heart:
> "My children, gotten of a sinful father, if you will obey me, we should punish the vile outrage of your father; for he first thought of doing shameful things."[28]

These are the emotions of a mother who loves her children, though they be monstrous and *other* in the eyes of their father. These are the emotions of a victim of repeated sexual violence who has no choice but to literally turn her body into a weapon, as Gaia does when she crafts the sickle out of the flint of her Earth-body. Kronos, for his part, is cast unflatteringly in the myth as a hateful and conniving son, without acknowledgment that he has very good reason to hate his father who rapes his mother and imprisons his siblings. Perhaps it was not hate but love in Kronos's heart, love for his hurting mother and siblings, that moved his hand to take up the blade that freed them.* Perhaps it is not so strange, then, that the deity born of this act of violence and desperation, liberation and love is the goddess of love herself—a goddess who will go on to not only rule love but also *passion*, as in the irrepressible strength of feeling that motivates the heart to great deeds as well as horrible ones, and many that are both.

As a creation myth, Aphrodite's is one that acknowledges the nonbinary nature of love, desire, and the human condition. Love is not all perfume and pleasure, roses and wine; love is also grief, pain, longing, and sacrifice. Sometimes love is violent. Desire certainly can

---

* This reading is not without its complications, as in some tellings Kronos re-imprisons his siblings after he frees them, siblings who will only later be freed by Kronos's own son Zeus—interestingly with the help of Gaia, who finally gets to see her children free.

be. Aphrodite's powers to stir love and desire in the hearts of gods and humans alike also extend to powers of compulsion, inducing individuals to fall in love against their will or to harbor intense (and often transgressive) desire for people they would rather not. Humans are likewise a non-dualistic entanglement of feeling, of vices and virtues, of desires and deeds that don't always yield easily to tidy categories of sacred and profane, evil and good. Perhaps, as Nietzsche famously wrote, "What is done out of love always takes place beyond good and evil."[29] Aphrodite's birth via castration does not demonstrate a binary of love and beauty versus hate and violence, but a *simultaneity* of them.

Aphrodite wakes desire in both humans and animals; she is the procreative impulse that begets all living things. But the passions she stirs also lead to death: It was Aphrodite, after all, who stoked Paris's desire for Helen, which led to the Trojan War. As Pat Benatar sang, "Love is a Battlefield," and was it not love that laid the trail for so many tragedies, from *Tristan and Isolde* to *Romeo and Juliet*? The experience of love, too, can be as unbearable as it is blissful. The famed Lesbian poet Sappho, a devotee of Aphrodite, described the lovely, horrid, and, perhaps most importantly, inevitable grasp of love: "Now Love masters my limbs and shakes me, fatal creature, bitter-sweet."[30] Across millennia of myth, religion, art, and pop culture, it is apparent that love is wonderful and horrible simultaneously. Love begets life and sometimes ends it. But love also overcomes death, as in the Christian tradition of Jesus's sacrifice: "For God so loved the world, that he gave his only begotten Son, that whosoever believeth in him should not perish, but have everlasting life."[31] But the love that Aphrodite represents is greater than that between humans or even gods. As Baring and Cashford remark, in positioning Aphrodite's birth at the moment when Heaven and Earth are divided and creation ensues, "Love is drawn in the greater perspective of humanity's longing for reunification with the whole." In that love is what brings us together, "Aphrodite is 'born' when people joyfully remember, as a distinct and sacred reality, the bonds that exist between human beings and animals and, indeed, the whole of nature."[32]

Aphrodite troubles the modern mind that seeks to separate all things into dualisms, re-entangling them and delighting in their slippery complexity. She disrupts coherent categories of gender and sexuality, purity and perversity, beauty and monstrosity, sensuality and spirituality. She represents a love that encompasses heterosexual love and homosexual love and is bigger than sex. Hers is a desire that is human and more than human, animal and vegetable and divine, a desire that is perhaps as grand as the vivifying urge of life itself. By "urge of life," I do not mean solely the procreative urge to create babies or the sexual urge to fuck, but the *erotic* (from Eros, or "Love") urge to feel, experience, connect, taste and touch and smell and sense. Hers is not just the desire to create life, but the desire to *live*.

Goddess of Transgender Beauty and Self-Love

Aphrodite's conception and seafoam birth is far queerer than cisgender, heterosexual penetrative intercourse. By one line of thinking, the one that has dominated interpretation of the myth thus far in scholarship, Aphrodite is the child of a dismembered penis that "fertilizes" the "womb" of the sea—a body of water that is frequently feminized even though it has no sex or gender, being a mass of liquid H_2O filled with all manner of plant, animal, and microbial life— reducing her strange, unruly, inhuman birth to nothing more than a metaphor for cis-heterosexual, penis-in-vagina sexual intercourse. This interpretation whiffs of patriarchal scholarship struggling to grapple with a disorderly creation myth that defies gender essentialist, binary modes of sex, gender, and creation. At the very least, it lacks imagination. By another (an-*other*) line of thinking, if we back up to the manual action that catalyzes her conception, Aphrodite's parents are freedom and a knife. Indeed, one way that we might queer Aphrodite (even more than she is already) is by rereading her birth as a *re*birth, one that transcends gender. One that is, perhaps, *transgender*.

It begins with an act of self-ownership. We've already discussed the castration of Ouranos as an act of love and liberation. And now, as the male genitals dissolve into the ocean, a woman emerges from the froth. What if we read another layer in the story's current, a queerer mythology turning in those saline waves? What if Aphrodite is a trans woman? I do not mean to insist that a trans Aphrodite is the historically "accurate" interpretation of the ancient myth, nor do I care. Accuracy is not our concern here, and it is not entirely possible to achieve an empirical "accuracy" in the figurative terrain of myth anyway, a story-form that functions not through fact but through symbolism. The 21st-century concept of "transgender" did not exist as such in ancient Greece, but neither did our modern conceptions of masculinity, femininity, and heterosexuality—although we apply them to ancient myth all the time with little protest. Instead, I'm interested in unlocking Aphrodite's creation myth as a potential site of queerness for modern trans, nonbinary, and/or gender-nonconforming people to find ourselves reflected and affirmed in, which we deserve just as much as cis and straight people do.

Through a trans hermeneutics, we can (re)read Aphrodite's birth as paralleling the modern experience of gender transition. The removal of the male genitals, their transformation inside the sea, and the emergence of the goddess from the foam could be read as a metaphor for male-to-female gender affirmation surgery. A woman crafts a blade of her own body and, with some surgical help, frees herself.* Life flourishes. The myth can also be read as *any* transition from one gender to another, transitions which often involve removing, adding to, or transforming some part of one's form through surgery or hormone replacement therapy (HRT) or expressing one's identity through nonmedical means like changing one's name, pronouns, or gender expression through clothing, hairstyle, and makeup—Aphrodite's favorite sacred art of beauty and adornment.

Aphrodite is the goddess of beauty, after all, and what is beauty except what makes us *feel* beautiful, whether that's a glittered eyelid or a muscular chest, a plush belly or a butch haircut? The goddess is associated with beauty in the human form, in nature, and in art. If we pierce beyond the skin-deep formula of beauty as aesthetics, or what is pleasing to the eye, we can conceive of beauty as an *expression* of something spiritually true. When we make or encounter art that deeply affects us, it expresses or touches something that feels realer than reality. When we observe beauty in the natural world, in a sunset or a mountain pass or heat lightning on a summer night, it stirs

---

* I've always thought the detail that Gaia makes the sickle of flint from her own body to be significant, because although her son Kronos wields the weapon, the blade is of Gaia; it is her decision and her agency. She frees herself.

21

awe-inspiring feelings of the sublime. When we decorate our bodies and feel beautiful, it transcends the physical and reaches toward euphoria. When trans and genderqueer people can express our gender in ways that make us feel beautiful or sexy or, simply, *good*, we bring our embodied reality into closer harmony with our soul-felt truth. Beauty—not magazine beauty or normative gendered beauty, but *beauty*—is not merely aesthetic; it's divine.

The idea of transgender Aphrodite-Venus is not a new one: *Venus* has been the name of many drag queens, ballroom queens, and trans women, such as Venus Xtravaganza of *Paris Is Burning*, the 1990 documentary film on New York City ballroom culture. A 2017 photo spread in *ELLE Brasil* recreated Sandro Botticelli's famous painting *Birth of Venus* with transgender model Lea T standing in for the dewy fresh-born goddess on her half shell. But a gender-transcending Aphrodite has even deeper roots as well, ones that stretch back before the emergence of the goddess on the shore of Cyprus.

Aphrodite's Queer History of Gender Expansion

Like most deities, Aphrodite is a syncretism of preexisting goddesses. Her direct predecessors were the Phoenician Astarte, a goddess of love, sex, and war who had gender-nonconforming aspects in that she was a hunter and warrior, occupations not assigned to women in her culture. Astarte, in turn, was a descendent of Sumerian goddess of love, sex, and war Inanna, who had the power to change women to men and men to women and who was thought to have a masculine side and presentation as well as a feminine one. One of Inanna's hymns describes a parade in her worship where "women adorn their right side with men's clothing" and "men adorn their left side with women's clothing,"[33] a practice meant to help them embody the fullness of their goddess, who was both.[34] All three of these goddesses—Inanna, Astarte, and Aphrodite—were associated with the star we call Venus today and were known by the same epithet, "Queen of Heaven." The Virgin Mary is another "Queen of Heaven" who retains syncretized aspects of these goddesses to this day.

Aphrodite also has associations with the ancient Anatolian mother-goddess Kybele. Kybele was a goddess of power, fertility, nature, and wildness, who was depicted with predator animals and whose sacred place was Mount Ida. Aphrodite, too, is associated with Mount Ida, as in the "Homeric Hymn to Aphrodite," wherein she ascends Mount Ida accompanied by predators reminiscent of Kybele's own: "After her [Aphrodite] came grey wolves, fawning on her, and grim-eyed lions, and bears, and fleet leopards, ravenous for deer: and she was glad in her heart to see them, and put desire in their breasts, so that they all mated, two together, about the shadowy coombes."[35]

Kybele was a goddess who, like Aphrodite, Inanna, Astarte, and the whole gang, transgressed and transcended gender norms of her day. In some stories, Kybele was abandoned at birth, raised by wild animals, and became pregnant out of wedlock, positioning her well outside the accepted patriarchal establishment. In another, Kybele, under her closely associated Phrygian name Agdistis, was described as androgynous and intersex, having both female and male sexual characteristics. Kybele's/Agdistis's intersexuality was threatening to the other gods, so they tricked Kybele/Agdistis into accidentally castrating themself,[36] a cruel and tragic maneuver that may resonate with the injustice of sexual reassignment surgeries forced on intersex infants by the 20th- and 21st-century patriarchal medical establishment. Where Kybele's/Agdistis's severed genitals fell to Earth, an almond tree emerged and bore fruit, which was eaten by a nymph who then gave birth to the god Attis[37]—an interesting inversion of the sea-birth of Aphrodite from the castration of Ouranos.

The priesthoods of Kybele, Inanna, and Inanna's Akkadian equivalent, Ishtar, also included priestesses who transcended gender roles. The priestesses of Inanna and Ishtar, called *gala*, were assigned male at birth but performed traditionally feminine roles in singing and worship, assumed feminine dress and sometimes names, and additionally seem to have practiced homosexual intercourse (the Sumerian word *gala* itself was written using the cuneiform signs for *penis* and *anus*).[38] Kybele's priest/esses, the *galli*, adopted effeminate dress and mannerisms, participated in ecstatic dance, and some even castrated themselves in service to their goddess and her son-lover, Attis, who legendarily also castrated himself upon witnessing Kybele/Agdistis in their full divine splendor.[39] Much of the surviving information on the galli come from outside sources, particularly early Christian authors who were disturbed by the gender-transgressing pagan priest-hood, so we don't know how the galli thought of themselves, but contemporaneous writers referred to them as a *"medium genus* or a *tertium sexus*—representatives of a third gender."[40] Whether these priest/esses pursued their path based purely on religious devotion or because they felt an unlanguageable pull to live a different life than the one assigned to their sex at birth, we can never know. One can imagine it may have been some of both. What we do know for sure is that Kybele's priesthood in particular lasted into the days of Christian Rome, persisting even through their criminalization and persecution, so whatever it is that the galli felt, it must have been powerful indeed.

To return to the trans/cendent Aphrodite herself, our goddess of love and beauty has a documented queer history of her own. In her sanctuary at Amathous on Cyprus, Aphrodite was worshiped as a bi-gendered deity called Aphroditos. Images of Aphroditos show her/him/them as wearing feminine clothes, sporting a full facial beard, and carrying a phallic scepter.[41] Others depict the femme-presenting deity raising their skirts to reveal a penis. Elsewhere on Cyprus, the god/dess is represented by a herm, a boxy column topped with a head, a type of icon usually associated with strongly phallic, masculine deities.[42] Figures of nonbinary or androgynous priests of Aphrodite have also been found on the deity's most sacred island, and worshippers of Aphroditos were said to have practiced ritualized cross-dressing.[43] These aspects of Aphrodite-Aphroditos's worship may have been hold-overs from their ancestors Inanna, Ishtar, and Astarte, but they also might recall the circumstances of the goddess's birth. According to Hughes, "Some believed that the young goddess kept her father's castrated male sex organs within her." This gives her well-known epithet *Aphrodite Ourania* (the feminine form of *Ouranos*, her father's name), or "Heavenly Aphrodite," a potentially new meaning. Hughes additionally connects Aphrodite to a prehistoric Cyprian fertility deity who appears in figurines unearthed from archaeological digs on the island, curvy figurines with breasts, a vulvic triangle, a pregnant belly, and a long, erect phallus for a neck and head. Aphrodite-Aph-roditos could be a memory of this prehistoric bigendered deity, or, as Hughes notes, "simply an early recognition of the nonbinary nature of sex and desire."[44]

So what does Aphrodite have to teach us today? The goddess of love and her predecessors teach us that love, sex, gender, and life are *and have always been* so much wilder and queerer than our narrow modern categories allow. Born of bloody liberation and stinging salt, of love and fury and a blade's edge, she demonstrates the revolutionary and transformative power of choosing oneself. Far from the proper, demure paragon of femininity, as she would later become objectified, Aphrodite is a being of sensuality and orgiastic ritual, rutting animals and shifting genders. Her Orphic Hymn rejoices that she "like[s] the night-long revel" and "delight[s] in festivities;" her "joy is in the bed of love."[45] One of her bawdy epithets was *philommêdês*, "fond of genitals."[46] Her devotees are the virginal maiden and the sex worker, the sapphic poet and the transgender priest, dancing unashamed in ecstatic desire.* Draped in an ambrosial robe and wearing a flower crown, with fluttering eyelids and a thick facial beard, she shows us that beauty is whatever makes us feel pleasure, that gender is not a physical characteristic but a spiritual expression of the feeling of the soul. Aphrodite is our trans goddess of transition, our euphoric deity of gender expression's sacred beauty, and our virile mixtress of queer desire and unruly passion. She invites us into an embodied, transcendent, liberating love. A love wet with the foam of living. A love that creates the world and a love that transforms it.

QUEER DEVOTIONS

Queer Contemplations

- Define beauty. What makes something beautiful? Why?
- Where did you learn about standards of beauty? (Family, social media, magazines, school?)
- Are you beautiful? Write down all the ways that you are beautiful.

---

* Though its historicity is contested in modern scholarship, Aphrodite was known in the ancient world to have sacred prostitutes in many of her temples, where sex and pleasure were practiced in worship to her.

- Is the Divine beautiful? What does the Divine look like? How do you know?

- Where are you able to see the beauty of the Divine in nature, art, music, or other people?

Devotional Tool-Kit: Building an Altar

You don't *have* to build an altar, but it can be helpful and rewarding to have a dedicated spot for your queer devotions. When we think of the word *altar*, we might think of something stacked with drippy wax candles and arcane religious or ritual objects, but altars can be as elaborate or as simple as you please. An altar is simply a dedicated space for devotion.

To build your altar, all you need to do is choose a spot (a bookshelf, side table, corner of your dresser, windowsill, or wherever you have room), clear and clean it, and place images and objects on it that have sacred meaning to you. Leave small offerings every now and then—flowers collected on a walk, a bowl of water, incense, a pretty rock, a sweet snack. Clean your altar and spruce it up every so often so it doesn't get stale. Upkeeping your altar also shows the deity or spirits that you remember and respect them—no one likes to be forgotten! If you're working with a specific deity, you can find lists online with suggestions for what scents, colors, flowers, herbs, and offerings they like. That said, give yourself the freedom to get to know your deity and find out what they like yourself. If you're not feeling called to working with a specific deity, consider making an altar to the Queer Divine and fill it with whatever speaks to you of queerness, reaffirms or inspires your queer spirit, or makes you feel connected to the divine of your understanding.

For example, my altar to the Queen of Heaven (which includes Mary, Aphrodite-Venus, Astarte, and Inanna) holds a dry fountain of the Virgin Mary that I found at a thrift store, the basin of which is filled with smooth ocean stones and seashells that I've gathered on the coast while singing songs to the sea. Remember: Aphrodite was born from the sea-foam; also, Astarte was a protector of sailors and appeared as the figurehead on Phoenician ships, and Mary is associated with the sea in many places. I keep a silver goblet filled with fresh water and a few generous splashes of rose water constantly on the altar, refreshing it often, and I burn rose-sandalwood incense in offering. The rose is sacred to Aphrodite-Venus and Mary, and the rosette was a primary symbol of Inanna and Ishtar. I often leave fresh flowers for her that I've picked on walks, and sometimes I leave a shot glass of rosé champagne on her altar when I have something special to celebrate or thank her for. The altar also holds active prayer or spell candles, and my rosaries hang from a set of antlers on the wall nearby. It is standard in witchcraft and ceremonial magic traditions to have representations of the four classical elements of earth, air, fire, and water on the altar. Notice that my devotional objects do double duty as the elements: sea stones (earth), incense (air), candles (fire), and a goblet of water.

Over time, your altar will begin to feel like a sacred space, because it is. When we come to a spot regularly for devotion, prayer, ritual, or any spiritual pursuit, that space becomes special, even consecrated, by the spiritual energy we've invested there. The repetition can affect us on a cognitive and somatic level, too, so when we approach our altar space, we are automatically shifted into a state of spiritual awareness, reverence, or connection. Decorating your own altar can also be a powerful and healing way of rewiring harmful conditioning around what the Divine is, what They look like, and what are the "right" and "wrong" ways to worship. In setting up your altar, you are setting up a new space for your own, self-discovered and self-directed spirituality, a place where only you—and the Divine of your understanding—make the rules and you can nurture your intimate connection to Them in the ways that feel sacred to you.

Devotional Tool-Kit: Affirmations

Affirmations are positive statements that encourage, empower, and challenge yourself, magical statements of intention to help you focus your consciousness, build self-esteem, and achieve goals. But most importantly for our purposes, affirmations can help LGBTQIA2S+ folks rewire harmful internalized conditioning received from the cis-heterosexist world and replace it with self-love.

Affirmations are usually short statements focused on the self and worded in present tense; for example, "My beauty is an expression of the Divine," "I love the Divine by loving myself," or "When I trust myself, I am divinely guided." Today, try writing an affirmation for Aphrodite-style self-love, even and especially if it feels difficult. Put a hand over your heart and repeat your affirmation to yourself. How does it make you feel? It may bring up tender or difficult emotions at first, and that's normal. That's your affirmation dislodging all that negative conditioning you've internalized. Try to call up the feeling of love, or if that's too hard, the feeling of warmth, and let it radiate from your heart all over your body as you say the words. Take your time, and don't rush it. Eventually, it will get easier, until one day you may find that you believe the affirmation and don't need it anymore.

If you have an altar, place the affirmation on it and return daily to repeat this process—placing your hand over your heart, repeating the affirmation, feeling the love or warmth. If you don't have an altar, place your affirmation in a location where you'll see it frequently—on a mantle, a mirror, taped to the coffee pot, or set a photo of it as the background on your phone. Repeat your affirmation to yourself every time you see it for a week or for as long as you need.

Daily Practice: Tiny Acts of Self-Devotion

Self-love can be hard for some queer and trans folks, and so can feeling like our bodies are divine, especially the parts of our bodies that we struggle with. Building a love relationship with our bodies can feel overwhelming or even triggering, so it's best to start small. Here's a tiny, simple practice that has helped me in big ways from Eli Lawliet, whose business The Gender Doula offers support for individuals who are questioning, exploring, or transitioning genders. Every day, choose one part of your body and thank it for what it does for you. Thank your toes for helping you balance, or your eyelashes for keeping rain and debris from your eyes, or your butt for providing a cushion to sit on, or the freckle beside your mouth for being an attractive, decorative feature of your face. That's it. One bit of thanks a day. Over time, it can help build a relationship of loving awareness and appreciation for the body.

Recommended Reading

The Body Is Not an Apology by Sonya Renee Taylor is an essential book for unlearning body shame and understanding body shame's roots in white supremacy and fear of difference.

CHAPTER 3

Díonysos, Two-Shaped, Thrice-Born

Queer Liberation with the Ecstatic Goddexx of Drag

Dionysos arrives in a riot of purple and green. Ivy slithers over walls and grape clusters drip from fences. Springs of wine and milk spout from bare rock and honey leaks from trees. The bull-horned god of ecstasy and transformation is preceded by clashing symbols, piping flutes, and pounding drums while wild things howl from the sylvan shadows. He comes naked or draped in a leopard skin, ivy twined in his long, perfumed hair. He lifts his thyrsus, an erect fennel stalk twined with ivy, dripping sweet honey from its tip. His face is girlish and blushed with wine, then bearded, then horned. Now he's a lion; now he's a goat, now a bull.

In town, the women, these wives and daughters and mothers turned maenad, leave their chores to drape themselves in dappled fawnskins, then rush from their homes to greet the lord of the dance. Dancing in wild ecstasy and frenzied song, they shout his sacred cry "Euai!" above their raucous music. They run wild through the forests and mountainsides, hunting wild animals with their bare hands, nursing wolf cubs, twining snakes in their hair, leaping and rejoicing until they must sleep, limbs tangled together in the shadowed groves.

Myth is full of such miraculous tales of Dionysos, also called Bacchus. Similar descriptions can be found in Euripides's *The Bacchae*,

Ovid's *Metamorphoses*, the *Homeric Hymns, The Orphic Hymns*, on numerous vase paintings and engravings, and in many more places besides. Dionysos is the goat-headed, bull-horned god of transformation, the gender-blurring god of wine and release, the ivy-draped, resurrected god of lusty vitality and green, living things. He is a marginal, outsider god, always considered new even though he was very old, always considered foreign even in Greece where he was born. But he is also an embodied god. At the height of their frenzied ecstasy, his devotees would experience enthousiasmos. The god would come to them, enter them. He approaches from the fringes, from the outside, an intimate stranger. He was sometimes called "the god who comes." Dionysos is a god of contradictions: male and female, human and animal, frenzied and peaceful, native and foreign, sacred and profane.

In his own time, Dionysos was known as a gender-bender and rabble-rouser. He was the god of many names, among them *Eleutherius*, "the liberator"; *Liber*, "the free"; and *Lysios*, "the releaser" or "the loosener." Indeed, his wine releases mortals from their cares and his ecstatic dance loosens limbs and frees spirits. He is the loosener of chains; in myth, he repeatedly frees himself and his followers from shackles and jails. His all-female maenads carry the phallic thyrsus, get wine-drunk, shout and run and hunt—a radical reversal of the typical gender roles of the time. As Athanassakis and Wolkow note, "Insofar as he is a god of transitions, he 'loosens' the moorings that tie an individual to any particular fixity."[47] Dionysos dissolves boundaries and binaries, flips roles, subverts rules, and laughs at civilized propriety. He is bestial, vegetal, human, divine, male, female, monstrous, beautiful, marginal, changing.

In so many words, Dionysos is pretty damn queer.

Considering who we're talking about, it should be no surprise that Dionysos's origin myths are queer. The god was born at least two times, sometimes three. In Orphic myth, Dionysos is first born as the infant Zagreus, child of Zeus in the form of a snake and Persephone. When the infant Zagreus is kidnapped by Titans, who summarily rip him apart and eat him, Zeus manages to save the child's heart—all that is left of him. He makes the heart into a soup and feeds it to a mortal princess of Thebes, Semele, who then becomes pregnant with Dionysos. But when pregnant Semele asks Zeus to come to her in his full form so she may truly know him, she is incinerated by witnessing the god's full power. Essentially, Semele is struck by divine lightning and dies. At the last second, Zeus saves Dionysos from her womb and sews the premature god into his own thigh to finish gestating. When it's time, Zeus undoes the stitches and gives "birth" to Dionysos. Hence, Dionysos is "thrice-born," once by Persephone, once by Semele, and once by Zeus. Dionysos was born of two female wombs and a male womb—indeed, sources such as *The Bacchae* call it exactly that: "male womb."[48] The *Orphic Hymns* more than once call him the son of two mothers—a queer family indeed.*

Dionysos's upbringing is also plenty queer. Hunted from birth(s) by Zeus's jealous wife, Hera, who generally sought to destroy all her husband's mistresses and bastards, Zeus had to hide baby Dionysos away for safety. In one source, Dionysos is raised as a girl by his aunt Ino.[49] He is also said to have been cuddled and nursed by foreign Nymphs in Nysa, or by Aphrodite, or by Penelope, or by satyrs. Other sources have him protected in a cave by Kouretes, armed Cretan men who dance wildly to pounding cymbals and drums, or Korybantes, armed ecstatic dancers who worship Kybele—male analogues to Dionysos's maenads.

As an adult, Dionysos is said to have traveled to Phrygia, where he learned the rites of the earth goddess Kybele and "adopted her accoutrements,"[50] suggesting cross-dressing. A 1st-century C.E. poem mentions Dionysos wearing a golden dress.[51] In Euripides's *The Bacchae*, Dionysos puts Pentheus in drag. The god is frequently described as looking like a girl, and his favored form seems to be effeminate, even while he is ritually celebrated with phalloi—gigantic, decorated phalluses on sticks,** sometimes with wings.[52] In The *Orphic Hymns*, he is repeatedly called "two-natured" and "two-shaped," and once as having a "three-fold" nature. "Two-natured" likely refers to Dionysos's androgyny, his fluid embodiment of masculine and feminine

---

* Dionysos's parentage is also interesting considering with his attributes as a god of transition, transformation, and vegetation. Snakes are ancient symbols of fertility and transformation, and this is the form Zeus chose to first conceive Zagreus with Persephone. Persephone is the lady of springtime as well as the queen of the underworld, making her a liminal goddess, border-crosser, and goddess of death and rebirth. Semele, while a mortal woman in these myths, may have been a remnant of older Thracian and Slavic earth goddesses by similar names.

** My spouse just now said, "A dick on a stick is a dildo," and he's not wrong.

attributes, while "two-shaped" probably references the god's ability to morph into human, animal, or monstrous, combined forms.[53] "Three-natured" may refer to the god's three births or his embodiment of the human, the bestial, and the divine.[54]

A 21st-century audience may hear an echo of nonbinary, intersex, or the Indigenous American Two-Spirit gender in "two-natured" or "three-natured" Dionysos. While it's important to remember that our modern concepts of gender—including modern masculinity and femininity—did not exist in ancient Greece, transgender and gender-nonconforming (TGNC[*]) people today can absolutely feel affirmed and represented by the gender-blurring god of transformation.

He is, after all, the god of changing forms.

Of Shapes Transformed

Ovid's *Metamorphoses* (8 C.E.), one of antiquity's most influential mythological works, is a veritable compendium of transformations. In the nearly 12-thousand-line poem, Dionysos is a prowling magnetism haunting the margins. The god appears directly in some of the stories, but in many more he revels in the green shadows beyond the city walls, calling his maenads into the fringes, into the dance. In addition to his own shape-shifting,[**] he transforms humans into dolphins, bats, doves, and oak trees. Sometimes these transformations are acts of rescue and deliverance, and other times they're punishments. But even as punishments, his transformations tend to have a poetic appeal. And if transformation begets liberation, one wonders if they are truly punishments at all.

In one tale, when pirates attempt to abduct Dionysos, in disguise as a beautiful boy, suddenly the ship's masts are twined in vines and draped in grapes, the deck awash with wine and honey. As the pirates attempt to escape, the god transforms them into dolphins who dance and leap joyfully, the seamen now at one with the sea. In another

---

[*] TGNC includes Two-Spirit, nonbinary, agender, and genderfluid people and anyone whose gender is not fully aligned with their assigned sex at birth.

[**] Admittedly, shape-changing is not unusual to the Greek gods, who frequently took on animal forms, usually to perpetrate rape, as in Zeus's numerous cases, or to commit some other mischief against humans or one another. But Dionysos never uses his transformative powers for these purposes.

tale, when the daughters of Minyas refuse to join the maenadic celebrations, calling them "false rites" and choosing to stay inside and weave at their looms, they are changed as well. At dusk, that liminal hour that belongs to neither night nor day, their looms suddenly turn green, their weavings sprout leaves and tendrils, phantom beasts howl in the hallways, and the sisters transform into bats. Having refused the wild dance to stay indoors at their domestic chores, the bat-sisters now abhor the daylight and haunt the rafters of homes.

As a vegetation god, Dionysos represents the wild life-force that animates all living things. Denying him is denying our own lusty pulse of life, denying our animal natures, and severing the mind from the body. When the god is rejected, it is often on some pretense of purity or self-denial, as with the daughters of Minyas, or else military self-control and trumped-up ego. But Dionysos knows that ignoring the body is not purity; it's abstraction. Nothing in nature is "pure;" all is infinitely and intimately connected, contaminated, interdependent, enmeshed. Riddled with microbes, minerals, spores. Everything is always living and dying, dissolving and coagulating, all the time. In these tales of transformation, we might read a message that none can escape their animal natures, none can slip the green net of life. No matter how civilized we may think ourselves, no matter how smartly we enforce our will over nature, in the end the wild always wins.

In other tales, Dionysos transforms humans in order to save them from death or grant eternal life. Such is the case with Dionysos's young male satyr lover, Ampelos. When Ampelos died, Dionysos loved him so much that he turned him into the first grapevine—which, by the way, also places homosexual love at the literal roots of the god's sacred drink, wine. In another story, the daughters of Anius are about to be captured by enemy soldiers and cry out to Bacchus (Dionysos) for help. The poet Ovid tells us that the god delivers aid, "if destroying [the daughters], in a wondrous manner, be called giving aid,"[55] by transforming the beleaguered women into another form entirely. They "lost their shape," the poet tells us, and turn into doves.[56] Thanks to Dionysos's transformative intervention, the dove-daughters evade capture and fly to freedom.

As we have seen, transformations are often used as punishments by the gods, including by Dionysos. But Dionysos the Liberator—loosener of chains and social codes, genderqueer teratomorphic shape-shifter, lord of the wild catharsis of ecstatic surrender—knows the healing power of "losing" one's shape. His devotees, too, know the freedom of becoming "lost." They frolic on mountaintops in animal skins, shouting, dancing, fucking (one hopes), hunting, dissolving into the wild landscape like the animals they—and all of us—truly are. The daughters of Anius are devotees of Dionysos. After their avian transformation, they never resume human form again.

Perhaps, as birds, the dove-daughters are not lost to themselves and certainly not lost to the god. They are only lost to cold civilization, lost to the defining expectations of society, lost to the violent clutches of war-making men whose grip they have blessedly flown. It is not insignificant that they are turned into doves, the sacred bird of Aphrodite, the goddess of love, and an emblem of peace. Perhaps, in having "lost their form," these women were finally, truly, free.

Madness and Disorder

Dionysos brought madness. The topic of "madness," of so-called sanity and insanity, is tender and complex. It's a topic very close to my own heart as a person with C-PTSD and generalized anxiety disorder who has family members with schizophrenia. The pathologizing and stigmatizing of different ways of thinking, perceiving, and being that are not privileged by the norm has done so much harm. Diagnoses of "hysteria" allowed husbands and parents to lock up noncompliant women in psychiatric hospitals. People diagnosed with mental or physical "defectiveness" by 20th-century American eugenicists were compulsorily sterilized, an inherently white supremacist project that disproportionately targeted Black, Latino, and Indigenous Americans. Diagnoses of "gender identity disorder" that have enabled TGNC people to access gender-affirming care simultaneously gatekeep it, hiding it behind arcane requirements, years of expensive therapy appointments, mazes of red tape, and that we submit ourselves to being labeled "disordered."* Diagnoses of autism, ADHD, or PTSD can feel validating or freeing for some but stigmatizing or confining for others. Sometimes medications are overprescribed. Sometimes medications are necessary, life-saving, or welcome.

To talk about Dionysos, we have to talk about madness. The madness the god brought was usually, but not always, a gift. As the god of intoxication, ecstasy, and, yes, madness, Dionysos was a god of altered states of consciousness. Through dance, music, and drinking, his worshipers could enter trance states or receive prophetic visions. Scholars have noted that elements of Dionysos's religion may have come from Indo-European invaders, potentially carried from the far North where shamanism was practiced.[57] In myth, the maenads in their ecstasy would experience their surroundings differently—for instance, perceiving men as boars or lions. In his Mystery religions, initiates would work themselves into ecstatic states and experience enthousiasmos, wherein Dionysos would enter them or possess them, blurring the lines between human and divine.

Woodruff notes that the "paradox of losing one's mind in order to gain it is fundamental to Dionysiac religion, even though celebrants evidently do not use words for madness (mania) of themselves."[58] This is important. Dionysos's devotees did not call themselves mad, yet mad is the word applied to them again and again throughout the literature. Like *crazy* today, the "madness" of Dionysos's followers was a normative appellation, applied by those with privileged or normalized ways of thinking and being to those whose ways of thinking and being they did not understand. To the maenads and celebrants themselves, their ways were perfectly well and sound.

Perhaps it is as Dionysos says in *The Bacchae*, "Speak wisdom to a fool and he'll think you have no sense at all."[59]

In a 21st-century world, we might also find threads between the "madness" Dionysos represents and the perspectives and lived realities of marginalized groups today. In a mad world, the only sane thing to do is lose your mind. At the same time, it is important not

---

* In 2013, the fifth edition of *The Diagnostic and Statistical Manual of Mental Disorders* (DSM-5) dropped the name "gender identity disorder" and replaced it with "gender dysphoria." It also specified that gender dysphoria is not a mental disorder. And yet, it still must be diagnosed for TGNC individuals to receive care, and the manual still clearly states "Mental Disorders" in the title.

to romanticize madness. Being neurodivergent can be extremely difficult in a society that treats it as an aberration. For individuals who experience psychosis, it can be debilitating and even dangerous—not dangerous for others, but for the person experiencing psychosis, who is statistically far more likely to be the victim of violence than the perpetrator. But perhaps Dionysos can provide an example of how perceiving, thinking, behaving, or *being* different—being in a way that the norm calls "mad"—can also be divine.

Queen Pentheus and the God of Drag

Theater in the West began with Dionysos. At his festivals, revelers donned costumes and enacted performances of his myths in celebration of the god. In Athens, his festival was the premier theatre event of the year, called the City Dionysia.[60] The City Dionysia featured theater competitions, wine-soaked revels, and parades involving elaborate costumes and fabulous phalloi sent in from every province.[61] It was here that tragedy and comedy developed, as well as a campy third genre called the "satyr play," which seems to be mostly composed of bawdy dick jokes. Fitting for the lusty and shameless god of merriment who nonetheless knows suffering and pain (let's not forget the Titans). In the plays, actors always performed in masks, and the iconic tragedy and comedy masks of the theatre can be traced back to these festivals. The masks bore highly exaggerated features to be seen from afar and to communicate emotion, establish character, and create mood. A sky-high lifted brow, an amplified lip, an emphasized winged eyeliner.

In addition to drama and camp, Dionysos might be the father—or mother—of drag.

Perhaps the most famous and enduring play that arose from the City Dionysia is Euripides's *The Bacchae* (c. 405 B.C.E.) in which Dionysos acts as a drag mother, albeit not the kindliest one. Throughout the play, Dionysos is arguably in drag himself as a god appearing in a human form—human drag, if you will. Indeed, he announces himself in the first scene with a bombastic charisma worthy of a queen entering the dressing room of *RuPaul's Drag Race*:

Behold, God's Son is come unto this land

Of Thebes, even I, Dionysus, whom the brand

Of heaven's hot splendour lit to life . . .

So, changed in shape from God to man,

I walk. . . .[62]

Dionysos's return to Thebes is not a happy occasion, however. He has come home because he heard that his aunts (the sisters of his human mother, Semele) and his cousin Pentheus have been denying his divinity. In an ancient form of slut shaming, his aunts have been spreading lies that his mom Semele was *not* pregnant with Zeus's child but someone *else's* (gasp!), and that's why Zeus smote her with lightning, for lying that she was pregnant with the son of the king of the gods.* As for cousin Pentheus, the ultra-masculine, misogynistic, militaristic, and autocratic young king of Thebes, he's been capturing and imprisoning Dionysos's followers and threatening to make war on the maenads, also known as Bacchae (from Dionysos's other name, Bacchus). Understandably, Dionysos is pissed. He also knows he won't be welcomed home with open arms, so he takes the form of an effeminate young man, posing as a devotee of his own religion, and lets Pentheus's soldiers "capture" him.

When Pentheus first meets Dionysos in disguise, who we'll call "the foreigner," Pentheus's appraisal of the foreigner's pretty looks rings with an undeniable homoerotic appreciation:

Marry, a fair shape for a woman's eye,

Sir stranger! And thou seek'st no more, I ween!

Long curls, withal! That shows thou ne'er hast been

A wrestler!—down both cheeks so softly tossed

And winsome! And a white skin! It hath cost

---

* Remember: Semele was incinerated by Zeus's divine lightning when she asked the god to show himself to her in his true form—and no mortal can survive perceiving the full divinity of a god. According to myth, Zeus cared for Semele and did not want to do this, for he knew the cost, but he had promised to do anything she asked; therefore he could not refuse.

Thee pains, to please thy damsels with this white

And red of cheeks that never face the light![63]

Pentheus lingers on the way the foreigner's tossed curls caress his rosy cheeks, even while he mocks their length as inappropriate for the manly sport of wrestling—a move that hints at desire swiftly buried beneath machismo. While Pentheus seems to revile the maenads, he also desperately wants to know their secrets. He tries to extract information from the beautiful foreigner, who answers his questions plainly, if somewhat cryptically. Their meaning escapes Pentheus every time. Pentheus asks what the god looks like, and the foreigner replies, "Whatever way he wanted."[64] Pentheus orders him to summon the god, and the foreigner says, "He is where I am."[65]

Pentheus cannot understand the foreigner's answers nor recognize the disguised god's true divinity because he's caught in a rational, literalistic, linear way of thinking and perceiving—what queer theorist José Esteban Muñoz called "straight time."[66] Straight time is the myopic organizing vision of cis-heteronormativity that insists it is the only reality, the only valid past, present, or future that exists. Nothing else is real—not gender variance, not queer sexualities, not minority experience, not fringe historicity, not magic, and not, in this case, a god. Anything that challenges the illusion of straight time is not treated with curiosity or wonder, nor as tangible evidence that other temporalities do exist, but is instead declared fake, an aberration, an abomination, a problem to be locked away or exterminated like the maenads. Pentheus peppers the foreigner with questions, but none of the disguised god's answers fit into the king's straight world order, none are what he wants (or perhaps expects) to hear, so he learns nothing.

Pentheus gets frustrated by his own impotence and overcompensates with threats of violence. He threatens to chop off the foreigner's long, flowing hair (which honestly he seems obsessed with). By the end of their exchange, when Pentheus orders his soldiers to tie the foreigner up, Dionysos seems truly surprised, even horrified. Not at being imprisoned—that's no threat to the Liberator. Instead, the god seems disturbed by Pentheus's total lack of self-knowledge.

This is the moment that seals Pentheus's fate. Dionysos cries: "Thou knowest not what end thou seekest, nor / What deed thou doest, nor what man thou art."[67]

Later in the play, Pentheus decides to hike up the mountain to spy on the maenads—despite his revulsion to them, he's fascinated. With clever talking and charisma, Dionysos-as-foreigner convinces the king to disguise himself as one of the maenads because the wild women are known to turn violent when their sacred rites are violated by men. And so, in short order, Pentheus ends up in drag.

What ensues is a comic scene at Pentheus's expense, which plays on gendered tropes and cross-dressing taboos to fabricate its humor. The audience of 5th-century B.C.E. Athens was no doubt meant to laugh at this manly man primping about the stage in ladies' clothes. At the same time, there is a real tenderness to the scene as Dionysos arranges Pentheus's hair and clothes, and as Pentheus finally gets to experience a repressed side of himself for the first time. When he practices dancing like a maenad—dancing so hard he musses his hairdo—he releases his self-restraint and maybe even experiences a taste of unfettered joy. When he asks the foreigner if he's holding the thyrsus right, if his stance is appropriately feminine, he softens in more than just mannerism. Dionysos clucks over Pentheus's dress like a mother hen, draping the skirt correctly, moving pleats into place. "In the hollow of thy hand, I lay me," says Pentheus, "Deck me as thy wilt."[68] Dionysos tells him he looks just like his mother and aunts, dressed so. He tucks a stray curl into Pentheus's headband.

Finally, in full drag regalia, Pentheus is able to perceive Dionysos, slipping sideways out of straight time and into queer time:

Yon sun shines twofold in the sky,

Thebes twofold. . . .

And is it a Wild Bull this, that walks and waits

Before me? There are horns upon thy brow!

What art thou, man or beast? For surely now

The Bull is on thee!

Dionysos responds:

> He who erst was wrath,
>
> Goes with us now in gentleness. He hath
>
> Unsealed thine eyes to see what thou shouldst see.[69]

In letting go of his authoritarian superiority and performative hypermasculinity, in destabilizing his own identity and donning a different form, Pentheus is finally able to "see." Only once he's in drag can he perceive the divine man-woman, animal-vegetal, alive-dead, new-old, familiar-strange, two-natured, two-shaped, androgynously hybrid Dionysos. He sees double. Through the magical art of drag, Pentheus sees God.

But Dionysos is a god of tragedy as well as comedy, and the play does turn tragic. In the end, Pentheus climbs the mountain and finds the maenads, his mother and aunts among them, who have been "stung" into madness by the god for spreading lies about Semele. In their madness, his mother and aunts perceive Pentheus as a wild beast and, along with the other maenads, tear him limb from limb. Pentheus had vowed to slaughter the maenads, after all, so in a harsh turn of divine justice, it is the maenads who slaughter him. Once his mother realizes what she's done, she tries to put him back together again but cannot.

It is interesting to note, though, that before they tear him apart, the maenads perceive Pentheus as either a lion cub or a young bull, two familiar forms of Dionysos. Likewise, Pentheus's fate appears a grim analogue of Dionysos's own dismemberment as an infant by Titans. In appearance, in dress, in fate, Pentheus in drag is aligned with the god—equated with him, even. Maybe the god of enthousiasmos, the embodied god, is with Pentheus in the end.

If we consider the myth through a queer lens, through a doubled vision, another ending emerges. Pentheus's dismemberment becomes not a literal rending of flesh, but a symbolic disintegration of identity. As queer and trans people, many of us know too well that finding ourselves requires a pulling apart of our former identities, our former selves. To figure out who we truly are, we must take on the terrible task of dismembering our own image—the one we created for society, the mask we wore to gain acceptance into cis-heteronormativity or earn the false love called approval—and dig to find ourselves among the bloody wreckage. Sometimes it is our parent, parents, or families who rip us apart for being who we are. And it hurts. But they're not the ones who can put us back together. Only we can do that. Remember, transformation always requires one thing first: losing our former form.

Earlier in the play, as Dionysos escorts Pentheus up the mountain, the genderqueer god offers the king in drag—Queen Pentheus—what seems, to my ears, to be a promise, a blessing, and a benediction: "You are wonderful and terrible; wonders and terrors await you / where you go. You will win glory towering as high as heaven."[70] There's a key there in the word *terrors*.* Dionysos is the ecstatic god, the god of altered perception, the god of transformation. In his rites, votaries lose themselves to find themselves. A process that must have been wonderful and terrifying.

Dionysos, before putting Pentheus in drag, before walking with him up the mountain, speaks of his plans for Pentheus and says this: "Then he will know the son of Zeus, / Dionysos, and realize that he was born a god, bringing / terrors for initiation, and to the people, gentle grace."[71] Terrors for initiation.

In donning drag, in losing his form, in facing the terror of the destruction of his former identity, Pentheus was initiated.

She's a maenad now.

The Ever-Dying, Ever-Living God of Liberation

Throughout his mythology, Dionysos does not seem to desire total chaos; rather, he opposes the violence of rampant civilization and human domination over each other and over nature. A god of contradictions and paradox, his rites bestow the peace of non-dualistic thinking on his initiates. He's a god of frenzy but also of comfort.

---

* In the original Greek, the word translated as "wonderful and terrible" and "wonders and terrors" in the previous line is *deinos*, which can additionally mean "fearful," "awe," "powerful," "marvelous," and "strange." Henry George Liddell and Robert Scott, *A Greek-English Lexicon*, revised and augmented throughout by Sir Henry Stuart Jones with the assistance of Roderick McKenzie (Oxford: Clarendon Press, 1940). Perseus Digital Library, Tufts University, https://www.perseus.tufts.edu/hopper/text?doc=Perseus%3Atext%3A1999.04.0057%3Aentry%3Ddeino%2Fs1.

Through the liberatory "madness" of ecstatic frenzy, his followers experience the simultaneous beauty and brutality of their god and of life itself, and they reach a place of non-dualistic acceptance of mortality. This life is pleasure and pain, wine and blood, vine and claw. There are no city walls high enough to keep life out—or death.

Dionysos, a god of vegetation and life who conjures vines from looms and milk from rocks, was also a god of the underworld. This chthonic, meaning "underworld," dimension is not typically listed as one of his domains, but being born three times gives a god a certain ease with death. Dionysos was the ever-living, ever-dying god. According to Heraclitus, Dionysos and Hades, god of the underworld, were one and the same.[72] In Orphic cosmogony, Dionysos is correlated with Phanes, or Protogonos, the androgynous primeval deity who hatched from the cosmic egg at the beginning of creation.[73] Dionysos is birth and afterlife, genesis and apocalypse, creation and destruction, alpha and omega. Initiates into Dionysian and Orphic Mysteries were assured of rewards in the afterlife. In Italy and Greece, numerous tombs have been found of Bacchic initiates buried with small leaves of gold inscribed with directions for navigating the underworld and passwords to give various guardians to ensure safe passage.[74] One 4th-century B.C.E. Thessalian woman was buried with ivy-shaped gold tablets reading, "Tell Persephone that the Bakchic one himself set you free!"[75] In Olbia, Italy, a 5th-century B.C.E. bone tablet was found that reads, "life, death, life, truth."[76]

Chthonic Dionysos reveals a truth that extends to far more than the god himself, a truth at the center of his Mysteries as well as the Eleusinian Mysteries in which he also plays a role: the truth that life is death and death is life. When cities fall, the vines and moss reclaim the stones. When we die, our bodies feed the worms, the fungi, the carrion birds, the roots of trees. Life becomes death and then feeds new life.

Some scholars argue that the festivals and ecstatic rites of Dionysos only served to provide a temporary state-condoned release to the people, after which they would placidly return to ordered civic life. In other words, Dionysos's liberation was a false one, just another way to yoke the masses. To a certain extent, this is certainly true. As so often happens, when the state cannot expunge undesirable elements from the populace, it tries to warp them to its own use. This is corporate Pride and rainbow capitalism in a nutshell. Sell rainbow-drenched merchandise at the big-box store. Take the queers' dollars and donate them to anti-trans political candidates. If you can't beat 'em, use 'em.

There was a point, however, when Dionysos was certainly a threat to the state. Bacchic rites were severely repressed by the Roman senate in 186 B.C.E. Why else would they be restricted, if not perceived as a danger to an increasingly militarized, colonialist, and authoritarian way of life? In *The Flowering Wand*, Sophie Strand points out that two of the most organized revolts against the Roman Republic were led or influenced by Dionysian devotees. The famed escaped gladiator Spartacus, who led the slave uprising of the Third Servile War, was married to an unnamed prophetess who Plutarch reports to have had "visitations of the Dionysiac frenzy."[77] She escaped slavery with Spartacus and traveled with him, and her prophecies may have influenced tactical decision-making.

Another priestess, Paculla Annia, led a popular revival of Dionysian worship that expanded initiation to include young men—previously, only women were initiated—which was perceived as such a threat to the state that Rome tried to wipe the cult from existence with mass trials and executions.[78] When the Senate harshly repressed Bacchic cults in 186 B.C.E., it was based upon allegations of disruptive conduct and organized conspiracy against Rome,[79] as well as crimes including murder and sodomy.[80] Whether initiates actually carried out such acts is unknown (though I'm rooting for sodomy). But as Sarah Iles Johnston notes in her study of Mystery cults in *Ancient Religions*, "The note of wild abandon that such stories strike does reflect a genuine element of Dionysiac cult: Dionysus released worshippers from everyday concerns and limits."[81]

Dionysos was called the Liberator for a reason. As Strand writes, "Mythically, his arrivals signaled the inversion of social norms and the blooming of unfettered, uncivilized celebration, often conducted by society's underdogs.* This behavior isn't just fermented ecstasy.

---

* Dionysian worship was led by women, and initiates were traditionally exclusively women. In the case of Spartacus's wife, we can see the god was worshipped by enslaved people as well. In his mythology, everyone from every class and walk of life left their work to join the ecstatic rites.

This is spontaneous, unruly revolt."[82] In the Roman Empire's culture of increasingly severe masculine military colonialism, the effeminate Dionysos and his slippery, gender-subverting ecstatic rites were a serious threat to Rome's repressive, absolutist civic control. We might hear macho, militaristic King Pentheus's words here:

> "What madness," says Pentheus, "has confounded your minds, O ye warlike men, descendants of the Dragon*? Can brass knocked against brass prevail so much with you? And the pipe with the bending horn, and these magical delusions? And shall the yells of women, and madness produced by wine, and troops of effeminate *wretches*, and empty tambourines prevail over you, whom neither the warrior's sword nor the trumpet could affright. . . . ?"[83]

Knowing Pentheus's fate as we do, the answer to his question is a resounding yes. Perhaps sharing Pentheus's fears, Rome was more successful in their war against Dionysos. When the Republic could not control the green god and his followers, they were banned, hunted, annihilated. Kicked out of the city gates and back into the wilds.

But the joke's on Rome, of course, just like it was on Pentheus. The wilds are exactly where Dionysos is most powerful. Bury a vegetation god, and he'll simply grow anew.

Dionysos is one of the oldest Greek gods. His name appears in the Mycenean Linear B tablets (c. 1400 B.C.E.), suggesting that the god was already known to the Greeks in the Bronze Age. Who knows how old he really is, our queer shape-shifting god of the unruly vine? Strand connects the bull god Dionysos to the bull-headed Minotaur and, through him, to the sacred bulls that the Minoans worshipped as fertility deities. The bull could not be kept in the labyrinth, it seems, much less slayed. After the Senate executed Paculla Annia's followers and repressed Bacchic worship, it didn't take long for the god of the vine to send up new, green shoots in Jesus of Nazareth, the traveling magician who turned water to wine and famously said, "I am the vine."

Of course, Christianity soon became anti-Dionysian, no doubt influenced by the Roman Empire under which it grew. But even then, the ever-dying, ever-living god could not be killed. He can be spotted

---

* "Descendants of the Dragon" refers to the soldiers of Thebes. In legend, Pentheus's grandfather, Cadmus, slew a great snake or dragon and planted its teeth in the ground, from which men grew. These men then helped Cadmus found the city of Thebes.

in the Christian Devil, which the Catholic Church created specifically to demonize Dionysian wild gods of pagan Europe, assigning him qualities of Dionysos, his satyrs, and his closely related wild god Pan.* The green god of the vine can be found in the Green Man figures of Europe and in Arthurian Romance as Gawain's Green Knight. In the 20th and 21st centuries, we can spy his leafy face unfurling once more in the Horned God of Wicca and other reconstructionist pagan religions and witchcraft traditions. Every theater, stage, and drag show is his temple. He still has a festival, a two-week-long one that attracts tens of thousands of people to New Orleans, Louisiana: Mardi Gras, of course. Bacchus has his own parade—one of the biggest, if not *the* biggest—but the god of intoxication, masquerade, and ecstatic inhibition is undoubtedly the presiding god of Carnival, dancing behind every mask and in every phallus-beaded plastic necklace.

But let us not forget that Dionysos is not merely the god of the party. He is Liber, the free. He is Lysios, the releaser. He is Eleutherius, the Liberator, and liberation means so much more than having a good time. Dionysos's liberation starts inside each of us, in releasing our knots of self-denial and repression, in reconnecting us to the ecstasy of feeling, in introducing us to the euphoria of being ourselves, in "losing our form" so we may (re)birth our truest form into the light. And then his liberation spills outside of us, into our communities, into the natural world, into all our diverse interconnected systems of life, love, and care, because having tasted liberation for ourselves, we know we must strive toward that sweetness of mutual liberation for all. The God of Liberation is not a dusty old god of the past and certainly not a dead god, but an extremely relevant, necessary, and alive god for today. And even when we are not free; when we are persecuted, marginalized, disenfranchised, and oppressed; when liberation seems a distant dream, we must remember that the God of Liberation is enthousiasmos, inside of us.

We have always been here, and we always will. We will always live, and always die, and always grow and grow and grow anew.

---

* There is no centralized personification of all evil in the Bible, just many different demons and spirits, and the figures of Satan and Lucifer are never described with Dionysian qualities in scripture.

QUEER DEVOTIONS

Queer Contemplations

- Do you think the Divine is in everything—plants, animals, minerals, rivers? How about created objects like a car, couch, or tub of estrogen cream?

- How does many-shaped Dionysos queer the idea of a fixed, static deity? How does Dionysos break down the divides between human, animal/vegetable, Divine?

- What is sacred about the ecstatic frenzy of the maenads? How can releasing inhibitions bring you closer to experiencing the Divine?

- Dionysos shows us that we have to "lose" our forms before we can find ourselves. Why might that be the case? How can getting a little lost help us find our way?

Journaling Prompt: Rewilding Gender

What's your gender? Pause to write down the first thing that comes to mind before you keep reading.

Done? Read on.

You probably wrote down an identity term, like *male, female, masc, femme, nonbinary,* or *genderfluid,* right? If you wrote something else or if you didn't know how to answer, congrats! You're ahead of the class. Because now I want you to put that gender identity term out of your head. Forget you ever learned it and all the qualities and attributes it describes.

Now describe your gender without using identity terms. What does your gender feel like? Taste like? Smell like? Sound like? What does your gender move like?

Now describe your gender in terms of the natural world. If your gender was a tree, what would it be? How about an animal? A mineral? A weather pattern? Is it fuzzy, sleek, sharp,

48

breezy, slithering, iridescent, humid, cool? Don't confine yourself to just one thing or theme, and don't try to make it make sense. Write down everything that feels right.

When you're done, revisit your original answer. In light of this exploration, do you perceive your original answer in a new light? Do you think other people who wrote the same identity at the top of the page described their gender in the same exact wild ways as you did? How does this expand your ideas about what gender is and how it's experienced by others?

Activity: Sacred Drag

Drag wears many hats. It's a form of art and entertainment. It can be a mode of personal expression or a political statement. It can be stunning, glamorous, acrobatic, comedic, or just plain fun. And it can be performed by anyone, gay or straight, trans or cis. Drag can break down barriers between gender categories and reveal the constructed nature of gender, and it can help people expand their minds around the possibilities of gender expression, bodies, and beauty.

Drag can also be a form of devotion, whether you're the drag performer or you're in the audience. If you've never been to a drag show, find one in your community to attend if you can. If you can't, watch one of the many popular drag shows on TV. (*We're Here* on Max is a personal favorite—prepare to cry happy tears.) Then answer these questions:

How might drag function as a devotional act?

How can attending a drag show be like going to queer church?

How is drag a reflection of the Divine?

CHAPTER 4

Infinite Trans Dignity and the Nonbinary Image of God

The Pluri-Queer God of Genesis, the Gnostic Mother-Father, Intersex Adam, and the Alchemical Jesus Hermaphrodite

On April 8, 2024, the Vatican, under the direction of Pope Francis, released a 20-page declaration on the doctrine of *Dignitas Infinita*, "infinite dignity," which declares, "Every human person possesses an infinite dignity, inalienably grounded in his or her very being, which prevails in and beyond every circumstance, state, or situation the person may ever encounter."[84] Sounds great, right? In some ways, it is. The declaration aims to "show that this [dignity] is a universal truth that we are all called to recognize as a fundamental condition for our societies to be truly just, peaceful, healthy, and authentically human." Unfortunately, the otherwise progressive (for the Church) document doesn't stop there. It slumps back into well-trodden Catholic territory, naming abortion and (this is new) surrogacy among these "grave violations," and adding "gender theory" and "sex change" to the list.*

---

* The terms "gender theory" and "sex change" are tantamount to anti-trans dog whistles. "Gender theory" is commonly used alongside "gender ideology" by trans-antagonistic entities that seek to discredit nonnormative gender identities and enforce an essentialist sex/gender binary. "Sex change" is an outdated term for medical transition that enforces normative binary sex/gender by implying a "switch" from one binary sex to another and implicitly locating gender in binary sex.

Funny how "infinite dignity" stops at trans people. Seems rather finite to me.

This stance comes as no surprise from the Catholic Church, which has long refused to see the inherent dignity in queer and trans people, murdered us for centuries in its Inquisitions, and continues to have our blood on its hands through doctrines like this one that bolster transphobic legislation and fuel hate.

The declaration is filled with so much doublespeak and so many rhetorical backflips that it would be funny if it wasn't so dangerous to actual trans lives, not least the lives of trans kids growing up in Catholic households. The Vatican asserts that "dignity is not something granted to the person by others based on their gifts or qualities, such that it could be withdrawn,"[85] even while it seeks to withdraw it from trans people. It declares that dignity is not conditional while placing conditions on dignity. To be more precise, the doctrine does (in its view) grant human dignity to people who are trans, but that dignity lies in the trans individual's assigned sex at birth, not in the authentic truth of who they are and what kind of life they are called to lead.

I don't need the Vatican to grant me my trans dignity. I already have that, and it *is* infinite. In its effort to marginalize trans people to the edges of infinity, the Vatican actually handed us some quite useful theological lenses for establishing the infinite dignity and even the *divinity* of transness, and they're the very same ones the Church employs to oust us from the Garden: the *imago Dei*, the nature of creation, and the unconditional and "unmerited" love of God. Through readings of Genesis and early Christian texts and the writings of Christian mystics and a bishop, we'll reveal that sex and gender have never been binary; that trans, genderqueer, and gender-nonconforming people are made in the image of God; and maybe even that God is Trans.

The Pluri-Singular Androgynous Image of God

The theological concept of the *imago Dei*, or "image of God," comes from the book of Genesis: "God said, 'Let us make man in our image, after our likeness' . . . So God created man in his own image, in the image of God he created him; male and female he created them"

(Gen. 1:26–27). These two lines are trotted out time and again to justify the Church's stance on binary sex and heterosexuality as the will of God ("God made Adam and Eve, not Adam and Steve"). The verse appears to present an indisputable sex binary that is not only ordained by God but is in the *image* of God himself. But scratch those verses a little harder and all manner of queer potentials tumble out. Why the plural first person, "*our* image, after *our* likeness" [emphasis mine] in the first verse, followed by the switch to the singular he/his in the second? If God created man, meaning "humankind," male and female in his own image, does that mean God is *both male and female?*

In the original Hebrew, the name used for God in Genesis is *Elohim*, itself a plural form of the singular *eloh* (god). The text literally says that Adam, Eve, and the entirety of creation was formed not by *God* but by *Gods*. But it gets weirder. In *Queer Ancient Ways*, Zairong Xiang breaks down the ungrammatical (one might say *queer*) confusion of singulars and plurals in the first part of Genesis 1:26. In the original Hebrew, *elohim vaiyomer na'aseh* ("God said, 'Let us make'"), "the pluri-singular *elohim* enunciate(s) through a singular voice (*vaiyomer* ['said'] is third personal singular) a collective invitation: *na'aseh* (let us make)."[86] The English equivalent would be something like "They says, 'Let us make.'" Funny how the monotheistic establishment insists that plural *Elohim* can be used for a singular god, but a nonbinary person can't use the singular *they* as their personal pronoun. As Xiang points out, "The biblical text seems confusing only to a mind that is trained to strictly compartmentalize everything, even divine beings, and to dogmatically follow grammatical propriety. *Elohim* is/are pluri-singular."[87]

So perhaps the God of Genesis is not a singular and masculine mono-God after all, but a male/female, plural/singular, all-gendered Goddexs.* Not a He but a He/She/They/Ze. A Queer Divine.

There's a second account of the creation of humankind in Genesis that seems to contradict the first. In Genesis 2, instead of creating Adam and Eve concurrently, as in Genesis 1, God creates Adam (*'adam* is Hebrew for *man*, as in *mankind*) out of the earth (Hebrew:

---

*   As previously noted, *Goddexx* uses the letter *X* to connote queerness, gender neutrality, or gender inclusivity. Here, I swap one *X* for an *S* (*Goddexs*) to suggest the pluri-singular dimension of the Divine as both one and many simultaneously.

adama), and later creates Eve out of Adam's rib (Genesis 2:7, 21–25). This second account has been used to justify women's subjugation for millennia. Since Eve came second and was made from a piece of Adam to be his companion, or so the misogynist thinking goes, women are inherently inferior to men and are put on the earth to serve them. It's only *Adam*, the (presumed) male, who is made in the "image of God," and Eve is but a weak carbon copy. And a flawed one at that, seeing as she was tempted into eating the forbidden fruit, the so-called original sin that precipitated humanity's expulsion from the Garden of Eden and fall from Grace.

However, some early Christians found quite a different meaning in Genesis 1 and 2. In their view, Genesis was not a story of masculine supremacy and feminine inferiority, but of *androgyny* as the true, sacred original state of humanity. Quoting from Hippolytus's *Refutation of All Heresies* (3rd c. C.E.), historian of religion Elaine Pagels recounts an early Christian writing that, "having previously described the divine Source as a 'bisexual Power,' goes on to say that 'what came into being from that Power—that is, humanity, being one— is discovered to be two: a male-female being that bears the female within it.'"[88] In this view, if Eve was made from Adam, then Adam must not have been solely masculine, but feminine too. Adam, the prototypical human, was not a *man* at all, but androgynous. Likewise, returning to Genesis 1, if man and woman were created in God's image, then it follows that God must be masculine *and* feminine, Father and Mother.[89]

Taken separately or together, both Genesis accounts of the creation of humankind are pretty damn queer. The institutionalized church eventually denounced these beliefs as heresy (more on that later), but Christian theologians were still arguing about the original, "true" nature of humankind—androgynous versus binary—until the end of the Middle Ages. Medieval Christian art had a fondness for portraying Adam and Eve as joined at the waist, sharing the same pair of legs, with their torsos sprouting from their shared hips in a Y shape.[90] Sometimes art depicted the moment Eve was "born" out of Adam's side, placing Adam in the "feminine" role of giving birth while Eve emerges headfirst from a vulvic opening in Adam's side.[91] Christians weren't the only ones to read a fused, double-bodied androgyny in

Genesis. In a Jewish midrashic tradition from late antiquity (3rd to 7th c. C.E.), the androgynous Adam was interpreted as two-sexed, with two faces and two sets of genitals, one male and one female each, until God split Adam in two to create Eve.[92] The concept of a two-sexed original human is also found in Plato's *Symposium* (4th c. B.C.E.), in the Myth of the Androgyne made famous (at least among queers of a certain age) by the 2001 film *Hedwig and the Angry Inch*. In Plato's account, delivered through a speech by Aristophanes, humans were originally double, possessing two faces and two sets of arms, legs, and genitals. Some were male-female, some female-female, and some male-male. Zeus split them in half because they attempted to overthrow the gods, and that's why we humans have been searching for our "other half" ever since. Those who descend from male-female protohumans are heterosexual; those from female-female are lesbian, and those from male-male are gay.

It wasn't only pagan philosophers, fringe Christians, and rabbis who pondered a nonbinary origin of humanity. Some of the Church Fathers, so called because they established the doctrinal foundations of the Church, believed the pre-fall, idyllic state of humanity was either androgynous or sexless. Historian Leah DeVun traces this concept of the "primal androgyne" into mainstream Christianity in the writings of bishop and theologian Gregory of Nyssa (c. 335–395 C.E.). For Gregory, Adam and Eve were *both* androgynous in that they were absent of sexual differentiation, not necessarily both sexes as much as sex*less*. As DeVun explains, "Adam and Eve were angelic androgynes, a lost prototype of human nature that reflected God's purity and simplicity and transcended the need for bodily distinctions."[93] Only after their sin did their sexual differences "activate," making binary sex a state of the Fall. DeVun continues: "For Gregory of Nyssa, the most elevated state of humanity was the *absence* of binary sex. Sexual difference, as he viewed it, was not an inherent part of human nature. . . . Humans had existed before differentiated sex, and they would exist after it."[94] This is a far cry from the Vatican's current interpretation of binary sex as the *imago Dei* that should not be corrupted. According to Gregory, binary sex *is* the corruption.

Gregory of Nyssa may have been onto something in his condemnation of the binary. His vision of a human future beyond binary sex may sound remarkably prescient of modern slogans like "The future is trans" and "Gender is dead." However, Gregory was talking about anatomical sex, not gender per se. In his vision, Adam and Eve are pretty much Ken and Barbie dolls with smooth plastic mounds downstairs. Or, if not that, they are completely innocent of any knowledge of sexual difference, like children who feel no shame or reservation about genitals—their own or anyone else's—until they are taught to by adults. And it must be said, Gregory's vision of ideal humanity is the *opposite* of sex-positive.

But I hear something queer here nonetheless, some undercurrent of recognition that the sex binary (and the Western gender binary that is predicated upon it) is not an inherent or requisite part of humanity. In other words, sexual difference should not define us or dictate our lives, and to insist that it does is to fall from grace, to depart from the Garden. The biologically essentialist gender binary only divides us further from each other and from ourselves by forcing us behind immutable gender lines that are forbidden to cross. And perhaps, by relegating each of us—cis and trans and gender-nonconforming alike—into these compulsory roles, it also divides us from discovering our truest expression of the all-gendered, non-gendered "image of God." For some, that image will be feminine; for others, masculine; for others, nonbinary, genderfluid, agender, or genderqueer. Relegating the "image of God" to binary sex and binary gender not only does disservice to the people of His/Her/Their creation, but disservice to the indescribable, indefinable fullness of God His/Her/Themself.

Gnosticism and the Mother-Father God

In the Egyptian hills around the Nile River outside the town of Nag Hammadi in 1945, a group of brothers was digging for soft soil to fertilize their crops when they struck a large earthenware jar. Inside were thirteen leather-bound papyrus books containing 52 texts that had been buried for more than 1,500 years. The texts, Coptic translations of earlier Greek writings, composed a hidden library of sacred literature, including several books—that are not in the Bible—purporting to contain the teachings of Jesus.

The texts discovered outside Nag Hammadi, along with other early Christian texts also discovered in Egypt in the late 19th and 20th centuries, compose what is now known as the Gnostic scriptures. Condemned as "false" and "heretical" by the Church, Biblical scholars were initially suspicious of their legitimacy, assuming they must have been written well after the canonical gospels of Matthew, Mark, Luke, and John that form the backbone of the Christian New Testament. However, more recent scholarship has revealed that while the Nag Hammadi manuscripts were translations from 350 to 400 C.E., the texts they copied were originally written *around the same time* as the canonical gospels and the other books of the New Testament, between 50 and 175 C.E.[95] The gnostic Gospel of Mary Magdalene, for example, was written around the same time as the canonical Gospel of Luke, between 100 and 125 C.E.[96] The gnostic Gospel of Thomas may have been written as early as 50 C.E., twenty years after Jesus's death, potentially *predating* the earliest of the canonical gospels, Mark (c. 70 C.E.). Further, the fact that the Gnostic scriptures are copies, not originals, has no bearing on their legitimacy. No originals exist of *any* of the books or letters in the New Testament; as professor of Biblical literature and early Christianity Hal Taussig puts it, they're all "copies of copies of copies."[97]

The discovery of the Nag Hammadi and other Gnostic texts has raised new questions for Biblical scholars and many Christian believers. Questions including: Why are some early Christian writings considered "canonical" and legitimate and others "heretical" and false? Who made those decisions? Why were these texts banned and buried? And could the teachings of Jesus, and the Christian God revealed through those teachings, be much different than what we've been led to believe?

The landscape of early Christianity revealed through the Gnostic scriptures shows a plurality of Christian traditions and beliefs in the first three hundred years after Jesus's death. The term *Gnostic* does not connote one, unified group of people or ideas, but instead describes any of a multitude of diverse early Christian sects whose beliefs differed from those of the *Catholic*, meaning "universal," church.[98] One of the primary divides between Orthodox and Gnostic Christians was the structure of church leadership and the role of women. The Gnostics tended to value women and men equally in their communities and worship meetings. Unlike in the swiftly institutionalizing Orthodox Catholic Church, in Gnostic meetings women could speak, teach, and even lead. The Gnostic sects abhorred hierarchical leadership as well as orthodoxy, instead prizing communal leadership, heterodoxy, and gnosis—a Greek word meaning spiritual knowledge that comes from personal experience instead of dogma—the root of the word *Gnostic*. One group of Valentinian Gnostics drew lots to determine who would fill the role of priest, bishop, and prophet in that day's meeting, with all members, women and men alike, participating equally.[99] The system decentralized leadership, fostered equality, and ensured a diversity of viewpoints to resist orthodoxy. Naturally, the burgeoning leadership of the orthodox church did not approve.

By the 2nd century, the growing Catholic Church turned its attention to eradicating the competition. Bishops like Irenaeus and Hippolytus wrote massive and scathing volumes exclusively dedicated to renouncing the "heresies" of the Gnostics. (Ironically, in doing so, they preserved much of what they intended to erase.) In 367, the archbishop of Alexandria, Athanasius, sent out an Easter letter ordering Christians across Egypt to reject all heretical writings—anything other than the list of 27 scriptures Athanasius approved, which later became the books of the New Testament.[100] Thankfully, some believers disobeyed. The location of the Nag Hammadi discovery was near the sight of the monastery of St. Pachomius,[101] and it's possible that one or several monks there found the sacred knowledge contained in those 52 texts too precious to destroy, so tucked them safely in a jar and hid them underground.

But what exactly *is* heresy? Somewhat like the word *queer* means anyone who's not both straight and cis, *heresy* is any belief that diverges from officially condoned orthodox doctrine. As historian of religion Elaine Pagels puts it, "A heretic may be anyone whose outlook someone else dislikes or denounces."[102] In other words, a heretic is anyone the status quo says it is. But what did the orthodox Christians not like about the "heretical" Gnostics? What was so dangerous about their teachings?

To start, the Gnostics believed in a feminine aspect of God.

Drawing from Genesis 1, many Gnostics believed in a dyadic god that was both masculine and feminine or a god that was *beyond* gender and was neither masculine nor feminine.[103] In Pagels's study of Gnosticism, *The Gnostic Gospels*, she pulls from a variety of Gnostic sources to build a picture of a group of Christians who believed in something much more than "God the Father." She devotes an entire chapter to it, appropriately called "God the Father/God the Mother." In it, she recounts a group of sources that claimed to have secret teachings of Jesus passed down through James (Jesus's brother) and Mary Magdalene.[104] This group prayed to a Father *and* a Mother: "From Thee, Father, and through Thee, Mother, the two immortal names, Parents of the divine being, and thou, dweller in heaven, humanity, of the mighty name . . ."[105] In the 2nd century, Valentinus, one of the most influential Gnostic teachers, taught that God was beyond understanding but could be imagined as containing both masculine and feminine aspects; as Pagels explains, they are "the Ineffable, the Depth, the Primal Father," and "Grace, Silence, the Womb and 'Mother of All.'"[106] While these ideas still seem to exist very much within a gender binary, the presence of a Divine Being who is not one nor the other but *both* is queer indeed.

It gets more subversive: Marcus the magician (2nd c. C.E.), a prominent follower of Valentinus with his own following, taught that the holy sacrament of wine given in mass represented the Mother's blood, not Jesus's. And it gets queerer: In Marcus's mystical gnosis, he, a man, *becomes* the womb: "Marcus calls himself the '*womb* and *recipient* of Silence' (as she [the Mother] is of the Father)" (emphasis Pagels's).[107] As the womb, he receives Silence, associated with the Mother. There is a two-part gender inversion here: Marcus becomes the feminine womb that receives the Mother, shifting a man (Marcus) into the feminine, receiving role, and the Mother into a masculine, "inseminating" role. As if to underscore things, Pagels draws the parenthetical comparison that likens Marcus to the Mother and, by implication, the Mother (Silence) to the Father. The slipperiness of gender here is, well, *divine*.

Other Gnostics perceived the feminine aspect of God as part of the Holy Trinity. In the Apocryphon of John,* copies of which were found at Nag Hammadi and elsewhere, the apostle John has a vision during his grief after the Crucifixion, in which he perceives an entity with three forms. The entity says to him, "John, John, why are you doubting? Why are you afraid? Aren't you familiar with this figure? . . . I am with you always. I am [the Father], I am the Mother, I am the Child."[108] The standard ("official") version of the Trinity is the Father, the Son, and the Holy Spirit, usually considered an all-male trifecta. But here we have a Father, a Mother, and not a masculine Son but a neutral, agender, or androgynous *Child*. A triple deity who is masculine, feminine, and both/neither: a child, an entity of possibility not yet gendered or still forming, neither and both and something else entirely. Not only that, this tri-gendered entity that has appeared to John is none other than Jesus Christ himself—situating Jesus, at least in his post-Crucifixion spirit form, as masculine, feminine, and androgynous or neuter.

I cannot help but point out that the colors of the trans flag—light blue, pink, and white—represent boys (masculinity), girls (femininity), and those who are transitioning, have a neutral gender, or are intersex, respectively. I can feel the hate mail flowing as I write this, but there's a similarity. Jesus is all of these—masculine, feminine, neuter, *and transitioning*. When Jesus appears to John here, as well as to Mary Magdalene outside the tomb, it is after the resurrection but before Jesus has "ascended," placing him in a liminal, *transitional* state.

Later in the Apocryphon, the feminine aspect of God, called "Barbelo" in this and in texts of the same vein, appears to John. She "precedes everything" and is described in gender-expansive terms:

> the Mother-Father,
>
> the first Human,
>
> the holy Spirit,
>
> the triple male,

---

*   Also called the Secret Book of John or Secret Revelation of John.

the triple power,

the androgynous one with three names,

the aeon [eternal realm] among the invisible beings,

the first to come forth.[109]

So even the feminine aspect of God is not exclusively feminine, but also male and androgynous. Attempting to make sense of the genders in the Apocryphon and other gnostic texts is a glorious mind-fuck—at least if you try to force them into a gender *binary*. Though the language of the gnostic scriptures uses gendered terms and replicates a masculine/feminine polarity to an extent, it also persistently and perpetually *destabilizes* that same binary, queering and complicating it till any fixed gendered meanings we try to apply slide right off like Jesus's shroud in the tomb.

There's no way the "image of God" can be relegated to a bio-logically essentialist sex or gender binary. The "image of God" is masculine, feminine, androgynous, neuter, intersex, and, yes, *trans*.

The Jesus Hermaphrodite and Nonbinary Body of Christ

Alchemy is perhaps best known as the ancient precursor to chemistry that sought to transform base metals into silver and gold. But there was another side to alchemy—a philosophical and spiritual side—which instead of transmuting metals sought to transmute the human body and soul. Western alchemy began in Hellenistic Egypt and the Islamic world of Southwest Asia and North Africa, and in 12th-century Europe, it experienced a resurgence thanks to new translations of much older Greek and Arabic alchemical texts. In Europe, the alchemists gave the ancient natural philosophy a new Christian spin, one that sought to unify the human soul through an entity that came to be known as the "Jesus hermaphrodite."

Before we dive in, it's important to note that *hermaphrodite* is an archaic word for an idealized half-and-half fusion of the male and female into one body, a construct of myth, mysticism, and outdated medical theory rather than physical reality. When used to describe intersex people or trans people, the word is generally considered to be an offensive slur. Here, I use it in the historical sense to refer to the alchemical-theological construct that merged the alchemical hermaphrodite with Jesus Christ in the late Middle Ages and early Renaissance.

Alchemy was, at its foundations, a science of balance. Alchemists believed in the theory of the microcosm/macrocosm, or "as above, so below," which held that the divine order is carried through the entirety of creation. Therefore, discrete actions on the material plane can affect similar changes on the spiritual plane and vice versa, and the process of turning base metal to gold can mirror the process of purifying the human soul. For the alchemists, ideas of purity and perfection were rooted in the concept of balance. Gold was thought to be a perfect balance of its constituent elements; so, likewise, the perfected human soul would be a perfect balance of masculine and feminine.

Harkening back to Adam as the primal androgyne, the alchemists believed that the human body and soul before the fall had been a harmonious mixture of masculine and feminine, therefore the process of alchemy could potentially offer *salvation*: a return to the perfect, prelapsarian ("before the fall") human state. The chemical agent that enacted this transmutation in metals was called the "philosopher's stone." One of its other names was the "rebis," from an untranslatable Arabic alchemical term that some Latin-speaking alchemists translated as "res bina" or "two thing," which led some alchemists to interpret the philosopher's stone as a "hermaphrodite."[110] Artistic representations of the "alchemical hermaphrodite" showed a bi-form figure with two heads or faces on one body that was female on one half and male on the other, or a Y-shaped figure joined at the waist in a similar manner to images of Adam and Eve from the same period, suggesting a connection between alchemy and divine creation. Containing a perfect harmony of masculine and feminine elements, the philosopher's stone possessed the ability to transmute other objects into this perfect—and essentially nonbinary—harmony.

It was only a matter of time before the philosopher's stone gained a theological dimension. By the 14th century, alchemist-theologians began to associate the alchemical hermaphrodite with Jesus Christ.[111] It makes a certain sense: Christ was deeply intwined with both transmutation and nonbinarism, after all. In the New Testament, Jesus is frequently the agent of transformation. He transforms water to wine, multiplies loaves and fishes, and heals the sick, transforming their bodies from ill to well. He is the agent and substance of the transubstantiation of the Eucharist: his body and blood become bread and wine, the wine and bread become his blood and body. Through the transformation of his death, he transmutes the sinner's soul from damned to saved. The resurrection is a transformation from death to eternal life, from body to spirit. Christ is deeply nonbinary as well, both fully human and fully divine. Fully imperfect and fully perfect. Immaculately conceived by no heterosexual act and born exclusively of the Virgin Mary, Jesus must be entirely female in his genetic makeup (XX chromosomes), and yet he is a man.

As DeVun explains, "Like Christ, the philosopher's stone was a combination of nature and divinity, of corporeality and incorporeality, of opposites united in one subject. Moreover, such alchemical 'mixtures' resulted not in impurity nor corruption but in . . . marvelous unities of high and low, spirit and flesh, heaven and earth."[112] Unlike earlier ideologies of the primal androgyne, the "alchemical hermaphrodite" was not purely spiritual but both earthly *and* spiritual. Likewise, the alchemical hermaphrodite was not un-sexed by its androgyny, but hypersexed.[113] One of alchemy's goals was not only the transformation of base metals into precious ones, but the *multiplication* of metals, i.e., growing or reproducing them. Therefore, the philosopher's stone also held associations with reproduction, both sexual and asexual.[114]

Eventually, these ideas coalesced in the "Jesus hermaphrodite." DeVun writes about an early-15th-century German text called *The Book of the Holy Trinity*, which developed the image of the "Jesus-Mary hermaphrodite." Like a reversed image of the much earlier gnostic idea that Adam held Eve inside of him before she was "born," the unknown author of *Holy Trinity* operated under the premise that Jesus held his mother, the Virgin Mary, within him.[115] The author states that "God was and is eternally his own mother and his own father, human and divine, his divinity and his humanity intermingled within. And he depends on that which he wishes to be hidden most of all within himself, the divine and the human, the feminine and the masculine."[116] The author extends this into the figure of Jesus-Mary, claiming that the two cannot and should not be separated, as Mary composes the part of Jesus that is his humanity.[117] As DeVun explains, "According to this view, Christ is the ultimate nonbinary figure, a unity of contrary parts—the human and the divine, the male and the female."[118] Here, the term *nonbinary* is not meant to signify the modern gender identity of being neither totally masculine nor totally feminine, but instead to describe a body that cannot be categorized into one binary sex, which may strike chords for some intersex, trans, nonbinary, or gender-nonconforming people. The author of *Holy Trinity* goes on to describe the Jesus-Mary figure in the language of the masculine-feminine, sun-moon philosopher's stone, explicitly linking the nonbinary Christ with the alchemical hermaphrodite, both of which are central to material as well as spiritual transformation, after all.

Nonbinary Christ was not only a product of the alchemical imagination. The (seemingly) masculine Christ was frequently depicted as feminine or as performing feminine acts in medieval texts. The writings of Cistercian monks showed a penchant for describing God and Christ—as well as abbots and other male church leaders—in feminine terms.[119] In his letters, Bernard of Clairvaux often described himself as a mother and as metaphorically nursing the monks in his care with his metaphorical breasts. He ascribed breasts and nursing to God and Christ as well, such as in one letter where he wrote, "If you feel the stings of temptation . . . suck not so much the wounds as the breasts of the Crucified. . . . He will be your mother, and you will be his son."[120] Here, Bernard refers to a second feminine attribute of Christ: his side wound.

The fifth holy wound of Christ (in addition to the four nail holes), the side wound was inflicted by the lance of the Roman soldier Longinus, who pierced Jesus's side to ensure he was dead after the Crucifixion. In the Middle Ages, the five holy wounds became the subject of "affective devotion," a contemplative practice wherein Christians would reflect on the Passion of Christ and attempt to feel his suffering, often with the help of visual aids that focused on his wounds. The bleeding side wound was frequently pictured up close and turned on a vertical axis, making it strongly resemble a vulva. This resemblance is not the product of a dirty modern mind either. As Sophie Sexon shows in her article "Gender-Queering Christ's Wounds," the side wound was illustrated on rolls of parchment or vellum meant to be worn around the belly during childbirth to aid the process and protect mother and child, aligning Christ's suffering with the pain of childbirth and the side wound of Christ with the birthing woman's body.[121] Images of Christ's side wound were also thought to ease pain and issues associated with menstruation.[122] As devotional aids, images of the vulvic side wound were often touched with the fingers, rubbed, or kissed, adding a potentially erotic edge to private devotions.[123]

Bernard of Clairvaux's somewhat-gory allusion to suckling on Christ's wounds is far from an anomaly. Caroline Walker Bynum traces nursing at the side wound and/or breasts of Christ to the writings of a number of medieval monks, including Aelred of Rievaulx, who refers to nursing on the milk from Christ's side wound.[124] According to the Gospel of John, when Jesus's side was pierced, it bled both blood and water (John 19:34). For Aelred, these transmute to wine and milk: "The blood is changed into wine to gladden you, the water into milk nourish you." Aelred writes of entering the body of Christ through his wounds, "In which, like a dove, you may hide while you kiss them one by one. Your lips, stained with his blood, will become like a scarlet ribbon and your word sweet."[125] Aside from reading like a scene from an Anne Rice novel that I most certainly would have dog-eared, the mixture of sacred nourishment and mystic eroticism in this passage makes clear the visceral reverence the side wound of Christ commanded in the medieval mind.

According to Bynum, writers such as Aelred and abbess St. Hildegard of Bingen imagined "that the soul enters Christ's side, nurses from it as if from a breast, and is born from it as from a womb."[126] DeVun references an illumination from a 13th-century Bible that shows Christ on the cross giving birth to the Church in the form of a woman through his side wound in the same manner of Adam and Eve.[127] Feminine in its ability to be penetrated and entered, maternal in its flow of milk and ability to give birth, and associated with the vulva in the iconography and use of devotional images, Christ's side wound transfigures his otherwise masculine body into a nonbinary body that cannot be legibly defined as masculine or feminine, male or female.

Speculative Thinking About Bodies

In the 9th century, Irish philosopher and theologian John Scottus Eriugena wrote about a misogynistic version of the primal androgyne in which Adam was originally androgynous and Eve was made for him to satisfy his lusts. Like Gregory of Nyssa, John's view was wholly sex-negative, viewing not only binary sex but sexuality as part of the "fallen" state of humanity. According to John, sexual reproduction was not a necessary, and certainly not a sacred (as "Infinite Dignity" would have it), human act.[128]

For the 21st-century reader steeped in Church teachings about sacrosanct binary sex and the "miracle" of cis-heterosexual intercourse (as long as it's for procreation, not recreation), these theories of the "primal androgyne" are surprising and problematic. While releasing heterosexual intercourse from godliness might counteract compulsory heterosexuality (and even feel affirming for some asexual folks), positioning sexuality as part of the fall makes all sexuality sinful. While an androgynous version of creation might make room for some nonbinary and intersex people in the "image of God" in theory, in practice actual intersex people have been marginalized, treated as aberrations or medical oddities, subjected to surgeries, and/or divorced when their nonnormative sex characteristics were "discovered." Although theologians speculated on androgyny as humankind's true spiritual state, binary gender roles were nonetheless rigidly enforced. In fact, transgression of gender roles was so egregious, especially during sex, that the medieval meaning of "sodomy" was not anal intercourse, as it is today, nor even same-sex intercourse, but any inversion of gender roles during sex. If women took the active, "masculine" role during sex, even heterosexual sex, that was "sodomy." If men took the passive, "feminine" role, whether penetrated or not, that was "sodomy."[129]

So the theology and philosophy of sacred androgyny did not elevate the actual, living people who blurred the lines of binary sex and gender to any state of privilege or acceptance in the Christian world. As DeVun shows in *The Shape of Sex*, thinking around the primal androgyne and hermaphrodites vacillated between idealization and condemnation at various times from antiquity to the Renaissance, with plenty of Church Fathers and theologians vehemently renouncing theories of primal androgyny to preference binary sex, the heterosexual family unit, and the inferiority of women. At the same time, DeVun notes, "Speculative thinking about bodies and the ways in which those bodies are genuinely experienced cannot be entirely separated."[130] The centuries-long discourse around binary and nonbinary sex has indelibly shaped the lives and bodies of actual people.

We can observe this in history and in action today. Deifying binary sex erases intersex people from "natural" creation, which in turn leads to involuntary surgeries to "correct" perfectly healthy bodies. Transphobic doctrines like "Infinite Dignity" inform ideas about "right" and "wrong" bodies and genders, further complicating the experience of embodiment for trans Catholics and providing ammunition for anti-trans legislation to prevent trans youths and adults from accessing gender-affirming medical care. In preventing us from shaping our bodies, it shapes our bodies against our will.

Even though figures like the primal androgyne and Jesus hermaphrodite do not offer exact corollaries to the bodies and lived experiences of transgender, nonbinary, gender-nonconforming, or intersex people, these historical Christian ideas about sex and gender can provide a much-needed check to the totalizing immutability of the sex/gender binary presented by Christian institutions today. As DeVun writes, "Our sense of what qualifies as an acceptable human subject, a natural human body, or a proper human desire has much to do with the ways in which prior theorists solved problems of sex and gender over the centuries. Perhaps our task, then, is to let the past intrude, to be attentive to its iterations, and to keep the future open."[131]

The Infinitely Dignified Transgender Image of God

In the declaration on "Infinite Dignity," the paragraph titled "Sex Change" states:

> The dignity of the body cannot be considered inferior to that of the person as such. The Catechism of the Catholic Church expressly invites us to recognize that 'the human body shares in the dignity of "the image of God."' Such a truth deserves to be remembered, especially when it comes to sex change, for humans are inseparably composed of both body and soul. . . . Constituting the person's being, the soul and the body both participate in the dignity that characterizes every human.[132]

Confusingly, the paragraph ends with an allowance for "corrective" surgeries in cases of "genital abnormalities," by which they mean intersex bodies. So bodies born legibly male or female are "the image of God," but people with intersex variations are not? Just who gets to decide when the body is "dignified" as it is or requires corrective surgeries? The declaration specifically attacks medical and surgical transition, saying that changing our bodies is "to make oneself God," but the Vatican does not have this reservation about playing God with the bodies of intersex people, who are frequently subjected to nonconsensual surgeries to assign a binary sex in infancy.

Abortion is also included under the "grave violations" of human dignity, perhaps suggesting a theme: body autonomy. When a person has the power to choose what they do with their own body, that's a "grave violation" of the body's dignity, according to the Vatican. Somehow the body's dignity is only intact when its autonomy is taken away.

Turns out the "infinite" dignity of the body is finite.

Trans people, more than most, have an intimate knowledge of bodies and souls. It's common to hear trans people describe their experience as being "born in the wrong body." For other trans people, the "wrongness" doesn't lie with the body, but with the compulsory cultural roles and meanings that society inscribes on the body according to assumed sex. When we make efforts to align our bodies with our souls via clothing, hormones, or surgery, we are not "disguising" ourselves, but *revealing* our authentic truth, making visible a projection of our soul. Transition is not an escape from the body, but a self-loving effort to *embody* it. Transition is not refusing the body, but *choosing* it, not violating the body but *dignifying* it by loving it enough to transform. Through this lens, transition can be perceived as the pursuit of unifying the body and soul—the goal of the alchemists. Transition, like alchemy, is the chemical and spiritual science of transmuting the body and soul into harmonious balance.

In her essay "The Authentic Lives of Transgender Saints," M. W. Bychowski coins the term *imago transvesti*, "transvestite image," to give a name to the legitimate and authentic transgender reflection of the *imago Dei*.[133] Bychowski purposefully uses the out-of-date term *transvestite* in reference to sexologist Magnus Hirschfeld's groundbreaking 1910 book, *Die Transvestiten* (*The Transvestites*), in which he examines the lives of so-called medieval transvestite saints (they exist!) to establish a deep history for trans existence—which, then (as it is now), was erroneously considered "new." Drawing on Hirschfeld's observation of cross-dressing as "an unconscious projection of the soul" and the life of "transvestite" St. Marinos the Monk, Bychowski establishes that to transition, or to live in a way that aligns with one's gender identity, is to live an authentic life in alignment with one's soul. She writes that this is a saintly act because it strives for authenticity despite risk and sacrifice, and because it inspires others to live in authenticity—both established features of the lives of saints. Bychowski cites Augustine's 5th-century *On the Trinity*, in which he argues that "the image of God" begins as a seed. Building on his foundation, Bychowski writes, "The process of constructing the self authentically, then, can be a co-creative act of affirming the *imago Dei*. Initially present only as a seed, this *imago Dei* is revealed as each person affirms the internal logic of their creation" through social or medical transition, "marking the living out of authentic truths, trans *imago Dei*."[134]

Christian writings reveal that the sex and gender binary are not nearly as biblical as the church would have us believe. Bychowski draws on the concept of the *imagines mundi*, or "images of the world," to "critically name the socially assigned images of the self which contrast with those made by God."[135] If anything, the "images of the world" are the sex and gender binary, the former of which is proven a lie by God's own creation of nature in its prolific and queer sexual variety, and the latter of which is a modern social construct that did not solidify into its current binary state until the last few centuries, and then as an arm of white supremacy and colonization. Gregory of Nyssa wrote of binary sex as a corruption, and the sex/gender binary *is* a construction of the cis-heteronormative white supremacist capitalist colonialist patriarchy. Not the *imago Dei* at all, but the *imago mundi*.

What if there is nothing "wrong" with us as trans people? What if we were born not only into these bodies, but into these *experiences*? The Church acknowledges that the "image of God" isn't just a material, physical, corporeal image, but also an emotional, experiential, spiritual one. If God wills us into being exactly as we are with unconditional and unmerited love, then that must, of necessity, include our transness, our gender-variance, our gayness, our queerness. If every person exists because they are "willed, created, and loved by God," to use the Vatican's phrase, then God willed and created us as trans and loves us for it.

In a class on transcestors (trans ancestors) led by Eli Lawliet and Isazela "Zel" Amanzi over a live video call in 2023, Zel said something that irrevocably changed the way I relate to my body and my transness. Zel said that they were "born into a body meant to be an altar to transition."[136] In that simple statement, Zel articulated something I'd been feeling but unable to put into language, something about transness not as aberration, not as being born *wrong*, but as being born into a body *meant to transition* by divine design. Born into a body meant to transform, a body meant to be Trans. This is Trans not as a state that needs correcting, but as a living altar to fluidity, to plurality, to liminality, to transformation.

We've lived for so long in a paradigm of trans experience defined by being born wrong, treated as a tragedy, an oddity, a mistake. But we are not mistakes. It's time to shift that perspective from transness as cosmic joke to transness as cosmic gift, one that introduces us in no uncertain terms to the substance of our souls and the authenticity of our truth, no matter what religious or secular institutions think about it. Trans is a beautiful and worthy—and *dignified*—state in and of itself, no qualifications or quantifications (or pontifications) needed.

Our dignity *is* infinite, and it cannot be taken away by doctrine or legislation, no matter how hard they try.

I'm not trans as a transitive state, but a permanent one. I'm Trans as the journey and the destination. Trans as unifying body with soul every day. Trans not as *imagines mundi*, not as construction even if gender is a construct and my body is constructed by a surgeon's knife. Trans not on accident, but by the blessing of God. Trans as holographic. Trans as immanent. Trans as destiny. Trans as worship. Trans as androgynous Adam birthing Eve from their side. Trans as Christ the Mother-Father-Mary-Jesus-God-Human-Child. Trans as pluri-singular Goddexs molding a body out of the all-gendered, no-gendered primordial clay and calling it "good." Trans as created by God, in Their image. Trans as the image of God.

QUEER DEVOTIONS

Queer Contemplations

- What if "God" or the Divine of your understanding made trans people on purpose, as one expression of Their divine image? If you identify as trans or include yourself under the trans umbrella (as many nonbinary and gender-nonconforming people do), spend some time considering how your unique experience as a trans person might have a spiritual dimension or be a sacred experience.

- Imagine the Divine looking like you. How does that feel? How would it have changed your experience of religion or spirituality growing up if "God," or whatever name They went by where you lived, looked like you? What does reflecting on your own image reveal to you about the *imago dei*, the image of God?

- Do you believe, as many Gnostics did, that God or the Divine of your understanding has both masculine and feminine qualities? Does God have a gender?

- What is heresy? Is heresy an affront to the Divine, or to human institutions?
- How does living in accordance with your authentic inner truth bring you closer to the Divine?

Devotional Tool-Kit: Prayer

Prayer is a tricky topic for some of us, especially those who grew up in organized religion and left it. The way I was taught to pray was the exact same way I was taught to recite the Pledge of Allegiance. "I pledge allegiance to the flag" had the same emotional weight and resonance as "Our Father, Who art in heaven." Which is to say: none. Both had the same function as well, enforcing a mechanical, uncritical allegiance that I didn't actually feel.

Prayers can be powerful, but especially if we understand what we're saying and *mean* it. For this reason, I think the most powerful prayers are the ones you write on your own, though there is certainly power in traditional prayers that are recited by leagues of people every day. Prayer can seem intimidating, but it's really just talking to the Divine. I recommend starting by saying hi and introducing yourself, as ridiculous as that may seem, and then just talking to the deity about whatever's on your heart and mind. You can give thanks for things (that's just good manners), and you can ask for things. I don't think the main purpose of prayer is to flatter the deity or ask for what you want, however. Instead, I believe the main purpose of prayer is simply to connect with the Divine, even just for a few minutes a day. You can pray freestyle, write your own prayers, recite poems as prayers, sing songs as prayers, move your body in dance as a prayer, or "pray with your feet" in acts of service or activism. If you're working with the Greek pantheon, *The Orphic Hymns* are an essential source for prayers that real people used thousands of years ago, and you can also tweak and adjust them to better reflect your needs.

For those who are open to a little creative heresy, you can rewrite the institutional prayers you grew up with to be queer and/or more aligned with your true spiritual beliefs. This can be a powerful way to counteract negative associations with prayer by subverting the prayers that made you feel that way in the first place. It can also be its own act of devotion: In rewriting and *queering* these prayers, we reclaim spiritual space for our queer selves and for the Queer Divine. It has taken me a long time to rehabilitate my relationship to prayer—to feel safe and loved instead of judged when praying—but today one of my most beloved practices is praying a queered version of the rosary, though in a decidedly un-Christian context. For my own queered rewrite of the rosary prayers, see Appendix 1.

Don't put pressure on yourself to feel anything particular or have a spiritual experience every time you pray. I think of prayer as opening a door in my head and heart. Sometimes I feel the Divine meet me at the threshold, and sometimes I don't—but it's a lot easier if the door is open.

Ritual: Releasing Internalized Homophobia, Transphobia, and Queerphobia

For this ritual, you'll need a candle, a firesafe bowl, and a pen and paper. You'll be burning slips of paper in the flame, so make sure you have water or a fire extinguisher handy and that you're not near flammable objects. In a safe, private space, sit with the candle in front of you and light it. Watch the flame. Take several slow, deep breaths, and clear your mind. Feel where your body contacts the chair or the floor, the earth hugging you toward it with its gravity, and imagine yourself as physically connected to the earth through your feet or seat. Know you're safe and supported.

Now, gazing at the flame, ask yourself, "How do I feel about my queerness?" "How have people made me feel about my queerness?" "How have religious institutions made me feel about my queerness?" Write all the negative messaging you've received about yourself and your queerness down on slips of paper. If you're feeling anger, sadness, shame, rage, or other difficult emotions, let yourself feel them and flow through you into the earth, which sucks them up and filters them out.

Then, one by one, safely burn each slip of paper in the candle flame. (Drop the burning paper into the firesafe bowl before it burns your fingers.) As you do this, push all those negative messages, thoughts, and feelings about yourself into the flame, because none of them belong to you. None of them came from you. Push them into the very heart of the flame and let the fire burn them away. When you're done, imagine the flame glowing brighter, burning higher. Let its warmth spread throughout your body, starting in your chest and radiating through your limbs. Know you are divine and divinely loved. Thank the Divine for making you exactly as you are. Extinguish the flame.

The ritual is complete. Dispose of the ashes outside your home or flush them down the toilet.

 CHAPTER 5

The Queer Devotion of Joan of Arc

Cross-Dressing, Class Warfare, and Trans Sainthood

For a while in elementary and middle school, my fellow students and I were tasked to read a biography and write a book report every year. While my peers read biographies on American presidents, famous scientists, and star athletes, I was only interested in two subjects: the Salem witch trials and Joan of Arc. It seems an odd pair: one a pious Catholic saint and the others alleged devil-worshippers. Maybe I was interested in the witchcraft angle; Joan was accused of witchcraft, though not convicted of it. Maybe I was attracted to stories of defiant women and girls persecuted by religious patriarchal authority. Maybe I sensed something in their contrary spirits that sung to something in mine. Or maybe I was projecting. Whatever the case, I read a different book on Joan or the witch trials every year, alternating subjects so my teachers wouldn't catch wind. My plot wasn't to cut corners or turn in repeat book reports, but genuinely because I was on a quest to know everything I could about Joan and the witches. Something in me hungered to know what the Salem witches knew, to possess the defiant confidence Joan possessed, to be free enough to dance naked with devils or wear boys' clothes and fight for a higher calling.

What was it that made me crave devilry in a strongly Christian household in Alabama, in the veritable buckle of the Bible Belt in the American Deep South? What made me hope for magic? I now believe my attraction to Joan had everything to do with being a trans and nonbinary kid in an environment where binary biological gender norms were tightly enforced. Joan dressed like a boy, defied gender norms, was aggressive and brash and talked back to Church authorities—all the things I was scolded for doing, but that Joan was celebrated for. Until she was killed for it. My interest in witches ran along the same lines: Witches stepped boldly outside the oppressive Christian order and found power in the margins, in the shadows, in the forbidden and taboo. The power of a witch was not in following the rules, but in defying them.

Long before I had words for it, I knew I didn't fit in with the other girls, knew I was different in a way that was unacceptable in the Protestant religion and conservative culture in which I was raised. At the same time, I sensed that there was more to the world and to "God" than what I was taught. Perhaps it was my awareness of my difference, my inability to fit comfortably in the gendered mold, that also made me aware of these other spiritual currents. When the shoe doesn't fit, you go looking for other shoes, and sometimes those are pointed like a witch's, and sometimes they're for boys.

Every year, I read a new book. Every year, I was disappointed when the Salem witch trials turned out to be nothing more than mass hysteria incited by a misogynist culture and the accusations of four young girls portrayed as petulant and attention-seeking. Every year, I was bothered when Joan turned out to be a staunch royalist and pious Catholic woman whose cross-dressing was brushed off as utilitarian. Nevertheless, I kept reading, following the scent of something I couldn't yet name between the lines of print. Joan was not a witch; she was a social radical who broke the barriers of gender and class. The Salem witches were not witches either, as in none were Satan-worshippers. Some, though, were outsiders who did not fit into conventional Puritan norms of womanhood and were thus considered threatening to the establishment. Maybe what I was searching for was evidence of people like me in history, people who resisted patriarchal authority and defied the social constraints placed on their gender assigned at birth. People who chose authenticity and loyalty to themselves, their truth, their "voices," over the orders of a church that told them there was only one "right" way to be. People who risked heresy and hellfire in order to be themselves and follow what they knew was right. People who could inspire me to be strong enough, brave enough, to do the same.

Jehanne the Maid, Daughter of God

Joan of Arc was a controversial and category-defying figure in her lifetime, and she continues to be so today. She was an illiterate peasant who rose to the office of general and was revered as a folk saint in her own lifetime. She was executed as a heretic by the same church that later canonized her as a saint. She is revered as a trans and gender-nonconforming saint by many, including myself, but at the same time has been coopted by the transphobic alt right as a symbol of French nationalism. She was a girl who heard divine voices that told her to cross-dress as a boy, or maybe they weren't a girl at all.

To honor Joan's gender-nonconforming complexity, I will use both she/her/hers and they/them/theirs pronouns to refer to Joan here. Sometimes I will alternate, and other times I'll use one or the other as feels appropriate. The name "Joan" is an Anglicization of the French "Jehanne," the only name they ever went by in life, and the title "of Arc" was only added after their death. In life, Joan gave no surname, calling herself only "Jehanne the Maid, Daughter of God." The name "Jehanne," while predominantly a feminine name in French, sounds more androgynous to me and my English ears than the overtly feminine "Joan," leaning toward "Jean" or "Johann," depending on one's pronunciation, perhaps capturing a bit of Jehanne's gender-defying complexity. So from here forward, instead of the more common name Joan of Arc, I will refer to them by their name, Jehanne.

Jehanne was born around the feast of Epiphany in 1412 near the town of Domrémy in the Lorraine region of northeastern France. Lorraine in the 15th century was a borderland in more ways than one. Technically in the French kingdoms, Lorraine bordered and overlapped in some parts with the Holy Roman Empire; the Duchy of Bar, where Domrémy was located, was of uncertain feudal allegiance and was surrounded and then overtaken by pro-English Burgundian forces in Jehanne's lifetime. Though mostly loyal to France, residents of Lorraine didn't tend to call themselves French, but "Lorrainers,"[137] and when Jehanne speaks of leaving for her mission in trial transcripts, she says the voices told her to "go to France," placing Jehanne and Domrémy on its margins. The region of Lorraine was also notorious for being a holdout of pagan ways, where the people still held on to some old beliefs and practices and preserved some matrilineal traditions.[138] Though nominally Christian, the peasants of the region practiced a highly syncretized version of Christianity that enfolded the local spirits, folklore, and sacred places, much to the displeasure of the ecclesiastical authorities.[139]

In his introduction to Jehanne's trial transcripts, T. Douglas Murray writes, "She came from Lorraine, out of which no good thing could come, as proverbs taught; for Lorraine had ever been branded as false to God and false to man. Ambiguous in its relations to France and to the Empire, it had, like most borderlands, the unstableness of character which comes of social and political insecurity."[140] It was into these ambiguous borderlands of war and culture, where political borders were lost in the rural woods and Christian religion twined with Celtic beliefs like the meandering Meuse River that wound its way through the valley, that Jehanne d'Arc was born.

In her essay "No Savior," Sophie Strand notes that to the medieval European peasantry—who could neither read the Bible nor understand the ecclesiastical Latin spoken in church—Bible stories were another kind of folktale, repeated orally, misheard, and combined with local folklore and legends into a deeply relational religion.[141] Their version of Christianity emphasized a "cult of saints" that combined Catholic saints with pre-Christian land spirits and local deities, and it retained Celtic holy places such as sacred springs and groves.[142] Two of these sacred places were not far from Jehanne's childhood home: the sacred oak woods of Bois Chenu and the "Fairies' Tree."[143] Of the oak woods, there was a prophecy attributed to Merlin that a young maid would come from the woods to save France.[144] Jehanne's interrogators attempted to use the prophecy against her in trial, likely so they could accuse her of placing herself above God, but she insisted she was unaware of the prophecy and put no stock in it. As for the Fairies' Tree, Jehanne was more familiar. She described it during her trial:

> Not far from Domremy there is a tree that they call 'The Ladies' Tree'—others call it 'The Fairies' Tree'; near by, there is a spring where people sick of the fever come to drink. . . . It is a beautiful tree, a beech. . . . I have sometimes been to play with the young girls, to make garlands for Our Lady of Domrémy. Often I have heard the old folk—they are not of my lineage—say that the fairies haunt this tree. . . . I have seen the young girls putting garlands on the branches of this tree, and I myself have sometimes put them there with my companions. . . . I may have danced there formerly, with the other children. I have sung there more than danced.[145]

Like many pagan sacred spots, the Fairies' Tree had been absorbed into Christianity, its pagan powers transferred to Our Lady of Domrémy. As with many syncretic practices, this meant the locals could leave offerings of flower garlands in the tree's branches and drink from the sacred spring as they had always done, though now it was the Virgin Mary from whom the miraculous healing flowed and for whom the children left flowers—not the fairies, land spirits, or Celtic gods. Younger generations, including Jehanne, may have thought nothing at all un-Christian about such practices; for them, the Lady of the tree and the Virgin Mary were one and the same.

The first time Jehanne heard voices from God, she was 13 and terrified. In the transcript of her trial, she says that it happened around noon in the summer in her father's garden. The voice came from her right side, accompanied by a light.[146] Eventually, Jehanne would be able to differentiate three voices among what she called her "counsel": those of St. Catherine, St. Margaret, and the archangel Michael. She heard them most easily in the woods, she said in trial.[147] She also heard them when bells rang and was known to drop to her knees at the peal of church bells. Many assumed she was praying, but she was listening to her voices instead.[148] She also saw her counsel visibly and was even physically touched by them on occasion. Jehanne heard these voices and saw these visions for almost four years, telling no one—potentially because they'd think her mad—until finally, at around age 16, their heavenly counsel instructed them to cut their hair short, dress in men's clothes, and set off to free France from the English.

The Hundred Years' War had been at Domrémy's doorstep since 1419, and in 1425 the town was attacked and cattle stolen. In 1428, a town not far from Domrémy was under attack by English forces, and Jehanne made her first attempt to leave home for the court of the Dauphin Charles, the yet-to-be-crowned heir to the French throne. She convinced her uncle to take her to nearby Vaucouleurs, still under French control, where she petitioned the garrison commander Robert de Baudricourt to send her with an armed escort to the Dauphin's court at Chinon. Robert strongly refused and sent them home. Shortly after, Domrémy was attacked and Jehanne and their family were forced to flee. When they returned home, their town had been burned and the crops destroyed. Jehanne made two more attempts to persuade Robert, and on the third, he acquiesced. One of his soldiers furnished Jehanne with men's clothing, and she set out for Chinon with an armed escort in February 1429.

In Chinon, Jehanne told the Dauphin Charles they were sent by God to liberate France and put him on the throne. Moved by Jehanne's religious conviction and uncanny ability to inspire the trust and devotion of the soldiers in their company, and in a rather desperate position politically and strategically, Charles wanted to believe them. He had Jehanne examined by a council of theologians and lawyers at Poitiers to verify their good Christian faith and ensure they were not in league with the Devil. When Jehanne passed their tests, Charles commissioned a suit of plate armor for Jehanne while she designed her own battle banner: two angels holding up a globe on a field of fleur-de-lis, bearing the words *Jhesus Maria* (Jesus Mary).

Guided by their counsel of angelic voices, Jehanne directed that an ancient sword be retrieved from a hiding place behind the altar in a church they'd never been to. The sword was found precisely where they said it would be. At the end of April, Charles sent Jehanne to relieve the siege of Orléans with an army, and by May 8, the siege was broken and the English in retreat. Jehanne went on to be instrumental in liberating other French towns and strategic bridges and roads in order to clear the way to Reims so Charles could be coronated. While Jehanne was never given troops to command by themself, they turned out to be a brilliant military strategist and advised the commanders. One knight who fought alongside Jehanne at Orleans described her thus: "Apart from affairs of war, she was simple and innocent; but in the conduct and disposition of troops and in actual warfare, in the ordering of battle and in animating the soldiers, she behaved as the most skilled captain in the world who all his life had been trained in the art of war."[149] Jehanne was fearless in battle, known for staying on the front lines and charging into the most vicious fighting to rally morale. She was injured in combat several times, but claimed to have never killed a man in battle. On July 17, 1429, Charles was crowned king of France in Reims, with Jehanne standing in a place of honor by his side.

In short: In just a few months, an illiterate, cross-dressing peasant who heard voices rose from obscurity, turned the tide of a war, earned the heart of a nation, and crowned a king. Tragically, the very same qualities that made Jehanne an inspiring, God-sent hero for the French would be interpreted as signs of the Devil by the English. In May 1430, Jehanne was captured by Burgundian forces, allies of the English, and in January 1431, Jehanne was put on trial in a pro-English ecclesiastical court for having demonic visions, refusing to submit to the authority of the Church, and blaspheming by wearing men's clothing. The trial was transparently politically motivated. In convicting Jehanne of heresy, the English would invalidate Charles's coronation and potentially break the *spirit* of France. In those aims, the English would not succeed. The English fortunes in France would rapidly decline from then on, in no small part thanks to the actions of Jehanne d'Arc. But the English would succeed in murdering Jehanne.

She was burned at the stake in Rouen on May 30, 1431, at age 19. Not for witchcraft, as is often assumed today, but for refusing to submit to the will of the Catholic Church, and for cross-dressing.

Feminist Icon or Transgender Saint?

At trial, Jehanne was charged with a number of heretical crimes, among them witchcraft, divination, conspiring with demons and evil spirits, talking to fairies, consorting with prostitutes, inciting men to murder, seducing people into idolatrous worship of her, and various other sacrileges and blasphemies. But one item the court seemed particularly hung up on, and the one that would eventually give them reason to sentence her to death, was the charge of cross-dressing. This charge seems to have especially infuriated her judges, as the trial transcript reveals:

> You have said that you wore and still wear man's dress at God's command and to His good pleasure, for you had instruction from God to wear this dress, and so you have put on a short tunic, jerkin, and hose with many points. You even wear your hair cut short above the ears, without keeping about you anything to denote your sex, save what nature has given you. . . . And although you have many times been admonished to put it off, you would not, saying that you would rather die than put off this dress, unless it were God's command. . . . You say also that nothing could persuade you to take an oath not to wear this dress and bear these arms; and for all this you plead divine command.

> Regarding such matters, the clergy declare that you blaspheme against God, despising Him and His sacraments, that you transgress divine law, Holy Scripture and the canons of the Church, that you think evil and err from the faith, that you are full, of vain boasting, that you are given to idolatry and worship yourself and your clothes, according to the customs of the heathen.[150]

Jehanne saw no conflict in wearing men's clothing because they were directed to do so by God. In her view, it could not be improper or indecent because God willed it; to put on women's clothes would be a betrayal of God's will. The interrogators persistently used Jehanne's faith against them, forbidding Jehanne from attending Mass and receiving the Eucharist as long as they wore men's clothing. At multiple points, Jehanne entreated their interrogators to allow them to hear Mass in their chosen clothes, saying, "I beg of you, my Lords, permit me to hear Mass in man's dress; this dress does not weigh upon my soul" and "Neither for that nor for anything else will I yet put off my dress. I make no difference between man's dress and woman's dress for receiving my Saviour."[151]

To the very end, Jehanne asserts their preference for dressing as a man. One of their last recorded statements on the subject demonstrates a remarkable ambivalence on the subject of gendered clothing in general. Jehanne says "it is more lawful and suitable" for them to wear men's clothing because they are among men.[152] Men's clothes were simply better for traveling and fighting. These certainly may be reasons for Jehanne's choice of clothing, but they do not have to be the *only* reasons, to the exclusion of any potential transgender or genderqueer feelings. A person who puts on men's clothes as a religious duty and wears them not only in battle, when men's clothing would be a more practical choice, but *all the time*, in every hour of their life, even on pain of death, just might be trans. In their perspective, the clothes one wears should not be dictated by one's sex but by one's role and company, which is just about the closest one can come to a 15th-century declaration that gender is performative.

Still, most historians and academics tend to gloss over Jehanne's cross-dressing and refuse any possibility that they might not be cisgender. However, assuming cis-hetero identity for Jehanne is just that: an assumption. She showed zero interest in any sort of sexuality, refused marriage when offered, and gave numerous indications that their gender was at the very least—and by sheer definition—*nonconforming*.

There are other dynamics to consider, not least that wearing men's clothing helped to desexualize Jehanne, deflecting the gender-based violence they might suffer among male soldiers to a certain extent. Men's tightly laced breeches and underwear made rape functionally more difficult. Tragically, reports from Jehanne's retrial 25 years after their execution reveal that Jehanne was likely raped in prison once they briefly resumed women's clothing in their final week of life. It is possible that their decision to resume men's clothes was in reaction to that assault.

The way Jehanne comported themselves was also known to be masculine. Aside from learning to wear armor, use a sword, and ride a horse like a man, Jehanne responded to their interrogators boldly and with rebellious attitude—or, as my grandma would say, "gave them lip." At a few points, Jehanne admonishes the judge, saying, "You say you are my judge. Take care what you are doing; for in truth I am sent by God, and you place yourself in great danger."[153] When Jehanne refuses to answer their questions about the appearance of her angels, she says, "There is a saying among children, that 'Sometimes one is hanged for speaking the truth.'"[154] When they ask if Jehanne will submit herself to "our Holy Father the Pope," Jehanne replies, "Take me to him, I will reply to him."[155] When her interrogators read Article XVI against her, which indicts her for refusing to wear women's clothes and "disdain[ing] also to give herself up to feminine work, conducting herself in all things rather as a man than as a woman," Jehanne replies, "I was invited to take a woman's dress; then I refused, and I refuse still. As to the women's work of which you speak, there are plenty of other women to do it."[156]

Further, Jehanne's queer gender subversion is not a modern anachronism. In their own time, Jehanne was called *homasse* by their captors, a French slur for "man-woman" or a masculine woman,[157] something like being called a *dyke* today. (Like the word *queer*, some butch lesbians have reclaimed *dyke* with pride.) A Parisian journal of current events treated Jehanne with dehumanizing language, calling them "a creature in the form of a woman, whom they called the Maid—what it was, God only knows."[158] There was enough question around Jehanne's gender that at their execution, once they were presumed dead and their clothes were burned away, the flames were banked so the crowd could see Jehanne's partially burnt naked body and know their sex.[159]

Commentators who aim to minimize Jehanne's choice of male clothing and habits tend to cite a moment at trial where Jehanne says they would have rather stayed home spinning wool than taken up arms to liberate France, but they were commanded to do so by divine providence and could not refuse. They take this to mean that Jehanne was a woman interested in womanly things.

But I hear something different. In Jehanne's words, I hear every time a transgender or nonbinary person, struggling under the weight of a society that makes existence very hard, remarks that they wish they could have been born a "normal boy or girl." Meaning they wish they didn't have to suffer such hardship and hatred for being who they are. But they *are* who they are. We are who we are. Jehanne was who Jehanne was. Not out of choice, but because of divine providence.

Of course Jehanne was not transgender in the way we conceive of it in the 21st century. But their chosen gender expression was masculine, and they certainly did not fit the normative mold of a 15th-century woman. Moreover, part of what made Jehanne such a monumentally powerful figure was precisely her unlikely gender subversion. A 16-year-old peasant boy taking up arms and joining the army would be nothing unusual, but for a *girl* to do it, in that time, was scandalous.

Christine de Pisan, the predominant female writer in France at the time, published a poem praising Jehanne's heroism after the victory in Orleans and King Charles's coronation in Reims, which Jehanne was instrumental in orchestrating. Historian Anne Llewellyn Barstow describes the war poem: "Comparing Joan to Moses, Joshua, Gideon, Hector, and Achilles, she claimed that Joan's fame should be greater than theirs because she is 'only a little girl of sixteen.'"[160] According to Barstow, who otherwise situates Jehanne firmly as a woman and female mystic, Christine's poem describes Jehanne in both masculine and feminine terms, conjuring "Joan the androgyne."[161] According to Arthur Evans, "Whenever she appeared in public she was worshipped like a deity by the peasants. . . . The peasants believed that she had the power to heal, and many would flock around her to touch part of her body or her clothing (which was men's clothing). Subsequently her armor was kept on display at the Church of St. Denis, where it was worshipped."[162]

This is not just a simple case of a cross-dressing girl or a gender-queer general, but a gender-transcending folk hero who was revered as a folk saint in their own lifetime. Crowds flocked to touch Jehanne's clothes, *men's* clothes worn by a teenage unmarried girl that were called an "abomination" by the clergy at Jehanne's trial, believing the garments had magical healing properties due to their proximity to Jehanne. This is not dissimilar to the way followers of Jesus touched his robes and were healed, or the way pilgrims touch or look upon the relics of saints to be healed. As Jehanne saw no difference between a man's dress and a woman's dress for receiving their Savior in communion, perhaps the French peasantry saw no difference between men's and women's dress for venerating their folk saint Jehanne. Probably anything Jehanne wore would have been made holy by its proximity to Jehanne, and yet the fact remains that Jehanne's cross-gendered expression was a monumental part of their ability to capture the heart of a nation and was instrumental in their uncanny rise—and fall.

There is no "Joan of Arc" without gender nonconformity. It's an intrinsic part of who she was and what she accomplished for France.

Cross-Dressing and Class Warfare Among the Fairies

At trial, it was not only the masculinity of Jehanne's clothing that angered their interrogators; it was its finery. Article XIII of their indictment complains about Jehanne's "sumptuous and stately raiment, cloth-of-gold and furs," as well as "short tunics," "tabards, and garments open at both sides."[163] It concludes:

> In one word, putting aside the modesty of her sex, she acted not only against all feminine decency, but even against the reserve which beseems men of good morals, wearing ornaments and garments which only profligate men are accustomed to use, and going so far as to carry arms of offence [weapons]. To attribute all this to the order of God . . . is to blaspheme God and His Saints, to destroy the Divine Law and violate the Canonical Rules; it is to libel the sex and its virtue, to overturn all decency, to justify all examples of dissolute living, and to drive others thereto.[164]

So, Jehanne's cross-dressing was not only a crime of gender, but also one of class. Leslie Feinberg notes that "beneath this outrage against Joan's cross-dressing was a powerful class bias. It was an affront to nobility for a peasant to wear armor and ride a fine horse."[165] Knighthood was not a profession but a hereditary rank of nobility, and for a peasant to assume fine clothes and plate armor was not only an offense to the nobility but a threat to the feudal hierarchy. And if Jehanne was allowed to do it, then others could too. Strand connects Jehanne's donning of armor to the peasant uprisings and outlaw activity in Europe in the 14th and 15th centuries, in which participants "often signaled their subversion of the dominant order by breaking sumptuary dress laws."[166] According to Strand, Jehanne "was invoking this radical trope when she put on armor as a peasant."

Indeed, the links between cross-dressing and popular rebellion and protest run deep, especially among peasants and laborers in the once-Celtic areas of Europe like Jehanne's native Lorraine. In *Transgender Warriors*, Feinberg catalogues cross-dressed rebels from 16th-century France to 19th-century Wales. In 16th- and 17th-century Dijon, Mère Folle ("Mother" Folle) and her "children," a cross-dressed carnival society similar to a modern-day Mardi Gras krewe, took advantage of festival days to protest war, deforestation, the cost of bread, and in one case to instigate an uprising against royal tax collectors.[167] In England in 1629, a "Captain" Alice Clark led a mob of male and female weavers, all dressed as women, in a grain riot, and in Montpellier in 1645, a "virago," or masculine woman, named La Branlaire led a primarily female tax revolt.[168] In the 19th century the Welsh "Rebeccas," men dressed as women on horseback, destroyed turnpike toll barriers that were choking the poor.[169] In 1812, during the Luddite rebellions in England, two men dressed as women and calling themselves "General Ludd's wives" led hundreds of exploited weavers in Stockton to destroy the looms and burn down the factory.[170]

Sometimes, the cross-dressed rebels associated themselves with fairies. In France in the 1770s, cross-dressing peasant men attacked surveyors scoping out their land for a landlord, and when the law came around to question their families, their wives said it must be the "'fairies' who came from the mountains from time to time."[171] The 18th-century Whiteboys of Ireland wore feminine white smocks over their clothes and leveled enclosures, targeted landlords, reclaimed confiscated property, and fought for the rights of tenant and subsidence farmers.[172] The Whiteboys pledged their allegiance to Queen Sieve Outlagh, a mythological Irish figure, and purportedly called themselves "fairies."[173] Later guerilla movements such as the Lady Rocks, Lady Clares, Ribbonmen, and Molly Maguires would grow from this rich tradition of militant cross-dressing.[174] The Radical Faeries, founded in 1979, is a loosely affiliated countercultural group whose worldwide members blend queer consciousness with secular, often earth-based, spirituality, anarchism, environmentalism, and social activism, continuing the connection between fairies and a certain queerness of positionality—one that recognizes gender subversion and anti-authoritarian, anti-colonial, anti-capitalist resistance are naturally linked—into the modern day.

In addition to cross-dressing and "driv[ing] others thereto," Jehanne d'Arc was also accused of consorting with fairies. Central to the witchcraft allegations against her were her childhood games at the Fairies' Tree, perhaps suggesting certain queer connections to the 21st-century ear. *Fairy* is a well-known slur for gay and/or effeminate men that came into use in the last few decades of the 19th century,[175] long after Jehanne's trial, but the association between fairies and queerness is much older. Social and literary historian Rictor Norton notes a play by Mary Pix, *The Adventures of Madrid*, performed in 1706, in which "a girl dressed as a boy is pursued by a man named 'Gaylove' who calls her his little 'Ganymede' [one of Zeus's gay male lovers] and 'fairy.'"[176] For centuries after Christianization, and sometimes still today, Europeans believed children with unexplained diseases, disabilities, or behavioral differences—children who were "odd" (queer) or "other" in some way—were "changelings," fairy children who had been swapped for the "real" human child. The Church officially considered fairies to be demons, and association with fairies was frequently trotted out by the Church as proof of witchcraft, as it was at Jehanne's trial. Fairies were implicitly linked with paganism and "unnatural" or "heathen" ways, as was homosexuality and gender nonconformity.

In the Middle Ages, the connection between homosexuality, sodomy (which, remember, was any sexual act that transgressed Church-approved binary gender roles), and paganism was so strong that mere charges of sodomy could be considered proof that a person was a witch or a heretic. This was the case with the Cathars, a medieval descendant of Gnosticism* whose members believed in spiritual equality of the sexes, the androgynous nature of the human soul, reincarnation, pacifism, asceticism, and communal living. Catharism became so popular in France and Italy that the Church waged the Albigensian Crusade against them and targeted them with Inquisitions, resulting in thousands of deaths. Among the primary charges against the Cathars: sodomy.** Whether or not the accused

---

* For more on Gnosticism, see Chapter 4.

** There may be credence to these claims, since Cathars believed procreation trapped souls into bodies on the "evil" material plane and therefore generally avoided sex acts that could lead to pregnancy but permitted other, nonprocreative sex acts, potentially including homosexual ones. Whether this is true is debated among scholars, but it is certainly true that the Church used allegations of sodomy to persecute the Cathars.

Cathars were actually gay (though it's reasonable that some had to be, statistically speaking), the Cathar heresy and sodomy became so synonymous in the cultural mind that the pejorative epithet *bugger* arose from *Bulgari* ("Bulgarian"), referencing the Balkan region that was believed to be the origin of Catharism. The epithet was used then as it still is today, to mean sodomite.[177]

Another slur for gay men, *faggot*, also has an uncanny link to the Church's inquisitions. Though the word's use as a slur for gay men did not arise until the 1920s and follows a different etymological path (likely tracing back to a 16th-century pejorative for a "worthless woman"[178] or "harlot"[179]), *faggot* originally meant a bundle of sticks of the kind that fueled bonfires—and the pyres that witches and heretics were executed upon. Those accused of sodomy were sometimes burned, occasionally at the feet of alleged witches, with the kindling.[180] According to Evans, the popular speech of the time included phrases like "fire and faggot" and "to fry a faggot," which to Evans suggests "that the victims themselves were called 'faggots.'"[181] Evans also notes that bundles of sticks were sometimes embroidered on the sleeves of heretics who had recanted and were thus allowed to live,[182] like a medieval precursor to Hester Prynne's scarlet letter, or perhaps more like the pink triangles gay people were forced to wear in Nazi concentration camps. The word *faggot* perhaps comes from *fagus*, the Latin name for the beech tree.[183] The sacred Fairies' Tree where Jehanne played as a child, as she attests in trial, was a beech tree.

In the end, Jehanne's interrogators could not drum up enough evidence to convict them of witchcraft. But they did not have to. They had her on heeding her voices above the authority of the Church and on cross-dressing as a religious imperative. At the time, cross-dressing did not carry a death penalty, but relapsing into heresy after recanting did. After months of questioning, starvation, painful imprisonment, and a tour of the torture chamber and gallows, Jehanne agreed to wear women's clothing on the condition that they be released from irons and allowed to go to Mass and receive the Eucharist. When her captors did not follow through on their end of the agreement, Jehanne resumed men's clothing, and the judges deemed her a relapsed heretic—a capital offense. They had their excuse to kill her.

Jehanne was not a rebel of the same sort as Mére Folle's Children, the Rebeccas, or General Ludd's wives, who staged protests and demonstrations, led peasant and laborer uprisings, and waged guerilla class warfare. Jehanne was quite the opposite: a royalist who fought to secure the French monarchy. But in Jehanne's world, fighting to secure the French throne was tantamount to fighting to secure the welfare of her people, Lorrainer peasants and French nobles alike, who had suffered under English occupation. Though Jehanne rubbed elbows with nobility and wore fine clothes, Jehanne also fought with regular men in the mud and blood of battle while the nobility surveyed from a safe distance. The army that Jehanne rallied was composed of peasants and laborers who fought to rid themselves of English colonization. The only thing Jehanne asked of Charles in return for her service was that the people of her hometown of Domrémy be permanently free from paying taxes, having observed the harsh burden they placed on her townspeople. Jehanne may have been individualistic to a fault, but the only thing they ever asked for was greater financial freedom for the peasants of their hometown.

Though a brilliant military strategist and charismatic leader, Jehanne was in many ways naïve; she believed Charles and the French nobility would continue to support her, a brash and independent peasant girl in boy's clothing who didn't even know how to read or write, after she served their purpose. Leading up to Jehanne's capture, she had lost a series of battles and had argued with Charles over strategy. After her capture, there is no evidence that Charles did anything to try to ransom or rescue her. The English were in retreat, Charles was crowned, and Jehanne's usefulness had run its course.

But the people of France continued to love and venerate Jehanne d'Arc as a hero and folk saint. Twenty-five years after Jehanne's death, Charles would order a retrial and find Jehanne innocent of all charges, functionally affirming that Jehanne's cross-dressing was indeed ordained by divine providence. This was, of course, self-serving for Charles, as Jehanne's conviction of heresy could undermine his claim to the throne, which she had been instrumental in orchestrating. But for the French people, as well as Jehanne's mother, Isabelle, who first petitioned the king to overturn the conviction, this was a victory and vindication. Nearly five hundred years after their death, in

1920 Jehanne would finally be canonized as a saint by the Catholic Church, the same church that executed them.

Jehanne in Transition

When asked what they called themself, Jehanne replied, "Jehanne la Pucelle, Daughter of God." *La Pucelle* means "the Maid," a term sometimes also used for the Virgin Mary. *Maid* in this instance means maiden or virgin, but not solely in the sexual sense. Whereas virginity has become synonymous with never having had penetrative heterosexual intercourse, it once had less to do with sexual innocence and puritanical ideas of "purity" and more to do with female autonomy. Marriage was an ownership contract where wives became the property of their husbands, so to be a virgin meant to be unmarried and thus the property of no man. So, la Pucelle connoted independence and self-sovereignty. Strand points out a transitional property of the word Pucelle in that it also implied the passage into sexual maturity. By choosing the title Pucelle, Strand writes, "Joan portrayed herself not as a static virgin, kept separate for God, but as a potent and dynamic figure in movement, in transition. . . . Joan made the choice to position herself 'between' countries, genders, mystical states, and social classes. The pucelle was transitioning between girl and woman. Between woman and man. Between the Lorraine and France. Between peasant and nobleman."[184]

Too often, cisgender feminists and transgender people clash over historical figures like Jehanne, insisting they must be a woman or they must be transgender or nonbinary in order to better suit the causes of one group or the other. But Jehanne was an actual person who lived and breathed, hoped and dreamed, who danced and sang under a fairy tree with their friends and made flower garlands for the Virgin Mary. In the socio-cultural matrix of the time, Jehanne was a woman who used feminine pronouns and used the gendered title "the Maid." *And* Jehanne dressed as a man and comported themself in masculine ways from the moment they left their father's house in Domrémy until they were burnt in Rouen, only lapsing into feminine clothing for a brief time under torture and threat of death. Jehanne can be a role model for feminists looking for bold women in history *and* Jehanne can be an inspiring genderqueer saint. Jehanne was—is—both. La

Pucelle. A living person who cut their hair and took up a sword, who rallied an army of laborers and liberated a nation from occupation, who heard voices, who believed in themself, who was betrayed by the nobility they liberated, who knew God loved them, who did not abandon themself, and who died too soon. Jehanne was killed by powerful people who hated them for who they were and what they represented: a way of living outside the lines of gender norms, a threat to patriarchal power, and a personal connection to the divine that needed no churchly middleman.

Jehanne saw no conflict in wearing men's clothing because they were directed to do so by their inner voices, their personal mysticism, their inherent channel to God. To put off men's clothes and put on women's would not only be a betrayal of themself, but a betrayal of God's will. Likewise, denying her angelic counsel would be heresy— contrary to the clergy in Rouen who attempted to convince Jehanne that heresy was denying the will of the Church. Joan's faith was in God and her counsel of angelic voices first, and the institution of the Church second. When asked if they would submit to the decision of the Church, Jehanne replied with their characteristic pious insubordination: "I refer myself to God Who sent me, to Our Lady, and to all the Saints in Paradise. And in my opinion it is all one, God and the Church; and one should make no difficulty about it. Why do you make a difficulty?"[185]

Jehanne faced judgment, hateful accusations, and authoritarian manipulations, and they were not broken.

As I write this in 2024, more judgments are being passed down by conservative judges and bigoted politicians on trans health care, trans sports, trans bathroom access, trans protections under anti-discrimination laws, and whether or not trans people have civil and human rights. In times like these, Jehanne d'Arc is a powerful saint and transcestor to call on. I wear my Jehanne saint medallion when I need an extra boost of strength, when I need to face something scary, when I need to root into my inherent dignity and stay true to my authenticity. They've lent me strength at protests, marches, and vigils, at family events where I know I may be repeatedly or purposefully misgendered, and on regular days when the weight of being trans in this world feels like too much to bear. Jehanne rallied a movement, and we can call on her to aid our fight for LGBTQIA2S+ rights, women's rights, the human right to bodily autonomy, as well as struggles against colonization and occupation and for freedom and liberation worldwide. Jehanne stayed true to themself despite horrible persecution and listened to their voices despite the noise of powerful people who told them they were evil and wrong. Under Jehanne's banner, we can find the courage, confidence, and queer devotion to do the same.

QUEER DEVOTIONS

Queer Contemplations

- Were you surprised to learn that Jehanne was not executed for witchcraft, but for the relapsed heresy of cross-dressing? Why do you think this detail is not common knowledge?

- Some believe that Jehanne may have been neurodivergent, that her angelic voices were in fact schizophrenia or a neurological disorder. What do you think? Could it have been both? If Jehanne's voices were both angelic *and* a neurological symptom, what implications does that have for the way we treat people with neurodivergence and mental "illness" today?

- Wearing clothes typically assigned to the other binary sex has a long history in spirituality and religion, as we've seen with Jehanne and with worshippers and priest/esses of Inanna and Kybele in Chapter 2. Is there a spiritual or devotional element to cross-dressing? Cross-dressing has a potent history in activism and resistance movements. Do you sense a relationship between spirituality and activism? What about between heresy and resistance or protest movements?

- How can "heretics" like Jehanne, the Cathars, and the Gnostics help you rethink what you thought you knew about God, religion, or the relationship between institutions and believers? Do you think personal spiritual knowledge (or *gnosis*) is more or less important than institutional religious dogma?

- How can heresy be a sacred act of queer devotion?

Devotional Tool-Kit: Listening to the Divine

Most of us don't "hear" and "see" the Divine with the clarity of Jehanne, and figuring out how to "listen" to the Divine can take time and feel confusing or frustrating. The first step is to release expectations around how the Divine communicates. It probably won't be a clear voice in your head, and it probably won't answer at your beck and call, if at all. Instead, it might be a feeling, an emotion, an impression, a dream, an image that pops into your head during prayer or meditation, a song that plays on the radio, a fox or hawk or deer that crosses your path, a lone playing card face up on the pavement, a poem that pops on your social media feed, a luna moth that lands on your chest.

The second step is to believe yourself. This might be the hardest part. Materialist, empirical culture teaches us to trust only what we can see, touch, measure, and prove, making it tough to believe our own spiritual experiences and divine impressions. Unlearning that conditioning takes practice. In *Rebel Witch*, Kelly-Anne Maddox suggests practicing a "magician's mindset" for 10 to 20 minutes a day when you're feeling spiritually disconnected.[186] I like to do this when I'm having my morning cup of coffee, walking my dog, or winding down in my favored chair where I can watch the sunset at the end of the day. During this time, I'll open my senses and simply pay attention to the world. I'll try to perceive anything that sticks out as a sign, a love note, a scrap of the pattern of the Divine. Granted, not everything is a sign or message, but practicing this suspension of disbelief can help you gradually unlearn materialist conditioning and learn to believe yourself instead, and eventually you'll build the skills to discern spiritual encounters from random events. Opening your senses to the spiritual in the mundane is essential for building a relationship with the Divine and living a life infused with meaning.

Devotional Tool-Kit: Working with Transcestors

The term *transcestor* is a portmanteau of *trans* and *ancestor*, and it's exactly what it sounds like. Transcestors are the dearly departed trans people who came before us, who paved the way for us, who fought with their activism for our rights and respect, or who simply did their best to live and love as their truest selves in an unfriendly world. Transcestors do not have to be blood relations because we are connected by a different kind of blood: the blood of experience, the blood of love, the blood spilled in struggle and pain, the blood-singing and bone-echoing knowledge of our authentic truth. Transcestors may have lived before the term *transgender* was invented, but if they lived outside of or across binary gender lines, we can still consider them a transcestor. For a people too often disconnected from our families of origin, transcestors are a vein extending like a root into the past, connecting living trans people to a deep and supportive lineage of trans existence and trans wisdom.

If you'd like to work with transcestors, a great starting point is to research their lives and learn who they were and what was important to them. It can be hard to find trans people in the archives of history because the gatekeepers of history have suppressed and erased us, but they do exist. Well-known recent transcestors include Marsha P. Johnson and Sylvia Rivera, who co-founded the Street Transvestites Action

Revolutionaries, were self-professed drag queens, and were instrumental in the Stonewall uprising that resisted police and mob persecution of queer and trans people and started Pride. There is also, of course, St. Jehanne d'Arc, a transcestor beloved by many.

You can find photos of the transcestors you want to honor, print them out, and add them to your altar, where you can venerate them much like you would a saint. (Indeed, Marsha P. and Sylvia are considered modern trans saints by many.) You may also want to research the Transgender Rite of Elevation, an annual nine-day ritual beginning on or around November 20, the Trans Day of Remembrance, to honor the transgender dead, including transcestors of the past and transcestors who have been killed by transphobic violence during the year. You can find more information at trans-rite.tumblr.com.

There are lots of reasons to work with transcestors, but one that feels especially necessary right now is the resilience and support they can lend us in challenging times. During the onslaught of anti-trans and anti-queer legislation over the past several years, I have felt the presence of my transcestors, lending me the strength to persevere, the attitude to fight back, and the hope and faith to keep living and loving as who I am. For me, transcestors are the firm, stable ground that I can root into in times of fear and crisis, because they remind me that trans, nonbinary, and genderqueer people have always been here—and that we always will be here no matter what.

CHAPTER 6

Liberating Sir Gawain for a Green Night

Gay Kisses, Soft Masculinity, and Queer Nature

The first time I read the 14th-century Arthurian romance poem *Sir Gawain and the Green Knight* in high school English class, I thought it was horribly silly. A vapid knight accepts a pointless challenge to prove his manliness and satisfy his inflated ego, even though it might kill him. Later, having nothing better to do, two men in a castle play another pointless game involving hunting and flirting for sport. The gay kisses were interesting, but they were largely unexplored in the text and outright ignored in English class. In the end, the hero proves himself a lying coward and gets celebrated for it. And the meaning of the poem? The triumph of Christian virtue and civilized order over wicked human nature. Booooring.

Then I watched David Lowery's film adaptation, *The Green Knight* (2021), and things took on an altogether different, greener hue. The film highlights the exact attributes I found annoying in high school, turning Gawain into a bumbling antihero and exposing his cowardice in ways that made him plainly unchivalrous but also human, sympathetic. The film departs from the original poem at times to tweak and amplify themes present in the original for modern, 21st-century relevance, themes including the doom of destructive, extractive patriarchal civilization and the patient inevitability of nature.

For most of this chapter, we will stick to *Sir Gawain*, the 14th-century romance poem, and explore the queerness teasing and troubling its civilized borders. But we'll also venture into *The Green Knight's* cinematic interpretation, because modern retellings have value. No texts, no religions, no gods are dead. They are alive and in conversation. If you don't believe that, then why are you reading this book?

After I watched *The Green Knight*, I returned to *Sir Gawain* with refreshed eyes and was pleasantly surprised to find the green god Dionysos—or something like him—winking back at me from the tangled hedgerows of verse.

The Middle English poem begins with curious lines having to do with Troy—that's right, the one from the Trojan War in Greek mythology—that ostensibly link the legendary King Arthur with the esteemed emperors of Rome. Then we are dropped right into Camelot, into Arthur's banquet hall, where the Green Knight crashes the king's 15-day-long Christmas festivities on New Year's Day. It's a dramatic moment; the music stops and everyone goes silent to stare at the strange stranger who enters: a gigantic man "from neck to loin so strong and thickly made," riding an equally giant horse, and all of them—man, horse, clothing, saddle—entirely green.[187]

The Green Knight's hair is worn long and loose around his shoulders, and his beard is "thick and green as a bush,"[188] and together his hair and beard cover his arms to his elbows like the cloak of a king. He wears no armor and no shoes, but his clothing is rich and bejeweled "with fair stones set upon silken work" and embroidered with "birds and insects in gay gauds of green and gold."[189] In one hand, the Green Knight bears a holly branch, and in the other, a mighty axe four feet wide, made of green steel and gold set into a strong, straight staff, with a strap twined about the head and handle, "clasped with tassels on buttons of bright green richly broidered."[190] The Green Knight is described in a juxtaposition of brutality and finery, green and gold, monstrosity and beauty. King Arthur's court gazes speechless upon the knight, wondering at "what it might mean that a knight and his steed should have even such a hue as the green grass; and that seemed even greener than green enamel on bright gold."[191]

What might his greenness mean indeed? Green is the color of nature, of the evergreen trees of winter and the holly bough the knight holds, as well as of the fresh, new leaves of spring. Green is the color of life, of renewal and rebirth. At the same time, green is associated with devils, who are often portrayed with green skin in medieval art, and with death through the green of infection and the greenish skin of a corpse. The green color of the knight and, later, the location of his "Green Chapel" under a grassy hill in the woods align him with fairies, who were thought to live underground in fairy mounds. Indeed, the people of King Arthur's court conclude that the strange knight is of "phantasm and faërie."[192]

Everyone in the hall, including Arthur himself, is speechless—and probably afraid. Finally, the Green Knight speaks. He has come to the greatest court in the land with a festive challenge, an exchange of blows. The terms are this: One of Arthur's revered knights will take the Green Knight's giant axe and strike him one blow with it. Then, one year from that day, Arthur's knight will allow the Green Knight to return that blow to him in kind.

Of course, none of the supposedly bravest knights in the land want to take him on. The Green Knight taunts them, questioning their valor, and when Arthur moves to take the axe himself, his nephew Gawain steps up to the challenge to spare him. Calmly and with a little smile, the Green Knight bows his head, exposing his neck for the strike. Thinking that his best shot at survival will be to kill the Green Knight with one swing, and thus escape the return blow in a year, Gawain hefts the green axe and chops the Green Knight's head clean off.

The head rolls on the ground for a moment, spurting blood, and Gawain thinks he has won. But then the Green Knight's headless body moves gracefully forward and retrieves the rolling head. He mounts his horse, head in hand, unbothered, and lifts his head by the green hair to look at Gawain. The eyes blink and lips move, alive as if the head was attached to its body, and the Green Knight speaks. He directs Gawain to seek him at the Green Chapel in one year to receive his end of the bargain. Then the headless knight and his great green horse gallop out the doors.

This isn't in the text, but one imagines Gawain shit his pants.

The Green Knight's entrance into King Arthur's Camelot is akin to the intrusion of the wild into civilized order. No Dionysian mae-nads leap up to dance and hunt, no wine flows miraculously from bare rocks, but then again, we are not in ancient Greece. We are in medieval England, a Christian society much less liberal, much more repressive, than the one that birthed boundary-blurring Dionysos. Critics have interpreted the Green Knight as a pagan fertility symbol and as a force of nature and the vivacity of life personified. He bears a resemblance to the green men, or foliate faces (i.e. faces with leaves sprouting from them), popular in medieval art and architecture at the time the poem was written, an artistic device that likely inspired *The Green Knight's* vegetal costume design.

The idea of the Green Man was later incorporated into 20th-century reconstructionist neo-paganism as a face of the Wiccan Horned God and/or a corollary of the Greek god Pan. Additionally, the Green Knight may be influenced by "Wild Man" figures such as the Middle English woodwose, which we are told that Gawain encounters on his travels to the Green Chapel. Usually depicted covered with long body hair like a medieval European Bigfoot, Wild Men have been likened to satyrs and sileni, who were the attendants of none other than Dionysos in Greek mythology, as well as to the ultra-gay and horny Greek god Pan. However, the Green Knight is too refined (see all those tassels and gold embroidery) to be fully a Wild Man himself, but he plays a similar role in the romance poem, acting as a pagan-inflected, nature-aligned counter to Camelot's civilized Christian ways.

The Green Knight in his entrancing strangeness represents the challenge of queer nature always creeping in at the edges, trailing up the walls, reminding us that our (hu)man-made order is but a temporary delusion in the face of the Wild Queer Everything. Nature is queer because it is perceived as inhuman, as unknown, as Other by Western civilization. Nature does not abide by the laws of man but has its own strange rhythms and sense of justice. It's also queer *because it literally is*. Nature is not exclusively heterosexual—gay penguins and humping humpback whales can attest to that. Neither is nature cisgender—a human concept that is ridiculous to apply to nature in the first place—nor binary-sexed, as sex-changing clownfish, hermaphroditic nematodes, gynandromorphic cardinals, and female phallus-growing hyenas can prove. *Cis-heteronormativity is an invention of Western patriarchal colonialist civilization.* It holds no sway over nature, over life. It never has, and never will. Thinking otherwise is just more grandiose human delusion.

The Green Knight is not the Wild Man, though. He is a knight. He wears civilized clothes. But he is also *green*. As we will see in the poem, he laughs at death and has mysterious morals. He has one foot in civilization and the other in the wilderness. In this way, the Green Knight might be a bridge, a holy holly branch that reconnects humanity to nature, an axe that decapitates destructive patriarchal civilization, a Green Chapel that welcomes our spirits back to the Wild Queer Everything from whence we came and to where we always, forever, return.

A Gayme of Kisses

The year passes, and Gawain has ample time to reflect on his impending mortality. When it's time to depart for the Green Chapel, Arthur's court fits Gawain out in splendid jewels and armor, with a shield that bears the Virgin Mary's likeness on the inside (to give Gawain courage, we are told) and the sacred "pentangle," a five-pointed knot not unlike a pentacle or pentagram, on the outside as a symbol of his unimpeachable chivalric virtue. Due at the Green Chapel on New Year's, Gawain departs for the long journey into unknown lands on All Saints' Day (Halloween). Along the way, he faces many trials and challenges (including some woodwose), but no one he meets has heard of a Green Knight or a Green Chapel. Exhausted and despondent as Christmas nears, Gawain finally stumbles upon a castle in the woods.

The lord of the manor, Bertilak de Hautdesert, invites Gawain to spend Christmas with him and his beautiful wife, called only the Lady. Gawain, sore and frozen from his travels, gladly accepts. Lord Bertilak is a jolly host, generous with food, wine, and comforts, and perhaps a little wicked, quick to joke and instigate games. After several days of merriment, Gawain makes to leave for his appointment with the Green Knight, but Bertilak convinces him to stay a while longer. He assures Gawain that he knows where the Green Chapel lies, only two miles away, an easy half-day's ride. Gawain can rest longer and leave for the chapel on New Year's Day, refreshed and ready to meet his challenge. And in the meantime, Bertilak proposes a game. Every day while Gawain rests, Bertilak will go out on a hunt. Every evening when he returns, Bertilak will give to Gawain the spoils of his hunt, and Gawain will give to Bertilak whatever it is he has gained that day as well. An exchange of winnings. Gawain, thinking his will be the better end of the bargain, accepts.

On the first day, while Bertilak hunts, Gawain sleeps in. He is surprised when there is a noise at the door and Bertilak's wife, the beautiful Lady, enters his bedchamber. Gawain awkwardly feigns sleep, hoping the Lady will leave and spare him a tricky situation, but she crawls into bed with him. The codes of chivalry and courtly love dictate that Gawain cannot outright rebuff the Lady, lest he be considered rude, but neither can he accept her seductions, lest he dishonor Bertilak—a trap of manners of which the Lady is no doubt aware. She seems, at times, to toy with him. She has "captured" him, she says, and jokes that she will tie him to his bed so he can't escape.

The poem juxtaposes Bertilak's hunt with the Lady's seductions, positioning the Lady as huntress and Gawain as prey. Gawain spends the day walking a tightrope of chaste flirtation and polite deflection, until, finally, he accepts one kiss from the Lady. That evening, when Bertilak returns with a fine deer for Gawain, the knight must exchange his winnings. Gawain "clasped his hands round the lord's neck and kissed him as courteously as he might," adding that if he had received more, he would gladly give it.[193] Pleased, the lord declares it good and thanks him.

On the second day, the game repeats. This time, Bertilak brings Gawain home a boar, and Gawain receives two kisses from the Lady, which he eagerly gives to Bertilak, taking him around the neck and kissing him twice: "By [Saint] Giles," swears the lord, "ye are the best I know; ye will be rich in a short space if ye drive such bargains!"[194]

On the third day, Bertilak hunts a fox. Gawain receives three kisses from the Lady—and a little something else. The Lady entreats Gawain to accept a token of her love: a green silk girdle embroidered with gold. He staunchly refuses until she tells him that the girdle is magic: no man can be overcome or killed while wearing it. Fully expecting to die the next day under the Green Knight's blade, Gawain cravenly accepts the girdle.

That evening, Bertilak returns with the fox skin, and Gawain greets him happily in the hall, throwing his arms around the lord and kissing him thrice, "as solemnly [sincerely] as he might." Bertilak tells Gawain that his measly fox skin is "but poor payment for three such kisses as ye have here given me."[195] Gawain thanks him merrily.

Gawain does not give the girdle to his host, though by the contract he must. He keeps it secret, hidden beneath his robes.

The next morning, Gawain sets out for the Green Chapel, a pep in his step since he has the green girdle and no longer expects to die. When he finds the Green Chapel, it's not the fine or stately chapel that he expected, but a rugged, natural cavern under a grassy hill beside a bubbling brook. The Green Knight is there, sharpening his axe. He directs Gawain to remove his helmet and bend his head so he may fulfill their bargain. Gawain does so, refusing to show fear—after all, he has the Lady's magic girdle. But as the green axe comes down, Gawain flinches anyway. The Green Knight pulls his strike and makes fun of him for flinching. His pride stung, Gawain resolves to hold steady the second time. The Knight's second swing is a feint to see if Gawain would flinch—he does not, though he is annoyed with the knight for toying with him—but the third time the knight follows through. He swings his massive axe so it just kisses the flesh on the side of Gawain's neck, just enough to draw blood that dapples red in the white snow.

Jubilant at his escape from death, Gawain leaps back and unsheathes his sword, waving it at the knight with a threat if he tries for a fourth blow. But the Green Knight leans casually on his axe handle and laughs, as unconcerned with Gawain's threats as he was with his head rolling on the floor a year ago. He reveals to Gawain that he did not behead him on purpose. Instead, he gave him two blows without harm for the two days Gawain kept his covenant, giving Bertilak the kisses the Lady gave Gawain. But the third day, the Green Knight says, Gawain betrayed his promise, concealing the girdle, so he gave Gawain a nick in the neck for his failure.

As it turns out, the Green Knight is none other than Lord Berti-lak, who arranged the entire game with his wife as a test for Gawain. Also behind the scenes was Morgan le Fay, the pagan sorceress and Arthur's nemesis (and aunt), who the Green Knight/Bertilak rever-ently calls "the goddess."[196] For her part, it seems the sorceress mostly wanted to scare Arthur's wife, Queen Guinevere, with the headless Camelot stunt.

Gawain is furious at being tricked and then horrified by his expo-sure. He proceeds to rake himself over the proverbial coals for his cowardice and dishonesty, and then ruins any half-hearted account-ability with a misogynist monologue that shifts the blame for his inadequacies onto the Lady (basically, the "I wouldn't have done it if she hadn't tempted me" defense) and for all male weakness on women (because Eve ate the apple, etc.). One can't help but notice that Gawain is only aghast *after* the Green Knight/Bertilak reveals that he knows everything. Gawain was quite happy and smug when he thought he'd tricked the knight and escaped with his life. He's only remorseful after he gets caught.

Laughing, and perhaps rolling his eyes, Bertilak tells Gawain to keep the girdle as a token of his adventure at the Green Chapel. Gawain says he'll keep it, but as a symbol of his dishonesty and cow-ardice. Then, they part ways with an embrace and a kiss for the road. Gawain ties the girdle diagonally over his chest and travels back to King Arthur's court, where he tells the knights of the Round Table the shameful story of how he received it. Arthur declares that all the knights will wear a green girdle from that day forth in honor of Sir Gawain.

Slippery Genders and Green Morals

There's a lot going on there. We have a game-inside-a-game, an exchange of winnings inside an exchange of blows, perhaps inside another game of which only the Green Knight/Bertilak, the Lady, and Morgan le Fay are aware. We have kisses between two men, which some critics have argued are homoerotic and others strictly homo-social (of nonsexual same-sex affection), but either way definitely homo. And we've got the Lord and Lady Bertilak—swingers?—playing a seduction game with their guest. Oh, and then there's the green girdle, an article of women's clothing that becomes magic when a man wears it.*

A queer reading of *Sir Gawain* is not just possible; it's easy.

Granted, my language above is anachronistic, particularly in the case of calling the Bertilaks "swingers," but consensual nonmonogamy is older than the Bible. Is this what the anonymous author, called the Gawain-poet, intended? Highly doubtful. But then again, you never know.

Since the 1990s, critics have paid new attention to *Sir Gawain* through the lens of queer theory. While they detect homoeroticism in the poem, most tend to conclude that any gay tension between Gawain and Bertilak is used by the poet to reinforce the rightness and sanctity of heterosexuality and the heteronormative ways of a "good" Christian life. Of course, such a reading situates heteronormativity as firmly belonging to Christian civilization, with homoeroticism then belonging to the wildness of nature that civilization so fervently attempts to stamp out. Which way of life is the "good" one then depends on the allegiances of the reader, and which way of life "triumphs" is determined by who is the victor of the story—a topic of dispute in criticism. Some read the poem as a serious, pious reinforcement of chivalry and Christian ideals. Others read the poem as quite the opposite—a humorous critique of chivalry and Christian civilization and a playful ode to the old, pagan ways.

Though the poem is often interpreted as a reinforcement of chivalry and civilization, it seems to me that Sir Gawain and the Round Table's knights are the losers. The Green Knight/Bertilak wins the beheading game because Gawain cheats. The Lady wins the exchange of winnings because she finds Gawain's weakness—his fear of death. Morgan le Fay wins because Gawain falls right into her trap, and arguably so does the rest of the Round Table when they take up the baldric of the green girdle, wearing a symbol of pagan magic and knightly cowardice as a sign of pride.

One way to read the exchange of blows, a motif found in other folktales called the "beheading game," is as a kind of castration

---

* Girdles (cloth knotted around the waist as a belt) were worn by medieval men as well as women, but in this case the girdle is obviously a lady's.

metaphor.* The fear of losing one's head becomes the fear of losing one's masculinity becomes the fear of the impotence of socially constructed masculinity exposed. Indeed, the poem undermines chivalric masculinity at nearly every turn. A courtly bargain within a knightly challenge becomes a guise for a homoerotic game of exchanging kisses, the end game of which could have been homosexual lovemaking. If Gawain was to accept the Lady's seductions and have sex with her, he must then, by honor and the terms of the covenant, have sex with Bertilak too. This potential is never named in the text but is latently palpable, providing an erotic charge that pulses through the hunting and seduction scenes.

The poem reverses the typical gender roles of the time, making the Lady into the sexual aggressor, the huntress, while Gawain becomes the quarry, the prey. When the Lady kisses Gawain, she takes the masculine role and he the feminine, and then when Gawain gives the kisses to Bertilak, Gawain takes the masculine role and Bertilak the feminine. At the same time, feminist critics have argued that the Lady is used as a pawn—is "trafficked"—in a game between men. For her part, the Lady is never given the opportunity to inform the reader whether she was a willing or unwilling participant. Meanwhile, Morgan Le Fay, a woman, has apparently masterminded the entire situation. The entire poem, the entire story, is a push-pull tension wherein sexuality and gender roles continually wrestle each other, and the victor is anything but clear.

As scholars such as Carolyn Dinshaw and David L. Boyd have argued, in the late Middle Ages certain elements of the nobility and clergy were increasingly concerned with male effeminacy and queer behavior, and with the power of women—in other words, with queered gender roles.[197] They saw such behavior as driving the fall of a former, idyllic, chivalrous, and Christian way of life, and they used attacks on queer men and improper (i.e., masculine) women to shift blame for the problems of society and shore up the institutional power of the aristocracy and the church. There are clear parallels in the 21st century, with the rise of extreme rightwing homophobia

---

* Interestingly, the Green Knight arrives in Camelot on the Feast of the Circumcision, which could be a coincidence—or not.

and transphobia and the onslaught of legislation against queer and trans rights and abortion rights, all in a strategic political effort to resuscitate a dying conservative vote and consolidate the wealth and power of the capitalist ruling class. Not every story has been told before, but no story is new.

Sir Gawain seems to play on these sentiments, blaming male weakness on the machinations of women (the Lady and Morgan le Fay), but if its goal is to shore up chivalry, it does a confusing job of it. The story is ambiguous enough to be read a myriad of contradictory ways, and it is immensely unclear if the Green Knight is a villain or a savior. Indeed, while some read the Green Knight as a devil or a pagan fertility deity, still others read the Green Knight as a Christ figure who dies and rises to redeem Gawain by showing him the error of this ways.[198] As for Gawain, in the course of the poem, he fails nearly all of the five knightly virtues represented by the pentangle on his shield: (1) his five "faultless" senses fail him when he does not ascertain he's being tricked, (2) his faith in Christ falters when he accepts the pagan girdle, (3) the courage he receives from Mary is likewise shaken when he chooses cowardice as well as when he flinches, and (4) his virtues of honesty, fellowship, and courtesy go out the window when he lies and breaks his oath to his host. The only virtue remaining is "his five fingers which never failed him," but one wonders if that can be true when his five fingers eagerly grabbed the green girdle and tied it hidden beneath his robes.

In the Green Chapel, the Green Knight/Bertilak stands in judgment of Gawain, but if the Green Knight is a god, he is a merciful one. He forgives Gawain for his cowardice and deceit because it wasn't done for material gain or even lust, but, as the Green Knight says, "because thou lovedst thy life—therefore I blame thee the less."[199] Gawain made his choice out of desperation to survive, and according to the morals of the Green Chapel, there's nothing wrong with that. You can hardly blame someone for not wanting to die. That's only human. Only natural. The Green Knight finds little fault with him, declaring him the most worthy knight in the world, "as a pearl among white peas."[200] Perhaps this is meant to be read as humorous, as mockery, when Gawain has so clearly failed the knightly code, or perhaps it's a dig at knights in general—if Gawain is the finest, the rest must be poor indeed. But Gawain's failings weren't of compassion, kindness, or love; he only trespassed the rules of a frivolous game in order to save his own life, and in a way that harmed no one in any real way. Perhaps the Green Knight simply doesn't care for silly chivalrous codes. He's a different kind of knight, after all. Perhaps his codes are different too.

In Comes Green

In *The Green Knight*, writer-director David Lowery brings the question of the knight's color into dialogue that is not original to the poem but brings this central quality of the knight into focus. Lady Bertilak, played by Alicia Vikander, wonders aloud why the knight is green instead of another color. Gawain, played by Dev Patel, answers that he is green because he's unnatural, not of this world.* The Lady counters that green *is* the color of this world, of the earth, of life and living things, to which Gawain adds that green is also the color of rot, of mold and gangrene. The Lady agrees and then delivers a monologue that is equal parts disturbing and enchanting. The camera is rapt on the Lady's face as she speaks low and rhythmically, almost as if weaving a spell. She describes green as the color of life, and yet mankind has made green its enemy. When green vines creep over the walls and moss blooms between the cobblestones, we scrub, stamp, smother, cut it out. Though we chase after red—lust, blood, power—green wins out in the end, she says. The product of sexual lust is life—green—and once our red blood runs cold, green will grow over us all in death. Green will consume our bones, claim our swords, castles, coins. The Lady's dark eyes glitter in the candlelight as she ends her monologue with a prediction—no, a promise. Nothing you love will be spared, she tells Gawain, she tells *us*. Not our flesh, not our cities, and certainly not our virtue.[201]

To follow the Lady's color logic, Christian civilization, with its wars and cities, its purity codes and prideful quests and "virtue," would undoubtedly be the color red. Indeed, in the film, the magic

---

* Not of this world as in a devil from Hell or a fairy creature from another realm—though a 21st-century audience may also hear a reference to extraterrestrials, or "little green men."

of Morgaine (Morgan le Fay) is accompanied by vivid green lighting, while the magic of Merlin, representing the masculine civilization of Arthur's court, is all crimson red. And we know which hue always wins out in the end, at least according to the Lady.

In the 14th century, nature was an ever-present, lethal threat. Bears, wolves, storms, ice, famine, disease. Civilization offered an ordered respite, keeping the chaotic wilderness at bay behind the battlements. In the film, when Gawain leaves Camelot for his journey, he travels through acres upon acres of deforested land, tree stumps jutting from the landscape like tombstones. Then he comes to battle fields, strewn with the corpses of soldiers rotting where they fell, the earth charred and smoking as if a literal hell. Made for a 21st-century audience, these scenes hold an extra layer of ominous dread: We are viewing the beginnings of modernity, the world on a precipice of environmental destruction from which we will never return. When Gawain finally enters the forest, he asks a group of dirty, ragged, probably starving young people, little older than children, if they know the way to the Green Chapel. One replies, "You're in it." Then they attack and rob the gaily dressed knight, taking his jewels and smashing his pentangle shield down the middle, right down the center of the Virgin Mary's face. They steal his horse and leave Gawain tied up on the forest floor.

The attack portrays the wilderness, the "Green Chapel," as a lawless, brutal, and violent place where nothing, not even Mary, is sacred. And indeed it can be. But as the camera pans slowly from Gawain's prone form in a 360-degree arc around the forest, it's all blooming flowers and tender greenery, buzzing insects and calling birds, fruiting mushrooms and sunlight lancing between old-growth trees. It is peaceful. Contrasted with the fields of civilization that grow only stumps and bodies, one wonders which is more brutal and violent, which is sacrilege, which is evil: the Green Chapel or Camelot.

Sir Gawain is not a simple story of one knight's quest for honor, nor is it a simple competition between two different sorts of knight. What's at stake here is much larger. On one level, it is the story of a man coming to terms with his mortality, and on another, it is the story of humanity's attempts to dominate nature and triumph over death, attempts that are ultimately doomed to fail. As the Lady says, no swords nor battlements, no virtue nor religion, will beat back death—which is to say *life*—in the end. Perhaps we may read *Sir Gawain* as a darkly comedic exposé of the silliness of chivalry and the ravages of patriarchal civilization. When Gawain returns to Camelot at the end and confesses his shame, all the knights of the Round Table wind up wearing the girdle, the symbol of the failure of constructed heteronormative masculinity and the redemption of the wild, the magical, the queer, the green.

As for the Green Knight, he is a riot of contradictions, not unlike Dionysos. He is devilish and fae, but also knightly and masculine. He flits between Christian and pagan, courtly and wild, master and monster, human and vegetation. He returns from the manly hunt to be kissed like a woman by a man. He is a native of the landscape who is treated as Other by civilization. He is a jolly, dismembered god. He bleeds and resurrects, damns and saves, laughing all the while.

So let's give the Green Knight a double-headed labrys and wrap Gawain in pretty green garters. Maybe the thing that will save our lives is a garter belt, is a softening of the masculine, is the feminine on top, is kisses shared—sexually or platonically—among men, among lovers and friends alike. Maybe, to win the beheading game, we must decapitate the false superiority of "masculine" logic, "enlightened" civilization, and Christian "purity." We must run into the wilderness and metaphorically lose our heads. We must find our way (back) to the Green Chapel, to nature in all its queerness, and rediscover the sacred on our mossy knees. We must meet the Green Night, the verdant death, and bend the neck. It's the only way to live.

QUEER DEVOTIONS

Queer Contemplations

- In the poem, the Green Knight has mercy on Gawain, sparing him from losing his head even though he cheated. He seems to feel compassion for Gawain, saying he can't blame him for not wanting to die.

- Consider: Do you think the Divine is merciful? Do you think nature is merciful? Which is more merciful, civilization or the natural world? Which is more violent?

- Are you merciful toward yourself? If not, why? How can you extend more mercy to yourself or to the people around you? When people do harmful things (to others or themselves), how can you model the Green Knight and extend compassionate understanding?

• Morality and social codes come up a lot in *Sir Gawain*. What *is* morality, exactly? Is it divine? Cultural? Social? Natural? Is there a difference between morality and values? Is any of it ordained by the Divine?

• We have been reading a lot of stories that seem to pit civilization against nature. Does this have to be the case? Not all spiritualities believe that nature is divine, but a lot do. Does this mean that human society and civilization are, by necessity, not divine? Aren't humans a part of nature? What are some human creations that strike you as touched by the Divine? How can humans or our creations and technologies be useful in serving the environment and welfare of all life?

• Is protecting the environment a spiritual imperative?

• What (or where) is the Green Chapel for you?

Exercise: The Five Virtues of the Pentangle

The five-pointed star, or pentangle, on Sir Gawain's shield represented his five core virtues for a noble and godly life. Make a list of all the virtues or values that are most important to you—compassion, integrity, generosity, or creativity, for example—and then narrow them down to the five core virtues of your personal pentangle.

Why did you choose each of these virtues or values? How can you live your life in greater accordance with them? Remember that Gawain fails in all five of his virtues, but the Green Knight is still merciful to him. If you're not perfectly virtuous all the time, that's okay! The important thing is to know your values and do your best to live by them, even if you can't sometimes.

Draw your five-pointed pentangle in your journal and write your virtues beside each point. Check back every now and then to remind yourself of what's important to you.

 CHAPTER 7

Questioning the Grail

Perceval and the Fairy King
Heal the Wasteland

Perceval, le Conte du Graal [the Story of the Grail] has everything a good story needs: heroic quests and misadventures, magical objects and disappearing castles, a flawed but good-hearted knight, and a mysteriously wounded king who needs his help to lift a curse. It has everything, that is, except an ending.

Written by Chrétien de Troyes in the late 12th century, the Old French verse romance of *Perceval* is incomplete. It cuts off midsentence, either due to the death of the patron for whom Chrétien was writing it or the death of Chrétien himself. But the story enthralled readers; even in the Middle Ages, it seems, no one could resist a cliff-hanger. Multiple writers attempted to finish the story Chrétien started, adding approximately 50 thousand lines to Chrétien's original nine thousand, resulting in what are known as the Four Continuations, as well as two prologues, all inked by different hands in the 13th century. The Continuations attempt to pick up where Chrétien left off and fill in narrative gaps, but they frequently contradict each other or add elements, characters, and storylines nowhere in Chrétien's original. The result is a strange, sprawling cycle of stories that feels something like a fairy castle, full of unexpected rooms, distorted mirrors, secret passages, and hallways that lead to nowhere.

Chrétien's romance has further been adapted, retold, reimagined, and remixed in numerous variations across the centuries since. Wolfram von Eschenbach's early 13th-century *Parzival*, considered one of the masterpieces of the German Middle Ages, is a close adaptation of *Perceval*, but with an ending. Sir Thomas Malory's 15th-century *Le Morte d'Arthur* draws on the story of Perceval and the Grail, but with many liberties and alterations and significant Christianization. Richard Wagner's famous 19th-century opera *Parsifal* is directly inspired by Wolfram's *Parzival*, and T. S. Eliot's celebrated 20th-century modernist poem *The Waste Land* takes many of its themes and symbols from the whole cycle of works launched by Chrétien's unfinished romance. Perceval and his Fisher King have even appeared, in different forms, in an episode of *Doctor Who*, *The Witcher* books and video games, and characters from C. S. Lewis and George R. R. Martin. The grail itself has become one of the most well-known features of Arthurian myth, as well as the subject of much scholarly attention and just as many fascinating, if contestable, conspiracy theories revolving around certain Christian relics and royal French bloodlines.* The influence of Perceval and the story of the Grail on the Western imagination cannot be exaggerated.

What, exactly, is it about Chrétien's unfinished romance that has so enraptured readers, writers, composers, artists, and speculative thinkers for more than eight hundred years?

The tale begins with an inquisitive young man named Perceval, raised by his widowed mother in the rural countryside of Wales. One day, while going to check on his mother's fields, Perceval comes across a group of knights on the road. Never having seen knights before, at first Perceval thinks they're devils, making such racket with their loud, flashing armor. As they get closer, Perceval realizes they are beautiful, "more beautiful than God," and is convinced they must be angels instead. Upon learning that they're not angels but knights, Perceval peppers them with questions about their lances, shields, and armor, all while the leading knight attempts—unsuccessfully—to extract directions from the boy. "He doesn't know his manners, so help me God," the knight says, "because he won't answer anything I ask him in a straightforward way; instead he asks the name of everything he sees, and what it is used for."[202] Eventually, Perceval gives the knight

---

* I am, of course, referring to the theory that the Merovingian kings of France were descended from the secret child of Jesus Christ and Mary Magdalene, made famous by Dan Brown's 2003 novel *The Da Vinci Code*.

the information he wants, and then runs home to inform his mother that he's leaving to become a knight, himself. On hearing this, she promptly faints. Perceval sets off anyway, against his mother's wishes. Hijinks and quests ensue, and Perceval receives training in knightly conduct and courtly manners—including keeping his mouth shut and not asking so many questions.

Then, one fateful day, Perceval comes upon a fisherman sitting in a boat that floats perfectly still in the middle of a flowing river. The fisherman invites Perceval to stay the night at his nearby castle and provides directions to get there, warning that it's easy to become lost along the way. Perceval rides off in the direction of the castle and quickly becomes lost indeed. Just when he's cursing the fisherman for being a liar, he sees the castle's tower rising above the trees. Once he finally arrives, Perceval is warmly received, dressed in sumptuous crimson robes, and led to a grand banquet hall where his host waits. The humble fisherman has been transformed into a handsome nobleman with salt-and-pepper hair, leaning on one elbow on a daybed before a massive, roaring fire. As Perceval approaches, the lord apologizes that he cannot rise to greet him because he has difficulty standing, and invites Perceval to sit close beside him on the bed. As they chat, a squire approaches with a beautiful sword in an ornate scabbard with elaborate straps, which the lord promptly gifts to Perceval, saying it was destined for him.

Then a hush falls over the room and a strange sight appears: A young man enters carrying a white lance that bleeds from its tip, followed by two squires holding luminous golden candelabras, a maiden carrying a richly jeweled grail (a shallow serving dish), and another maiden carrying a silver platter. The assembly passes through the hall and exits into a dark room on the far side, without a word to explain the odd procession. Though he is curious, Perceval had been taught by the knight who trained him that talking too much and asking questions was rude. So he keeps his mouth shut and doesn't ask about the procession. After an exquisite and exotic meal, the lord bids Perceval goodnight, and they go their separate ways to bed.

Perceval wakes in the morning to find his clothing and armor laid out for him, his horse groomed and saddled in the courtyard, and the castle abandoned, not a soul in sight. Disturbed but taking the hint, Perceval dresses, mounts, and exits the strangely deserted castle. Behind him, the portcullis closes so quickly it almost snaps him and his horse in half. Soon, on the road, Perceval encounters a distraught maiden who tells him that the lordly fisherman was none other than the mythical Fisher King, wounded "between the thighs" and in constant pain. Nothing will heal the Fisher King other than being asked a certain question by a knight who has no knowledge of the king, the procession, or the curse. Tragically, if Perceval had only indulged his curiosity and *asked* about the strange procession instead of minding his manners and holding his tongue, the Fisher King would have been miraculously healed and much joy and abundance would have come to the land. But since Perceval failed, now the king's lands will turn barren and his kingdom cursed with death and sorrow.

Perceval goes on to have many more quests and adventures, but he carries a heavy regret. He later confesses to a holy hermit that he hasn't known where he was going ever since, almost like he is still searching for the fisherman's castle, lost in the woods. The remainder of Chrétien's original text follows the knight Gawain (yes, the same Gawain of the Green Knight), and cuts off midsentence before it returns to Perceval, as it had earlier promised to do.

We are left with an unhealed wound, an unasked question, and an unsolved mystery. Maybe the *Perceval* story is so enthralling because it emphasizes something we can all relate to: the agony of a missed opportunity. As scholar of medieval French literature Anna Roberts describes it, "The Grail Castle episode is a space invested with a negative charge, a melancholy space of regret—not a void, but a definite absence, not a staid silence, but a vibrant, unsettling 'un-said,' a screen onto which all readers can project notions crucial to their understanding of the romances."[203] When Roberts says "romances," she is referring to the genre of chivalric literature to which *Perceval* belongs. But I think it's fair to say that that void—that negative space of questions unasked, of things left unsaid—offers a screen that we readers can project our own grief and longing onto, all our what-ifs and if-onlys, all our missed kisses and questions deferred.

In Wolfram von Eschenbach's *Parzival*,* a close adaptation of *Perceval* written in the first quarter of the 13th century, contemporaneous with the Continuations, there is a pendulous "will they / won't they?" moment at the end of the banquet, when the Fisher King pulls Perceval aside to say good night. It's Perceval's last chance to *ask the question*—one imagines the Fisher King's candlelit eyes upon Perceval's mouth, waiting, hoping, perhaps unconsciously licking his lips—but the question does not come. The narrator voices the agonizing disappointment felt by the Fisher King and the readers as the two go their separate ways to bed: "Now here might I raise my war-cry at the parting betwixt the twain [the parting of the two], / For I wot [know] well that bitter sorrow each must from the venture gain."[204] I read a gay longing and anxiety in Perceval's unasked question: the longing of one man for another, and the anxiety of making a move for fear that you misread the situation, at best receiving rejection and at worst a fit of homophobic rage. So you hold your tongue, keep your hands to yourself, and wait for a familiar sign or signal, a direct question, an invitation to follow the queer procession into the darkened room.

But as most of us know too well, we can't always go back and grab the moment again once it's gone. In *Parzival*, the Fisher King's castle moves and disappears. It can only be found by one who isn't trying to find it. Somewhat like how life offers opportunities and invitations when we least expect it, often when it's least convenient—but when we're searching for them, they're nowhere to be found.

The authors who added to and adapted *Perceval* over the years have offered their own endings. In some, the Fisher King and his land are never healed. In others, Gawain or the chaste knight Galahad succeed where Perceval failed. In an attempt to answer the riddle of the lance and grail, later authors turned the lance into the Spear of Longinus that pierced Jesus's side at the crucifixion, and turned the grail into the Holy Grail, the fabled cup in which Joseph of Arimathea was said to have caught blood from Jesus's side wound. The ending eventually provided in the Continuations has Perceval healing the Fisher King not by asking the magic question, but by vengeance, by

---

*   *Parzival* is the German equivalent of the name *Perceval*.

tracking down and slaying the fiend who initially wounded the king. Other endings involve Perceval mending the sword the Fisher King gave him (in some tellings, it breaks at a pivotal moment and in others it was broken to begin with), and by doing so lifting the curse and healing the king in some act of sympathetic priapic magic. In another, Perceval takes over the throne after the Fisher King dies and heals the land in seven years with, one assumes, good old-fashioned hard work. Then he absconds to the woods to live out his final years as a hermit, taking the spear and Grail with him to heaven when he dies.

I prefer the ending in Wolfram's *Parzival*. After initially failing in the same manner as Chrétien's Perceval, Parzival eventually, much later, makes his way back to the Grail castle. He falls on his knees before the Fisher King and asks the magic question. In Chrétien, the question seems to concern the mysterious procession and its purpose. In Wolfram, the question is, simply, "What ails thee?"

A healing question indeed.

A Queer Wound

The Fisher King's wound has been the subject of much debate over the centuries, variously translated as a wound "through both thighs," "through the hips," "between the legs," or "between the thighs," to name a few interpretations. As is generally accepted by scholars of medieval European literature, a wound "in" or "between" the thighs or in the leg/groin area is a common medieval euphemism for infertility or castration. This seems especially true in the Fisher King myth, where the king's wound is magically connected to the fertility and prosperity of the land. If the wound is healed, the land will prosper, but if it is not, the land will be barren. Sterility was one of the worst things that could befall a king or a lord because it meant no heirs and an end to his bloodline, so it is no surprise that wounds in the thigh/groin area are plentiful in medieval literature and Arthurian myth.[205]

However, according to Roberts, the Fisher King's wound is queerer than it first seems: "One of the principal ways in which the medieval heteronormative imagination can conceive of queerness, is through the figures of the effeminate and the castrate, veiling the queer by substituting a cipher (castrate), and recalling the use of castration as a threat or punishment for homosexual acts."[206] As horrifying as that punishment may be, castration and effeminacy (as we have seen with Gawain in Chapter 6 and will see again with Loki and Odin in Chapter 8) are nonetheless what Roberts calls "queer thematic sites," veiled but detectable locations of queer representation in heteronormative texts.[207] They are breadcrumbs, ephemera, hints—Derrida's "trace" and Muñoz's "queer evidence"—that allow us to read queerness in oppressive heteronormative environments (like the Middle Ages or the present) that seek to erase, suppress, or argue historical queerness into oblivion.

Roberts points out that while the cause of the Fisher King's wound is not explained in Chrétien's *Perceval*, beyond it being a javelin wound sustained in battle, later addendums assign its cause to *sexual indiscretions* by the Fisher King. The king slept with someone he shouldn't have, either because it was outside of marriage, against the Grail's wishes (the Grail was said to choose its guardians as well as wives for them), or a violation of his celibacy as the Grail guardian, depending on the source. The wound is then sustained as a punishment for his indiscretions or self-inflicted in his own remorse. While the Fisher King's philandering is portrayed as heterosexual, the origin of the wound as a sexual *transgression*, combined with the location and queer connotations of the wound, leave plenty of room for a queer reading.

As we have already seen with Gawain and his Green Knight, medieval taboos against sodomy were predicated on fear of gender inversion—a woman on top, in a position of power and dominance, or a man on bottom, in a position of passivity and submission. A man being sexually penetrated was tantamount to becoming a woman, and in some versions of the story, the Fisher King is penetrated not just once in the initial injury, but multiple times. In *Parzival*, the queerly gendered nature of the wound is most apparent; the king has been "pierced through the testicles" and the wound is described as an orifice, as Roberts points out.[208] A series of physicians and healers penetrate and palpitate the wound with their hands in their attempts at treatment. They insert foreign objects into it including magic herbs and a mystical carbuncle from the base of a unicorn's horn. When the king's wound aches with cold, the bleeding lance itself is thrust into the wound to "warm" it, offering temporary relief. In medieval anatomy, female bodies were thought to be cold and male bodies hot, genderqueering the Fisher King's "cold," i.e., feminine, orifice further.[209] On top of that, the king's pain gets worse as "the moon draweth near to her changing,"[210] a rather menstrual turn of phrase. In some stories, the wound is inflicted *by* the Spear of Longinus, which, if you recall, is also responsible for the vulvic side wound of Jesus (see Chapter 4), who was also called the "fisher of men."* All in all, the Fisher King's wound locates him in an overlapping medieval space of queer sexuality *and* queer gender.

While the Fisher King offers a site of queerness in medieval legend, let us not forget that the Fisher King is also disabled. His queerness is veiled in the text, but his disability is clearly visible. Chrétien tells us that he has difficulty standing, must be carried to bed on a litter, can't ride a horse, and fishes to enjoy himself because he can't pursue the usual noble pastime of hunting. Later authors alter his disability, making it better or worse—he's perpetually bedridden or can walk about, his pain is constant or aggravated by certain activities or celestial events, he's injured or he's ill—but he always has a body that is, in one way or another, disabled. Chrétien describes his castle as comfortably built to suit his needs: "That is why he likes to stay in this hidden retreat, for there's no retreat in the world more suited to his needs, and he has had a mansion built that is worthy of a noble king."[211] While it's nice that the Fisher King's castle is the medieval version of ADA accessible, we can also read in that description an acknowledgment that the rest of the world is *not*.

Chrétien's Fisher King doesn't remain in his castle because he's bound there by some curse, but because the rest of the world is difficult or impossible to navigate with his disability. At the same time as he is described as having a disabled body, the Fisher King is also described as noble, good, kind, handsome, even holy. This is a marked departure from the usual medieval treatment of disability as pitiable, ugly, deformed, monstrous, or, worse, an external mark of some internal evil or sin. Then again, maybe the Fisher King gets to be disabled *and*

---

* There's a long history of scholarship on the Fisher King as Jesus, but that's outside the purview of this chapter.

good because he's a king. One doubts a disabled commoner would receive the same treatment.

However, the conceit that the Fisher King's disability is causing the land's devastation is deeply ableist. That the salvation of the land depends on him being "healed" into an able body is deeply ableist. If we read the king's wound as an indicator of queerness, then queerness becomes the affliction, the "curse," that blights the land. Then it's his queerness that needs to be "cured." In both readings, bodies (disabled, trans, intersex) and/or identities (gay, queer) that are perceived as "not normal" are punished, treated as afflictions in need of cures, and scapegoated for the ills of the entire kingdom. There seems to be no reading of *Perceval* that does not ultimately uphold able-bodied cis-heteronormativity as the life-giving idyll of health and "goodness" that brings prosperity and salvation to the land.

However, I think there's a different way to read it. I think we might have had it backward all along. What if the king's wound is not the cause of the wasteland, after all? What if his "wound" isn't even a *wound* at all?

Even more than the location of the wound in the king's groin area, its primary significator is the pain and suffering it causes him. Another word for suffering is *passion*, from the Latin *pati*, "suffer." The word *compassion* (*com*-passion) literally means "suffering-with." I propose that the kingdom is not suffering because of the Fisher King's wound, but the other way around. The Fisher King suffers *because the land suffers*. He hurts because his *people* hurt. The "wound" that causes the Fisher King such pain is not a wound at all, but the ability to feel, to empathize, to open to the experience of the land and its creatures with compassion. The Fisher King has the ability to hold space for a "suffering-with" that is bigger than him, to be open to a passion of suffering *and* ecstasy, pain *and* pleasure, grief *and* love, self *and* other. This interpretation need not erase our reading of the Fisher King as disabled, gay, or trans, either. He can be both/all: gay, trans, disabled, *and* compassionate. In our modern Western society—where emotion has been sidelined as weak and "feminine" and stoicism deified as strong and "masculine," where disability is treated as a flaw in need of fixing, where bodies that don't coherently fit into a binary gender

121

category are feared and pathologized—the Fisher King's suffering, emotional, compassionate, gay, trans, disabled, penetrated body is *queer* indeed.

Perceval and the Fairy King

The *Elucidation*, an anonymous Old French poem written in the early 13th century as a prologue to Chrétien's *Perceval*, offers an alternative backstory for the wounded king and the cursed wasteland. A highly eccentric text, the *Elucidation* has been largely panned by critics for being inexpertly written and confusing. It refers to stories that supposedly happen in the main text of *Perceval* and its Continuations but, for the most part, never do. It has spoilers. It spends a long time talking about what it's *not* going to talk about. But as Thomas Hinton points out, the confusing nature of *Elucidation*, which "invites its readers to accept contradiction and abundance as principles of narrative aesthetic," seems appropriate for the *Perceval* and its Continuations, in which, "no character, no storyline is allowed to define the narrative for any length of time; a minor plot strand can suddenly move centre-stage, before receding once more into the background, or disappearing altogether."[212] The most interesting part of the *Elucidation* for our queer purposes is the alternative background it provides for the barrenness of the land, a background that I find, well, *elucidating*.

Once upon a time, so the prologue goes, the land was populated by impossibly beautiful maidens who lived in its wells. Whenever a traveler needed food or drink, all they had to do was find a well and ask politely, and a well-maiden would appear with a golden cup brimming with bread and meat, not unlike the Grail itself, which in many stories magically provides endless food. But one day, a wicked king named Amangon raped one of the well-maidens and carried her off, along with her golden cup, forcing her to serve him. Seeing his example, the king's men and vassals did the same, taking what they wanted from the maidens by force, keeping them captive, and pressing them into servitude. The remaining maidens ceased to offer food and drink to the people of the land. They retreated into their wells, never to be seen again, and the landscape withered and dried up with them. No more trees bloomed or streams flowed. The land became a wasteland, and afterward the Fisher King's court, which the text tells us kept the lands fertile, cannot be found.

This alternative background the *Elucidation* provides potentially explains a lot. In my reading, the well-maidens, sometimes translated as "hill" maidens,[213] seem akin to spirits of the land from fairy tales and folklore. After all, fairies were known to live under hills or burial mounds, or near springs and wells, as with Jehanne d'Arc's Fairies' Tree beside a sacred spring. Like the bountiful land itself, the maidens provided ample sustenance freely—as long as they were treated with respect and no one took too much. The rape of the maidens is analogous to the rape of the land—overharvesting, overhunting, strip-mining, logging, damming and diverting rivers and streams, depleting the soil with the same crops year after year. Meanwhile, the Fisher King seems to have been wounded along with the land, and his castle recedes into hiding along with the maidens of the wells.

Despite their common title of "king," the text clearly treats King Amangon and the Fisher King as separate and distinct figures. For that matter, the Fisher King never truly functions as a *king*, with subjects and vassals, etc., anywhere in the *Perceval* text. In some retellings, the Fisher King has knights, but these knights' sole purpose is to keep the Grail safe—perhaps from people like Amangon who would steal it—not act as conquerors or cops. The Fisher King is not aligned with Amangon or, by extension, the dynasty of extractive, patriarchal colonialism-cum-capitalism that his actions and legacy represent.* Rather, the Fisher King seems aligned with the *land itself* and the spirits who once populated it. The maidens withdraw and so does he. The land becomes barren and so does he. The *Elucidation* describes him as a skilled magician and shape-shifter who could change into a hundred shapes. The magical shape-shifting Fisher King, with his parade of strange objects and his moving, disappearing castle, with his connection to the land and the well-maidens, is perhaps not a human king, but a *fairy* one.

---

* Amangon gets his comeuppance; the poem tells us that he and the others who wronged the maidens meet "a dreadful end" (*Elucidation*, lines 92-4).

Although writers after Chrétien applied a heavily Christian treatment to his romance, scholars have shown that Chrétien's source material was, more likely than not, pagan. The mystical objects have been linked with the treasures of the Tuatha Dé Danann,[214] a supernatural race in Celtic mythology who dwelt in the Otherworld and from whom the *aes sídhe*, or "fairies," descend in later Irish folklore. Their treasures are the Cauldron of the Dagda, the Spear of Lugh, the Stone of Fál, and the Sword of Light. The Dagda's cauldron, which never runs empty, may correspond with the Grail, which in many stories provides endless food (as do the maidens' golden cups). In Wolfram's *Parzival*, the Grail is not a dish but a stone, perhaps inspired by the Stone of Fál. The sword Perceval receives from the Fisher King may be the Sword of Light, and the Spear of Lugh may have inspired the bleeding lance.*

Further, the Fisher King himself may descend from figures from Celtic myth and legend. He bears similarities to Manannán mac Lir ("son of the sea"), a member of the Tuatha Dé Danann and Otherworld king in Irish myth who possessed a magic golden cup that would shatter into pieces if three lies were told in its presence and would re-form, healed, if three truths were told.[215] The Fisher King has also been connected to Manannán's brother in Welsh myth, Brân the Blessed, who was disabled by a wound to his foot and possessed a cauldron that could resurrect the dead.[216] Brân's cauldron offers another potential influence for the Grail, which in numerous stories has healing and life-sustaining properties. But there's a catch: Those resurrected from Brân's cauldron are returned without the power of speech. Voiceless.

The Fisher King is only healed if Perceval gives *voice* to "the question." In the *Elucidation*, when the maidens withdrew, the kingdom "lost the voices of the wells."[217]

Queers are familiar with silence. So are disabled people, neurodivergent people, women, survivors, People of the Global Majority, the houseless, the poor. Anyone whose body or identity has been marginalized by mainstream society has some experience with being silenced, with being punished for speaking out, with being called

---

* The Spear of Lugh is a spear of fire and lightning, not of blood, but the spear was said to have such a thirst for blood that it could only be kept under control by quenching it in a draught of poppy. The Luin of Celtchar, a similar spear often conflated with the Spear of Lugh, needed to be dipped in blood every hour (Loomis 267f).

"angry" or "crazy" or outright ignored. And sometimes we silence ourselves too. We know what it means to stay quiet like Perceval, only not out of politeness, but fear. Being marginalized means being subjected to repeated trauma by a society that perceives us as abnormal, lesser, broken, freakish, threatening, aberrant, confused. We feel that trauma like a wound reopened every time a family member misgenders us, every time there's no accessibility information on the event page, every time the cop's lights flash in the rearview, every time a car turns down the street and we reflexively drop our lover's hand. So many wounds, small and large, never able to fully heal.

In *Perceval*, the healing begins with a question. A question to the Fisher King, to the maidens of the wells, to one another, to us: *What ails thee?*

The Question

In Chrétien, the magic question is never asked, but we can surmise that it is some version or combination of "Why does the lance bleed?" "Who does the grail serve?" or "What is the purpose of all this?" Aside and apart from the Christian relics or gendered connotations usually applied to the objects (lance = phallic/masculine; grail = womblike/feminine), the lance is plainly a weapon and the grail a serving dish. The lance is an instrument of battle, violence, competition, and subjugation. The grail is an instrument of hospitality, a vehicle for serving food. The lance bleeds. The grail feeds. We need not gender either object because we are all, regardless of sex or gender, complicit in what the former symbolizes (violence, oppression, war) and capable of what the latter symbolizes (generosity, nurture, care). The kingdom is a wasteland not because its king is wounded, not because he's infertile or disabled or queer, but because the procession goes on endlessly, round and round, every day, and most of us have stopped asking why. Who is eating, and who is hungry, and why? Who is bleeding, and who is drawing blood, and why? *What is the purpose of all this?* The Fisher King directs our gaze to the arcane procession and raises an eyebrow as if to say, "Well?"

According to *Perceval*, the first step to healing is breaking our complicit silence and *asking questions*. It's reclaiming our voices and listening to the wells. As Chrétien himself writes, "It is just as wrong to keep too silent as to talk too much."[218] Misha Magdalene links the Grail question(s) to leadership and the civic responsibility of every person to pay attention, think critically, and ask the damn questions:

> Let's avoid the well-intentioned mistake of Perceval, who walked among wonders but failed to ask what and why they were for fear of seeming rude. Instead, let us practice discernment around what we do as individuals and as leaders in a group, a tradition, a community. Rather than accepting things as they are merely because they've always been that way or we don't want to rock the boat, let's ask why they are as they are, and who benefits by them being as they are. . . . In short, let us ask ourselves what these things mean, who they serve, and to what end.[219]

This is part and parcel of queerness. Queerness troubles, wonders, disrupts, experiments. Queerness questions. In her pivotal essay on queering medieval literature, Carolyn Dinshaw observes that "queerness works by contiguity and displacement, knocking signifiers loose, ungrounding bodies, making them strange; it works in this way to provoke perceptual shifts and subsequent corporeal response in those touched."[220] Questions also do this. They interrupt and unsettle, illuminate and deconstruct, cause trouble and make you think. And questions also connect, reach across space, invite a response, open a channel for empathy, for new perspectives, for new stories.

Let's also not forget that questioning is pretty canonically queer. Questioning one's sexuality, questioning one's gender, questioning what style of monogamous or nonmonogamous or queer-platonic relationships one wants to have. Questioning goes hand in hand with experimentation, with curiosity, with trying things out (kissing boys, testosterone, a haircut, lip filler, an open relationship, a new kink) to see if they work, and readjusting if they don't. Queer folks tend to be naturally gifted at the art of questioning, if only because we had to ask ourselves so many questions to find our way out of compulsory cis-heteronormativity.

In the fairy-tale logic of *Perceval*, a knight has to ask the question. If we follow the *Elucidation*, knights are the cultural descendants of Amangon, beneficiaries of his legacy of violence, extraction, and greed. Maybe that's why it's a knight who must ask the question. Not because he's special or pure, not because he's a hero or the Chosen One, but because he's none of those things. Maybe it's precisely because he's privileged, egotistical, complicit, and flawed—precisely because he doesn't *have* to ask the question, is *unlikely* to ask the question, but does it anyway—that the question gains its magical power. When a knight like that kneels to a queer, disabled fairy king and, unprompted, asks the question—*What ails thee? Why are you hurting? What can I do? What do you need?*—then maybe the healing can finally begin. Let's be clear: We're all knights. We're all Perceval. And we're also all descendants of the maidens of the wells.

A captured knight tells King Arthur in the *Elucidation*, "We are all offspring of the damsels," meaning the well-maidens, and that King Amangon's violations against them will never be rectified as long as *this* world—the world of oppression and extraction—lasts.[221] We are the children of knights and well-maidens, of civilization and the land. We are each wounder and wounded. Born into a legacy of injustice and oppression, we are each complicit in perpetuating that harm in our own ways, big or small, knowingly or unknowingly. And we are each responsible for, and will benefit from, the healing.

The Fisher King was never the cause of the wasteland. The "wound" was never queerness, homosexuality, transness, disability, or difference of any kind. To paraphrase Sonya Renee Taylor, difference has never been the problem; the problem is how we deal with difference.* We fear difference because we don't understand it. We're threatened by difference because it confronts us with the simple fact that our personal identity, or experience, or body, or beliefs are not the only ones in the world. Difference shows us that there's more than one "right" way to be. When we fear difference, we erase it, silence it, ignore it, attack it, subjugate it. We decide our version of reality, our ways of being, are the "right" ones. The wasteland's curse is human supremacy. Supremacy of one race, one religion, one kind of body, one sex or gender or sexuality or lifeway over another. Supremacy of humans over the land and its creatures. It has ravaged the land and wounded us all.

---

* "Rendering difference invisible validates the notion that there are parts of us that should be ignored, hidden, or minimized, leaving in place the unspoken idea that difference is the problem and not our approach to dealing with difference." Sonya Renee Taylor, *The Body Is Not an Apology,* 2nd ed. (Oakland, CA: Berrett-Koehler Publishers, 2021), 36.

Questions are one way to start the healing.

Questions are points of connection, how we reach across divides to ask, to empathize, to listen, to touch. Questions are fertile openings for new understandings, new worlds, to sprout. Writing about the empathetic magic of questions, Sophie Strand observes, "When Parzifal wonders about another being's experience, he opens up room in the romance for the real Grail: another story."[222] *Why do you hurt? What do you need? Who are you?* Another story opens, pollinates. The land blooms.

The authors who added to and adapted Chrétien's *Perceval* over the years have offered their own stories and penned their own endings. They've pondered the questions and arrived at their own answers, but whether they're the "right" answers is up to each individual to decide. Perhaps Chrétien did something unintentionally genius by leaving the question unasked, the romance unfinished. Because now we get to ask our own questions . . . and maybe even answer them.

If there's a moral to the tale of Perceval and the Fisher King, it's this: Always ask the question. Because the Grail was never a cup, or a dish, or a holy relic. The Grail was a question all along.

QUEER DEVOTIONS

Queer Contemplations

- How do you feel about people who look, act, or believe differently than you do? Are there some differences you appreciate and others you dislike or try to ignore? Are you comfortable talking or connecting with people who are different from you?

- The Fisher King is healed by a question, an invitation to conversation and connection. How can a question be healing? Is there a question that would feel healing for you? What is sacred about interpersonal connection?

- Questioning our assumptions makes us more self-aware. Asking questions of others (and listening when they speak) makes us aware of a diversity of perspectives and experiences. Questioning power and authority makes us aware of injustice and, when done en masse, can hold authorities accountable and potentially create more equitable change. What is sacred about questioning? Can questioning be an act of queer devotion?

- Are the public spaces, worship spaces, and businesses in your community accessible for people with disabilities? If not, can you advocate for accessibility as an act of queer community devotion?

Journaling Prompt: Asking the Question

What is the magic question you need to ask yourself? Maybe you've been afraid to ask it for fear of your answer. Maybe answering the question will unlock a radical transformation in your life, and change can be scary. Maybe it'll open the floodgates of pent-up emotion. If the question feels that big and potent, that means it's even more important to ask it. Ask yourself this question, and journal your response.

Activity: Passing the Grail

Have you checked in with your friends, partners, or loved ones lately? When was the last time you had a deep conversation with them? Instead of asking "How are you?," try asking "What ails thee?" Well, maybe not in those words. Start with something like "What's been on your mind lately? What's on your heart? What do you need?" and go from there. If you don't get a meaningful response, that's okay. The point is extending that bridge of connection. Next, try asking an acquaintance—chances are, they'll appreciate the opportunity to open up. If they decline, that's fine. Don't push it.

After that, try asking a stranger. The grandma next to you on the bus, a person visibly having a rotten day in line at the coffee shop, or the man who regularly sits in front of your grocery store with a cardboard sign that says *Anything helps.* Start with a simple "How are you today?" and go from there. You may get mixed reactions, but you might also get magical ones. For the magic of questions—of *connecting*—to really work, we need to extend our questions outside of our intimate friend groups and comfortable social circles. We need to step outside of our comfort zones and connect with more people in our wider communities, and even these momentary conversational encounters really do help.

Practical Devotion: Reviving the Wasteland

Small acts of service can be devotional: to others, to the land, to the divinity that's within you.

When you go to the beach, park, or a hiking trail, bring a pair of gloves and a plastic bag for picking up trash when you find it. Volunteer for a park cleanup or a community beautification project. Advocate with your town or city to plant trees, especially in dense urban areas where an abundance of concrete and asphalt create heat islands that pose dangerous health risks during heat waves for the people who live there. Beautify your own front yard, if you have one, by replacing lawns with native plants and wildlife habitats.

Learn about the Land Back movement and how Indigenous leadership and stewardship of the land is essential, not only for ethical reasons but for the care of the planet. Lend your voice, money, or presence at a protest for protecting the environment and its creatures. Research the local deities, spirits, and sacred places in your area, and if it is appropriate and welcome, visit those places. If appropriate and welcome, support the people who protect and care for those sacred places with your donations and/or service.

After doing some of these things, how do you feel? More connected? More in community? Devotion doesn't only have to be religious; it can be mundane and practical. Devotion isn't only about revering the Divine, but about respecting

Them and nurturing Them in ourselves, in others, and in all of creation. I find that practical devotions are the ones that make me feel most closely connected to the Divine, too, since putting our devotion into action bridges it from the spiritual plane to the earthly one—which is, if you think about it, magic.

CHAPTER 8

Marginal Gods at the End of the World

The Queer Magic of Loki and Odin and the Hopeful Norse Apocalypse

Loki: Gender-Fluid Trickster Deity of Queer Chaos

Of all the deities in this book, the Norse trickster god Loki is perhaps the most objectively queer. A shape-shifter, Loki morphs from male to female, from giant to fish to fly to horse, blurring lines of gender and species. Accordingly, I'll be using he, she, and they pronouns interchangeably to discuss the genderfluid goddexx. Though Loki can (and does) transform into birds themself, sometimes he borrows the goddess Freyja's feathered cloak that allows the wearer to fly. Why? Maybe Loki just likes wearing women's clothing. *Queerying Occultures* author Phil Hine additionally notes that "the bird-feather cloak is a recurring symbol for both shape-shifting and gender-variance in European traditions,"[223] so perhaps the cloak is something like a medieval rainbow flag. Loki also possesses magical shoes that carry them across the sky and sea, like fellow androgynous god Hermes's winged sandals.

Loki cannot be bound by gender, shape, or form, and certainly not by society's rules and conventions. Instead of using the usual Norse patronymic surnames, Loki adopts the matronymic *Laufeyjarson*, ("son of Laufey"), naming himself after his mother, the nature goddess Laufey, rather than his father, the jötunn (giant) Fárbauti. The etymology of the name "Loki" is disputed, but the primary contender connects it to tangles, knots, loops, and locks. Another possibility connects the name to keys, making Loki both tangle and untangle, trouble and solution, lock and key.

Loki's genderfluidity and shape-shifting are at the center of many of her tales. In the *Thrymskvida* ("Lay of Thrym") from the *Poetic Edda*, a collection of anonymous poems of Old Norse myth written between the 9th and 13th centuries, Loki helps the macho god Thor regain his precious, lost hammer with a little divine cross-dressing. The hammer has been stolen by the giant Thrym, who says he'll give it back in exchange for marrying the beautiful goddess Freyja. When Freyja soundly refuses, the brawny bro-god Thor begrudgingly dons bridal clothing while Loki shape-shifts into a female form, and the two infiltrate Thrym's hall to retrieve the stolen hammer disguised as Freyja (Thor) and her handmaid (Loki). While Thor throws a fragile-masculinity fit about wearing women's clothes, Loki volunteers for the handmaid role with, as one scholar puts it, "an alacrity that looks sexually questionable."[224] Thor's sullen bridal drag is given stereotypical comedic treatment: Thrym remarks that he's never seen any bride eat so ravenously or drink so much mead and asks why her eyes behind her veil are so terrifying, as if burning. Meanwhile, Loki's transformation goes unremarked upon and wholly unquestioned. She's referred to only as "the very shrewd maid."[225] We get the impression that gender-flipping and sex-changing is par for the course for the cunning god—or goddess, depending on the day.*

In Loki's most famous transformation, recounted by Snorri Sturluson in the 13th-century *Prose Edda*, Loki gets the gods off the hook for a pricey builder's fee—which would have cost them the sun and

---

* We also get the impression that Thor's drag is hilarious only because his hypermasculine ego is so threatened by it. Once he gets his hammer back, he kills all the giants in the hall with it–the Viking equivalent of swinging his dick around, which is to say overcompensating for his fragile masculinity.

moon (literally) and Freyja*—with a little creative sabotage. (Granted, as usual, Loki was partly responsible for the bad bargain in the first place.) Loki transforms into a mare (female horse) and seduces the builder's mighty stallion Svaðilfari, clomping around coquettishly until the lusty stallion gives chase, then enthusiastically wrecking the work site with their sexual exploits through the day and night. Horse-Loki and the stallion cause enough delay that the builder misses the deadline and the gods don't have to pay the bill.** In the process, equine Loki gets pregnant and sometime later gives birth to a child, the eight-legged horse Sleipnir. Sleipnir (the "slippery one") has the ability to fly and to slip freely between worlds, carrying riders into the other realms, including the land of the giants and the land of the dead. He becomes Norse all-father god Odin's favorite steed, lauded as the "best horse among gods and men."[226]

Loki is a boundary-crossing, genderfluid, ambiguous god, so it's appropriate that her children are similarly interstitial creatures. By the jötunn Angrboda, Loki fathers three children: the giant wolf Fenrir that plays a role in the apocalypse of Ragnarök, the Midgard Serpent Jörmungandr who encircles the world, and Hel, the half-blue, half-rosy-complexioned goddess of the underworld. Scholar of pre-Christian Norse religion and folklore H. R. Ellis Davidson, pointing to a line from *Baldrs Draumar* ("Baldr's Dreams"), suggests that Angrboda was actually a female form of Loki, making Loki both the father and mother of their three monstrous children.[227] It seems fitting that of Loki's kids, one rules the world of the dead (Hel), one crosses between worlds (Sleipnir), one circumscribes the world (Jörmungandr), and one instigates the end of the world (Fenrir).*** Loki seems to be connected to the primordial force of chaos itself, from

---

* This seems to happen to Freyja a lot. The good news is that the goddess almost always holds her own. She's a sexually liberated, horny goddess who seeks her pleasure as she pleases and refuses to be meekly trafficked by the arrogant gods around her. Frequently correlated with other love goddesses including Aphrodite/Venus (they share a day of the week–Friday, the day of Venus, is named for Freyja), I also find some of Artemis/Diana's fierce self-ownership and body autonomy in Freyja.

** Thor also smashes the builder with his hammer, which seems an unnecessary overreaction, as Loki had matters well in hand.

*** Loki has two other children by their wife Sigyn that are less attested in myth. One is said to have turned into a wolf, while the other's entrails are used to bind Loki while he is kept captive and tortured by the gods.

which all form arises and into which all form dissipates and returns. Indeed, some scholars have identified Loki with the obscure Norse creator-god Lodurr, who played a role in animating the first humans by giving them flesh, blood, or heat, depending on the translation. Fitting, perhaps, for a shape-shifting father-mother goddexx. Loki and his children also play a primary role in the apocalypse, placing the liminal god as instrumental in both the beginning *and* the end of the world. Mother and Father. Creator and Destroyer. Giver of Life and Bringer of Death.

Loki is not a force of evil, nor is she a force of good. He does good things and bad things and sometimes completely random things. Sometimes, they aid the gods and other times obstruct them. (And sometimes, obstructing the gods might just be the good thing to do.) They cause trouble and get the gods out of trouble, aid and antagonize, annoy and delight. Loki sees the narcissistic arrogance and hypocrisy in the so-called heroes of the Norse pantheon and delights in taking them down a peg. At the same time, Loki resists antihero idealization by doing plenty of problematic things herself. He takes pleasure in playing tricks and pranks to embarrass the gods, but will just as quickly embarrass himself for a laugh. In the *Skáldskaparmál* book in the *Prose Edda*, Loki is the only god to succeed in making the giant Skaði laugh, part of a bargain so she doesn't take vengeance on the gods for killing her father. Loki achieves this in classic slapstick comedy fashion, by tying one end of a leather cord around a goat's beard, the other end around his own testicles, and playing a game of tug-of-war.

According to Davidson, Loki exemplifies all the aspects of a quintessential trickster god:

> The tricker is greedy, selfish, and treacherous; he takes on animal form; he appears in comic and often disgusting situations, and yet he may be regarded as a kind of culture hero. . . . At times he even appears as a creator. He can take both male and female form, and can give birth to children. He is, in fact, a kind of semi-comic shaman, half way between god and hero, yet with a strong dash of the jester element, foreign to both, thrown in.[228]

In other words, Loki exists between hero and villain, male and female, god and mortal, dangerous and comic, creator and destroyer. They resist categorization, destabilize the status quo, and always remain intentionally imperfect. Loki disrupts and dissolves the binary categories of ordered society, proving their fixity a lie—and making us laugh while she does it.

Usually cast as the villain in retellings of Norse myth, and even equated with Lucifer and the Antichrist by Christian commentators, Loki's story arc in myth may be a relatable one to some queer folk. They are a god who doesn't fit in with the others, who is outcast, distrusted, derided, bullied. Loki's "monstrous" children are cast out of Asgard, the land of the gods, for fear of them—a theme which may strike close to home with the continued persecution of trans and gender-nonconforming youth in the U.S. today. The Aesir are genuinely afraid that Loki and their kids will bring about the end of the world. While ostensibly a member of the Aesir, the ruling gods of the Norse mythological cosmos, Loki's positionality is marginal. His parentage by a goddess and a giant—a race of powerful creatures that the Aesir tend to despise and frequently make war on—make him, in a sense, biracial. Loki is not the only Aesir with this biracial parentage (Odin and Thor are both children of giants), but he's the only one who is marked out for it and sometimes considered less than a god because of it.* According to Stefanie von Schnurbein's analysis of Loki's role in the *Prose Edda*, the Aesir's treatment of Loki can be boiled down to the fragility of masculinity in medieval Scandinavia: "He represents the 'effeminate' man and, for *that* reason, not necessarily because of his malevolence, is subject to derision and considered evil" (emphasis original).[229] Loki is not evil, is not even an adversary of the gods (not until the end, at least), but is treated as such because of plain, old-fashioned queerphobia.

Loki acts like he doesn't care about fitting in, and maybe he truly doesn't. But he sure hangs around Asgard a lot for someone who doesn't care about being included. For an evil antagonist, he spends a lot of time helping the gods. One wonders if Loki might not want

---

* Loki's mother, Laufey, was an obscure goddess who may or may not have been a member of the Aesir. There are other gods in the Nordic cosmos, including the Vanir, the earth gods with whom the Aesir fought an ancient feud. If she did not belong to the Aesir, this would *other* Loki even further.

to *fit in*, might not want to *assimilate* to the normative, but might still want to be *accepted* by the gods for who he is. This could be another reason for Loki using the matronymic surname Laufeyjarson. Naming himself after his goddess mother rather than his giant father may not have been picked only for genderqueer reasons, not just to be contrary to patriarchal conventions, but to align Loki more closely to the gods. Gender-ambiguous trickster and prankster though she may be, Loki wants to belong.

Though most of Loki's mischief-making antics are just that—mischief—the gods eventually feel so threatened by Loki that they overreact in a big way. The *Lokasenna* is a story of an epic "flyting," basically a contest of scathing insults exchanged between parties, kind of like a two-way roast. In it, silver-tongued Loki holds the starring role. She takes on a hall full of gods and ostensibly wins, pissing them off so thoroughly that they chase her from the building. Not all of Loki's insults are true, and the ones that are may be exaggerated, but there is enough truth in them that they hit their mark. The gods chase Loki down and capture them. They tie him up with his own child's entrails and torture him by dripping snake venom on his face in perpetuity.* In a classic misunderstood outcast-to-villain arc, it is only when Loki gets free of their bonds that Ragnarök, the end of the world, will begin.

After getting free from his endless torture at the hands of the Aesir, Loki understandably switches sides. In the prophetic vision of Ragnarök delivered by a dead seeress in the *Poetic Edda* and developed further by Odin in the *Prose Edda*, Loki is seen at the helm of the giants' ship, steering it into battle against the Aesir. After being so harshly treated by the gods with whom Loki tried to belong in his own chaotic way, it's no wonder that he will defect to the giants, his father's people and the enemies of the Aesir. Loki's children are also featured in the prophecy: Hel will lead her armies of the dishonorable dead to battle behind her father; the World Serpent Jörmungandr will battle with Thor and each will kill the other; and the giant wolf

---

* Loki's wife, Sigyn, holds a bowl over Loki's head to catch the burning venom, but when the bowl fills and she has to walk away to empty it, the venom drips on Loki's face and burns it. The entrails with which Loki is bound belong to one of his children by Sigyn, named Narfi or Nari, who otherwise goes mostly unmentioned in myth.

Fenrir will swallow Odin whole before being killed himself by one of Odin's sons. Loki will battle the watchman god Heimdall to their mutual death, and then the whole world will burn.[230]

This is where the mythology makes one of those brain-scratching chicken-or-egg time loops. If the seeress had never prophesied Loki's and his children's involvement in Ragnarök, then Odin and the gods may not have feared them to the extent that they did—imprisoning and torturing Loki, and exiling their children.* If Odin and the gods never went that far, Loki may not have defected to the giants, and their children may not have battled alongside them against the gods. The gods of Norse myth are essentially engaged in a doomed cycle of self-fulfilling prophecy: the gods' hatred and persecution of Loki and her children are exactly what causes Loki and her children to turn against the gods. In trying to escape the apocalypse, Odin and the Aesir create the circumstances to set it in motion. In the end, one wonders who the real heroes and real monsters truly are. Or maybe it's not so binary as that. Maybe they're heroes *and* monsters, all of them.

In the 2011 novel *The Witch's Heart*, author Genevieve Gornichec reimagines Norse myth from the perspective of Angrboda, Loki's giantess partner with whom he sires their three apocalyptic children Fenrir, Jörmungandr, and Hel. The tale is told from the literal margins, from Angrboda's cave in the woods at the edge of the world, where she hides from the gods and tries to raise her children in peace. In this telling, the gods are the monsters, and the "monsters" are just three kids trying to grow up in a world that fears and hates them. Loki flits in and out of the story in typical chaotic Loki fashion, at times a good father and good lover but more often an absent, unreliable one. (One of the things I appreciate about the novel is that it doesn't attempt to make Loki into someone he's not.) Gornichec's Loki says many irritating things, but occasionally Loki says something wise, such as these words to Angrboda: "It doesn't really matter where we came from, does it? We're here now. We're ourselves. What more can we be?"[231]

---

* The gods didn't exile Fenrir but tricked him into putting out a magical fetter that bound him, like his father, until Ragnarök.

Gods, heroes, monsters—maybe that's all beside the point. As Loki shows us, all we can be, the *best* we can be, is, simply, ourselves.

Odin on the Margins: The Transient God of Queer Magic

Odin is the patriarchal father-god of Norse mythology and Germanic paganism, but he's not your typical daddy figure. While other father-gods like Zeus are generally aggressive, domineering, short-tempered macho men, Odin is reserved, mysterious, and more than a little bit queer. Odin is a god of war and battle who has the power to strike his enemies blind and deaf, and who can instill in his warriors a battle-frenzy that makes them impervious to injury and powerful beyond defeat. In some stories, these warriors, called *berserkers*, were thought to literally transform into bears. Odin is also a death-god, particularly associated with the gallows, hanged men, and in some tales with burial mounds, who has the ability to speak with and maybe even raise the dead.* He is also a god of poetry, wisdom, and knowledge. He famously gave up an eye to drink from the well of wisdom and hanged himself from Yggdrasil, the World Tree, for nine days to gain the knowledge of the runes. He spoke only in poetic verse and was the best of all skalds (Scandinavian bards). Lastly, Odin is a god of sorcery and magic, but of a mighty peculiar sort for an all-father. Odin seems to have been a practitioner of seidr, a type of pre-Christian Norse magic practiced primarily by women.

The Old Norse *seidr*, meaning "cord, string, snare," is used as a synonym for *magic* in medieval texts that postdate Scandinavian conversion to Christianity, and there is not much known for certain about the particulars of how it was practiced in Iron Age Norse societies. Seidr seems to have mostly been a prophetic magic, geared toward uncovering unknown information or peering into future events with the aid of spirits or gods, but there are also accounts of it being used to harm or even kill.[232] Practitioners of seidr practiced in large groups but were also known to travel from village to village offering their divinatory and magical services, like a wandering magician-prophet.

---

*   In one tale, Odin claims to know a spell that can make hanged men walk.

What evidence exists points to a type of potentially shamanic magic, associated with altered states of consciousness, speaking to or commanding spirits, communication with animals, shape-shifting, and prophecy—all abilities exemplified by Odin. Historian of Nordic religion Thomas Andrew DuBois looks to the shamanic traditions of their northern neighbors, the Sámi, for clues. The shamans of the Sámi communicated with helping spirits in the form of birds, fish, or the reindeer bull, and their rituals involved entering an ecstatic trance state and making animal sacrifices to beseech the aid of spirits.[233]

Odin is strongly associated with ecstatic states: the wild, ferocious battle-frenzy of the berserkers, the intoxication of poetic inspiration, and the prophetic trance of seidr.[234] His name comes from a Proto-Germanic word for "fury, ecstasy, or inspiration."[235] (This wild divine possession strikes a parallel with fellow god of *ekstasis*, Dionysos.) Through this lens, Odin's seemingly disparate domains of poetry, battle, and magic start to make more sense. As professor of religion Kevin J. Wanner puts it, "The professional success of poets, warriors, and magicians depended, at least in principle, upon their accessing of otherworldly power and inducing states of inspiration or frenzy."[236]

Odin is also associated with gallows and hanged men, whom he is known to consult for knowledge of the future, as the dead are beyond the constraints of linear time. One of Odin's names is "God of the Hanged,"[237] and he famously hanged himself from Yggdrasil, potentially ritually dying (and then coming back to life) in order to gain the knowledge of the sacred runes.* He also frequently summons the dead to seek information. Perhaps the most important source for Norse cosmology is the *Völkasá* poem in the *Poetic Edda*, wherein Odin summons the spirit of a dead seeress, a seidr practitioner herself, to gather information about the end of the world. Elsewhere, he converses with the severed head of Mímir, a god of wisdom, for secret knowledge and advice. (Odin preserved Mímir's head and kept it around for exactly this purpose.) In the *Ynglinga saga*, a 13th-century history of legendary Norse kings written by Snorri Sturluson, the

---

* Odin is associated with the Hanged Man card in tarot, which shows a person hanging upside down from a tree or gallows. While the true origins of the card are most likely in Renaissance Italian "shame paintings," not Old Norse mythology, the card's meanings of sacrifice for enlightenment fit nicely with Odin.

author of much of the *Prose Edda*, Snorri writes that "Sometimes [Odin] called the dead out of the earth . . . he was called the ghost-sovereign, and lord of the mounds . . . and understood the songs by which the earth, the hills, the stones, and mounds were opened to him."[238]

As for animal communication, Odin is famously accompanied by his two ravens, Huginn and Muninn, which travel all over the world every day and bring back news to Odin, as if they are an extension of himself or his own consciousness. Indeed, their names translate to "Thought" and "Memory," and in the *Poetic Edda*, Odin says that when his ravens fly over the world each day, he fears that Thought might not return, but he fears even more for Memory.[239] Odin is frequently depicted with his two wolves Geri and Freki ("Ravenous" and "Greedy"), which eat all of Odin's food for him while the god consumes only wine and mead, potentially acting as another extension of Odin, as his digestive system. According to Davidson, his flying horse Sleipnir is "the typical steed of the shaman," who is often depicted as riding a bird or animal that can fly through the air.[240] Odin can shape-shift, which isn't very unique among the gods, but Snorri's description of the act in *Ynglinga saga* depicts the transformation in an unusual way: "Odin could transform his shape: his body would lie as if dead, or asleep; but then he would be in shape of a fish, or worm, or bird, or beast, and be off in a twinkling to distant lands upon his own or other people's business."[241] Loki wholly transforms in the blink of an eye, but here Odin enters a death-like sleep before transforming, suggesting a shamanesque trance state wherein the seidr practitioner projects their spirit from the body in animal form.

The *Ynglinga saga* is also where we find the strongest attestation of Odin's practicing the magic of seidr:

> Odin understood also the art in which the greatest power is lodged, and which he himself practised; namely, what is called magic [seidr]. By means of this he could know beforehand the predestined fate of men, or their not yet completed lot; and also bring on the death, ill luck, or bad health of people, and take the strength or wit from one person and give it to another. But after such witchcraft followed such weakness and anxiety, that it was not thought respectable for men to practise it; and therefore the priestesses were brought up in this art.[242]

But why did it cause such "weakness and anxiety"? Why is seidr only respectable for priestesses and, apparently, Odin? For one, among other things like singing, drumming, and mind-altering substances, seidr seems to have involved cross-dressing and activities considered "unmanly."[243] Quoting 13th-century Christian writer Saxo Grammaticus, Davidson describes the rituals of seidr-practicing male priests as incorporating "effeminate gestures," clapping and miming, and the "unmanly clatter of bells."[244] In Lee Colwill's study of transgender archaeological evidence in Iron Age Scandinavia, she examines three burials of potential seidr practitioners, describing them as containing an unusual mix of usually gendered items that can potentially point to a transgender or nonbinary gender identity. For example, one individual is buried in a steering position at the stern of a ship, potentially indicating a role as a guide to the afterlife. Beside them are a masculine axe-head and shield boss, and they are wearing a pair of feminine brooches and a "highly unusual" leather outfit, potentially a kind of androgynous ritual garb.[245] According to Colwill, this combination of multigendered grave goods "argues in favour of a memorial narrative for this *seiðr* practitioner that incorporated elements of masculinity and femininity, but which was also in some ways outside both."[246] Practitioners may have permanently occupied a gender outside of a male/female binary as a lifeway, or may have temporarily embodied one in ritual, potentially "gaining power for the duration of a *seiðr* ritual by 'transgressing' binary gender categories."[247]

In the *Lokasenna*, Loki accuses Odin of practicing seidr and traveling dressed as a wizard, also translated as "witch" or "fortune teller," as seidr practitioners were known to do. The implication is that Odin not only practiced women's magic, but also dressed as a woman.

> They say that with spells | in Samsey once
>
> Like witches with charms didst thou work;
>
> And in witch's guise | among men didst thou go;
>
> Unmanly thy soul must seem.[248]

The fact that this attestation occurs in a game of insults, the veracity of which is highly contestable, has led some scholars to discount Odin's involvement in such "unmanly" magics.* But Odin *was* a god of magic, and this is not the only source that attests to Odin's practice of seidr.

Significantly, the word Loki uses to accuse Odin of being "unmanly," also translated as "a pervert,"[249] in the original Icelandic text is *argr*,[250] and in the prior passage from *Ynglinga saga*, the word translated as "weakness and anxiety" is *ergi*.** *Ergi* (noun) and *argr* (adjective) are closely related pejorative terms associated with effeminacy and bottoming in same-sex male intercourse.[251] Calling another man *argr* was so offensive that in the Icelandic *Grágás*, the person who flings the insult can be exiled for life or even killed by the aggrieved party in recompense.[252] In addition to "unmanly" and "pervert," some of the various ways ergi/argr has been interpreted in translation include "craven" (cowardly), "sexually perverse," "effeminate," "emasculated," and, in the only instance where it is used to apply to a female (Freyja), "lust."[253]

Somewhat like the term "queer," *ergi/argr* seems to imply a reversal of "proper" gendered behavior, applied when a woman acts "unwomanly," as with Freyja's liberated promiscuity, but much more often when a man acts "unmanly," as with wearing women's clothing, taking the passive or penetrated role in sexual intercourse, or doing women's magic. According to Germanic historian Folke Ström, it is the occupation of a usually feminine role that causes the male practice of seidr to be branded *argr/ergi*, in the same way that taking the normatively "female" role of being penetrated during sex makes the homosexual male *argr/ergi*.[254] In other words, receiving the gods through seidr requires a passive openness to being entered, or penetrated, by the gods. Whether this penetration was ever literal is up for debate. In her discussion of the seidr-practicing priests with

---

* Loki's claim that Odin practiced seidr comes in response to Odin's claim that Loki lived underground as a milkmaid, milking cows for eight years, as well as giving birth to children. The subterranean milkmaid story is unattested elsewhere, but, as we know, Loki did enjoy morphing into female forms and gave birth on at least one occasion (Sleipnir).

** "Fylgir svá mikil *ergi*," sometimes translated as "follows so much *perversity*," as in Lee Colwill, "The Queerly Departed," 182, or "flows such great *effeminacy*," as in Kevin J. Wanner, "Cunning Intelligence in Norse Myth," 219.

their "unmanly" bells, Davidson draws a parallel to the transgender priestesses of Kybele who were known to engage in same-sex intercourse,* implying the *argr* priests may have done the same.[255] Hine brings it all the way home: "In surrendering themselves to passive intercourse, the *ergi* became a channel for the divine."[256]

For Loki to be called *ergi* and *argr* numerous times—thrice in *Lokasenna* alone—is perhaps no surprise for the genderfluid outsider-god of mischief. But for the patriarchal father-god to be associated with *ergi* and *argr*—not just once by the troublemaking tongue of Loki, but a second time in a text that otherwise sings Odin's praises in the highest order—is interesting, indeed.

Odin was said to have learned seidr from Freyja, the shape-shifting goddess of love and war who is credited with inventing seidr in the first place, and, if you recall, is the only female to be called *argr* in the eddas. While seidr was closely associated with Freyja, the male priests of Freyr, Freyja's twin brother and god of fertility, seem to have also practiced seidr. (These are the priests with the "unmanly" bells from earlier.) Colwill's archaeological analysis reveals that real-life seidr practitioners were buried in ships and wagons under burial mounds, burial practices particularly associated with Freyr. This is interesting because Freyja and Freyr are both members of the Vanir, gods of the earth who are old enemies of Odin's sky-gods, the Aesir. Throughout the Eddas, the Vanir are portrayed as passionate, lusty, intoxicating, emotional, and . . . backward. Though Freyja and Freyr were traded to live among the Aesir as part of an old peace agreement between the two rival groups, seidr is nonetheless a highly Vanir-coded, and thus foreign and Other, magical art. This adds a layer to Odin's subversive seidr. For the central god of the Aesir to practice Vanir seidr is not only a gender and/or sexual transgression, but treading quite close to a political transgression as well.

Then again, Odin was never the presidential type. He seems a reluctant patriarch much of the time, far more interested in pursuing knowledge and wisdom than heading the Aesir. Wanner argues that Odin is a marginal god, that his "character and activity are

---

* She is almost certainly referring to same-sex male intercourse, though she might be referencing the self-castration that Kybele's priestesses sometimes undertook. According to Hine, some of the seidr-practicing priests of the god Freyr may have been castrati due to descriptions of their voices (Hine 183).

fundamentally peripatetic," or on the periphery.[257] Seldom found where he should be, ensconced in his grand hall, running the realm, Odin is most often found in the territory of others, trespassing in the underworld, moving through the human realm, interfering in the land of giants.[258] Wanner lists some of the god's many names of wandering and travel—"Travel-Weary or Vagabond," "Wayfarer," "Way-Tamer," "Guest"—and names of enigma and disguise—"Masked One," "Changeable," "Concealer," "Long-Hood."[259] One of his most common depictions in stories and in art is as the cloaked stranger with a long, gray beard, his one eye peeking from beneath a deep hood or the wide brim of a Gandalf-like hat, leaning on a gnarled staff. An image more appropriate on the tarot's Hermit card than on a throne in Valhalla or a bloody battlefield.

I do not mean to draw a correlation here between Odin's queer qualities and deceptiveness—the idea that queer people are deceptive is one of the oldest queerphobic stereotypes in the book—but Odin's propensity for going incognito does displace him from the *axis mundi*, the center of the world, and set him somewhere on the wilder fringes. King of the gods or not, Odin seems to prefer the shadows to the spotlight—not exactly the shiny patriarchal figurehead he is sometimes made out to be. Though considered a god of battle, he more often achieves his ends via cunning and trickery than frontal assault. He might be more aptly considered a god of death than a god of warriors: he may grant his ecstatic gift of battle-frenzy, but he also interferes to turn the tide of battle in unexpected and counterintuitive ways and sends his Valkyries to pluck warriors, often his own favorites, from the battlefield according to his will and whim, sweeping their souls away to Valhalla. According to DuBois, "The shaman, the Germanic warrior class associated with battle fury and bear or wolf skins (the *berserkr* tradition), the *seidr* practitioner, and the holy hermit of Christianity all represented liminal figures in Nordic societies, beings whose sacral powers arose in part from their choice to assume a marginal, even pariah-like existence."[260]

For the central god of Norse mythology, Odin seems to draw the bulk of his power from the margins. A marginal god at the center of the cosmos.

The Gods and Us at the End of the World

Odin's insatiable search for knowledge and wisdom—whether through consulting the dead, sending out his ravens to scavenge the world for information, depositing his eye in the well of wisdom, hanging himself for the runes, wandering in disguise across the land, or practicing the women's magic of seidr—can be boiled down to a singular obsession: gathering enough information to avert the prophesied apocalypse. Odin's quest is futile, and yet he does it anyway: a corollary to the modern mortal predicament, perhaps. This is one of the things that makes Odin relatable, I think. He can't save the world, but he tries anyway. As Wanner puts it, "Odinn is not a savior or messiah who appears to lead alienated adherents out of present chaos or disenfranchisement into eternal order and power, but a god who joins his followers in an unrelenting struggle that all are aware can only end in their own destruction."[261]

Just like Loki, Odin is not a savior and is sometimes a villain. He tries—*really* tries—to save the world, but ultimately he can't. And in the process, he unwittingly sets up the apocalyptic dominoes to fall. Loki and Odin have many similarities. They are both tricksters and shape-shifters with cunning minds and silver tongues. They both queer their genders in some way: Loki with their genderfluidity and Odin by seeming to simply not care about gender whatsoever—maybe he's agender, or maybe he's just not about to let something as silly as *gender norms* get in the way of his quest. And Loki and Odin are sworn blood brothers. In *Lokasenna*, Loki says:

> Remember, Othin [Odin], | in olden days
>
> That we both our blood have mixed;
>
> Then didst thou promise | no ale to pour,
>
> Unless it were brought for us both.[262]

And Odin makes his own son get up so Loki can sit and join the fateful feast, after which he'll end up bound in guts, with venom burning his face. And the rest—that is, the future foretold—is history.

But Ragnarök is not the end. Along with all the death and fire, brother turning against brother, the destruction of heaven and earth, etc., the *Völuspá* prophecy foretells a beginning after the end. The earth will be reborn, green and new, complete with plunging waterfalls, eagles and fish, and fields that will magically grow crops without sowing. Two or three gods of the younger generation will survive (the names and numbers vary), and according to the *Prose Edda*, two humans will too. Their names will be Lif ("Life") and Leifthrasir ("Life Yearner"). They will eat morning dew for food, and from them will come enough descendants to repopulate the world.[263]

This may sound like a discount Christian apocalypse with a Norse spin, and some scholars have argued for Christian influence in the tale. But the story of Ragnarök differs from the story of Revelation in one hugely significant way. In Christian eschatology, the world burns and the people of the earth all die or are raptured to clear the way for the divine realm of heaven on earth. The mortal coil is ended and everyone (or the righteous, at least) is brought to live in perfect, eternal bliss in the presence of God. In the Norse version, however, the gods *die*. Almost all of them. Not in a righteous battle of good against some central, Luciferian evil, but in a stupid, tragic feud they are all complicit in, themselves. The heaven of Asgard and the afterlife hall of Valhalla is destroyed alongside the mortal earth. A couple minor gods and humans squeak through, it's true, but the new world that emerges is not heaven. It is not presided over by a ubiquitous, undying mono-God. It's not immortal, nor eternal. It may be idyllic, but it's only . . . the earth. The prophecy does not describe a consistent, organized utopia, but the very early stages of a couple people and a couple gods trying to rebuild, or start over, side by side.

This may seem bleak, fatalistic, even nihilistic, any sense of eternity or salvation via religion wrenched from mortal grasp, but I find it realistic and . . . hopeful. This world, no matter how bad or beautiful it is, will end. Our individual lives will end when we die, and humanity itself will eventually go extinct from climate apocalypse if things stay their current course. If we want to play it forward, eventually the Sun will inevitably explode, and the Earth itself will end too. But life won't. Life will go on. Here or elsewhere, with us or without us, life will live somewhere, somehow. That's for certain.

Nothing is permanent, not the Earth, not the gods, and certainly not us. Norse mythology offers a different kind of gospel than the Christian one, not a gospel of transcendence, permanence, and perfection, but a gospel of transience, impermanence, and imperfection. A far more realistic gospel. And maybe that's the one we need.

Wanner writes that Odin "is a vagrant god operating time and again on and from the margins, making the best tactical use of the situations that arise, and fighting a reactionary battle against eventual but certain defeat. There is nothing 'transcendent' about him."[264] In the 21st century, with the earth already burning, with escapism available on every phone screen, the *last* thing we need is transcendence. We don't need illusions of permanence and salvation, don't need a dissociative escape hatch to "rise above" our current situation or spiritually bypass our way out of facing difficult truths. What we need is to apply every scrap of our knowledge and cunning to avert climate apocalypse. What we need is to use all our cleverness and wiles to subvert the capitalist colonial powers that are relentlessly driving the earth to the edge. What we need is to summon a battle-frenzy, a poet-frenzy, to ecstatically fight for each other's rights to live as ourselves free of oppression and persecution. We don't need a transcendent god, but transient *gods*. Not a god for forever, but gods for right now. Not a divine masculine or feminine, but a divine whoever the fuck you are. Not a god of salvation, but gods of survival—crafty, cunning, determined, and able to laugh along the way—even if they, too, may succumb in the end.

Instead of perfect, eternal deities, magic-bullet one-act saviors, and all-powerful, infallible gods, maybe what we need are imperfect, transient, messy ones. Gods like Loki and Odin. Gods who fail and make mistakes, whose powers have limits, who wander the margins, who are heroic and monstrous, who struggle and strive just like us. Gods who see the end coming, who know it might be pointless, but who try—heroically, monstrously, divinely, humanly—to change the future anyway. Gods who try their best to live.

An Unfortunately Necessary Cautionary Note: Norse/Germanic Neo-Paganism and White Supremacy

Among modern-day Norse/Germanic neo-pagans, who often call themselves Heathens (followers of Heathenry), there are many wonderful people who are anti-racist and pro-LGBTQIA2S+, who are queer and/or BIPOC. As we've seen, Norse mythology holds gods who are queer and multiracial and stories that hold deeply resonant themes for the times we're living in today.

Unfortunately, Norse/Germanic neo-paganism has also been coopted by the far right. Those interested in learning more about Loki, Odin, and Norse/Germanic neo-paganism should be aware that these mythologies and their symbolism have been grossly appropriated by white supremacists, Aryan nationalists, and neo-Nazis who are active today. In the lead-up to World War II, the Nazis appropriated Northern European pagan iconography in their propaganda to create a false and idealized Aryan heritage and create a sense of white nationalist pride, which they then turned against anyone who did not fit their white supremacist Aryan delusions, targeting Jews and anyone else who wasn't Christian, white, and heterosexual. Though the Nazis lost the war, they did not disappear, and neo-Nazis still misuse Norse and Germanic paganism for their racist designs today.

A notorious recent example is the "QAnon Shaman" who raided the U.S. Capitol on January 6, 2021, dressed in a pseudo-Viking horned and furred headdress and patriotic face paint. The so-called shaman's shirtless torso was tattooed with Thor's hammer, Yggdrasil, and the valknut, a knot of three interlocking triangles associated with Odin that has been appropriated by white supremacists and is now listed as a hate symbol by the Anti-Defamation League, along with Thor's hammer.*

Some branches of the reconstructionist Norse and Germanic pagan religions are blatantly racist, transphobic, homophobic, and misogynistic, such as the Asatru Folk Assembly (AFA), which in 2016

---

* The Anti-Defamation League notes that the valknut may also be used by nonracist pagans, "so one should carefully examine it in context rather than assume that a particular use of the symbol is racist." Hate on Display™, "Valknut," Anti-Defamation League, accessed May 13, 2024, https://www.adl.org/resources/hate-symbol/valknot.

"declared point blank that non-whites and LGBT Heathens were not welcome in their tradition."[265] Siri Vincent Plouff, author of *Queering the Runes* and host of the *Heathen's Journey* podcast, identifies key terms associated with white supremacist Norse/Germanic religious groups to watch out for, including the term Folkish or Völkisch (as in Asatru Folk Assembly) and "metagenetics,"[266] a racist, pseudoscientific, and eugenics-adjacent concept that asserts culture is passed down in DNA, and therefore DNA dictates what deities one can connect to.[267] These "folkish" beliefs boil down to a "whites only" policy that goes hand in hand with conspiracy theories of "white genocide," the racist belief that the "superior" white race is being slowly and systematically erased via interracial coupling, immigration, and policies such as affirmative action. The authors of "Binding the Wolf" further identify the terms Odinism, Odalism, Wodenism, and Wotanism as being favored by extreme-right, white-supremacist Heathens—especially "Wotanism," which is also an acronym for "Will of the Aryan Nation" (WOTAN), according to the essay.

According to Plouff, Heathen groups that identify themself as "universalist" or "inclusive" tend to be explicitly antiracist and LGBTQIA2S+ inclusive, and Plouff offers a page of antiracist Heathen resources on their website.* In *Sacred Gender*, Serpentine offers a tip for weeding out transphobic Heathen groups, even among the inclusive ones: Ask how they feel about Loki.[268] If they're wary of the genderfluid god, chances are they may harbor some implicit transphobia, whether or not they're outwardly supportive. Whereas "where the attitude is closer to 'Loki? Heck yeah!', those are far more likely to be the groups where trans folks are loved and celebrated," says Serpentine.[269]

It's essential to emphasize that there is no intrinsic support for white supremacy or racism in the original source material for Norse and Germanic spirituality—no more so than there is in Greek mythology, Christianity, or the Hebrew Bible, at least. White supremacists latched on to the mythology and folklore of Northern Europe in order to provide "ancient" legitimacy to their ideas by instilling racist significance where originally there was none. (Christian nationalists

---

* https://www.sirivincentplouff.com/antiracist-heathen-resources

and Zionists have done the same.) But while it may seem safer or easier to write off Odin and Loki and ditch the whole pantheon, that would be letting the white supremacists win. And that's not an option. Fighting back against this hateful misappropriation of Norse/Germanic neo-pagan religion requires not only vociferously denouncing racist and white supremacist Heathen groups but doing our best to counter-act them through education (of ourselves and others) and real-world action. It also requires facing the racist past—and ongoing present—use of Norse/Germanic deities and sacred symbols to seed hate and provide a false basis for a sanctified white supremacy. But the most important and ongoing part of this work is learning about and practicing intentional antiracism in our daily lives and fighting against racism, transphobia, homophobia, and white supremacy wherever and whenever we find it.

QUEER DEVOTIONS

Queer Contemplations

- Is the Divine perfect? Are *deities* perfect? Is there a difference between the Divine and deities? What can you learn from Loki and Odin's *imperfect* yet still divine example?

- I grew up in a religion that believed God is infallible. Therefore, every tragedy and misfortune that befell us *must* have been God's will, usually because we have sinned or failed God in some way—a supposedly divine version of victim blaming. Do you believe everything happens for a reason? Is "everything happens for a reason" different from "everything is willed by God"? If everything happens for a reason, does that mean you believe in fate, and do you still have free will?

- The mythologies of Loki and Odin are caught in a self-fulfilling prophecy. Do you have any self-fulfilling prophecies in your life? What beliefs are keeping you circling the same cycles? Now extend that to a larger scale. Do you detect any self-fulfilling prophecies operating in your communities, in politics, in cultural thought?

- We usually think of the word "perfect" as meaning "without flaw," but it can also mean "whole." If you think of perfection in terms of wholeness instead of "flawlessness," how does this shift your ideas about the perfection of the Divine? Can one be whole and have flaws? How might this shift your ideas about your own perfection or imperfection?

Devotional Tool-Kit: Talking to the Divine with Divination

Odin legendarily hanged from the World Tree for nine days to gain the wisdom of the runes. Runes are the letters of the Germanic alphabet prior to the adoption of Latin letters with Christianization, but they were also used in spells and may have been used in divination too. Today, modern practitioners use them for magic and divination, as well as spiritual development.

Other forms of divination can be used in a similar way, such as my personal favorite: tarot. Rather than telling the future, I prefer to use tarot for personal development, introspection, and contemplation. I also pull cards when I'm feeling spiritually stuck or need a little extra guidance from the Divine. (The word *divination* actually comes from the word *divine!*) Divination is a great core skill to have in a queer devotional practice because it helps nudge us outside of ourselves to look at things from a new perspective. All you need are your tarot cards (or runes, oracle cards, or the divination medium of your choice) and a question.

My go-to questions for a general, everyday reading is "What do I need to know today?" or "What guidance do I need to have today?" You can also ask for a card for devotional contemplation. If you approach tarot for contemplation instead of as a Magic 8 Ball that's going to solve all your problems for you, tarot is a powerful way to foster spiritual growth. Critics may say we're making meaning out of random chaos, but hey, it *was* Chaos that birthed the cosmos in many world mythologies, so maybe we're onto something. For more on how to read tarot, check out my book *Radical Tarot*. Other queer and inclusive tarot favorites are *Queering the Tarot* by Cassandra Snow, *Tarot for Change* by Jessica Dore, *Seventy-Eight Acts of Liberation* by Lane Smith, and the classic *Seventy-Eight Degrees of Wisdom* by Rachael Pollack.

Practical Devotion: Activism as Devotion

Audre Lorde said the spiritual is political, and it's true. Not only do spiritual beliefs influence political opinions, as is plainly clear in the case of Christian extremists in the U.S. and abroad, but spiritual beliefs can either permission us to disengage into a privileged, escapist world of "love and light" and ignore the inequality and oppression all around us (this is called "spiritual bypassing" and is discussed in Chapter 9), or our spiritual beliefs can motivate us to show up for our neighbors and the global community through activism. As LGBTQIA2S+ people, we need to understand that our liberation is intwined with the liberation of all marginalized groups, and if we all band together in mutual solidarity, we can truly make strides toward collective liberation.

From a spiritual perspective, we can consider activism to be a tangible act of queer devotion. How can you get involved in the struggle for liberation in your local community? How about the international community? How can you make activism a sustainable part of your queer devotional practice? This might look like having conversations with people in your circles, writing letters or making calls to your representatives, donating to causes, participating in boycotts, showing up to marches and demonstrations, or supporting on the side by making signs or passing out water. You don't have to do *all* these things *all* the time—if you do, you'll burn out. Set a sustainable goal for yourself and make your participation a devotion to the Queer Divine of your understanding.

Recommended Reading

Ijeoma Oluo's *So You Want to Talk About Race* is a foundational guide to understanding how racism works in America, from cultural appropriation, to police brutality, to microaggressions, and what you can do about it. Austin Channing Brown's *I'm Still Here* is a powerful personal account of racism in white, middle-class, and Christian spaces that claim to value "diversity." *Tarot for the Hard Work* by Maria Minnis is an excellent guide for using tarot to confront and dismantle internalized racism and take action to fight racism in your communities. David Salisbury's *Witchcraft Activism* is a handy guide for using witchcraft for aid and protection in social justice and political activism.

CHAPTER 9

The Huntress and the Witch Queen

Sapphics and Survivors Hex the Patriarchy

Ancient Greek myth is a homoerotic cornucopia. Nearly every male deity has at least one gay tryst or love affair, including the ruler of the gods, sky-daddy Zeus himself, who whisks his boy-lover Ganymede off to Olympus in the form of a giant eagle. The gay love affairs of lyre-playing golden boy and unofficial god of twinks, Apollo, legendarily include Hyacinth, Adonis, and a dozen other men—not to mention just as many women, making him one of the most popular of bisexual gods. The priapic nature-god Pan famously frolicked around the wilderness, cavorting with anyone of any sex, gender, or species he pleased, including in one infamous statue, a goat. Greco-Roman mythology is, however, rather short on lesbian and bisexual goddesses and homoerotic affairs of the female heart.

Far from indicating that same-sex female desire did not exist in the classical world, the dearth of overtly sapphic goddesses indicates that patriarchy has been alive and well for a very long time. The phallocentrism of Greek and Roman society meant that the male writers of the epics, poetry, plays, and histories were mostly concerned with, well, penises. They seem to have had a hard time imagining that any sort of non-penetrative sex could be "real" sex, not unlike the heteronormative understanding of sex and virginity today, which still holds that one is a virgin until they've had penis-in-vagina sex.* The lesbian figures that are recorded in classical antiquity were mostly *tribades,* masculine women who took a dominant, penetrative role in sex—yes, ancient strap-ons existed!** The men who immortalized these lesbian lovers in writing seem to have held a low opinion of them, however, and they mostly appear in crude comedy plays.[270] The phallocentric bias extends to academia. When academics have gone looking for evidence of female homoeroticism in history, their standard of "proof" has more often than not imposed heteronormative standards on female homosexuality: for instance, by expecting to find one "active" partner and one "passive" partner.[271] While that is a dynamic in some female same-sex relationships, it certainly isn't the rule for all relationships, lesbian or otherwise.

If we read the classics not through a straight gaze but queer glance, one attuned to the queer hints and signals that the straight world seldom notices and almost never comprehends, then it becomes much easier to catch the sultry eye of a gay goddess across the smoky bar of history. And we may just find that these sapphic goddesses and legendary lesbos offer more than another way of loving, but another way of *living* as well.

Sappho, the Original Lesbian

While not a goddess, no account of female homoerotic love would be complete without the Mother of Lesbians herself, the original sapphic: Sappho. Little is known for certain about Sappho's life other than that she lived around 600 B.C.E. on the island of Lesbos (yes, that's where the term *lesbian* comes from, and *sapphic* is from *Sappho*)

---

* Over one thousand years later, the authors of anti-sodomy laws in Britain seem to have had the same prejudice. Male-male sexual activity was illegal (that's how Oscar Wilde went to jail), but female-female sexual activity wasn't. Mostly because they couldn't imagine how such a thing would work.

** In the 1st century B.C.E., Seneca the Elder writes about a married man who, upon catching his wife in bed with another woman, "looked at the man first, to see whether he was natural or sewn on" (Seneca the Elder, *Controversiae,* 1.2.23; quoted in Oliver 282f). A Greek dialogue from about 270 C.E. makes reference to "cunningly contrived instruments of lechery, those mysterious monstrosities devoid of seed" which women "strap to themselves" to "lie with women as does a man" (Lucian, "Affairs of the Heart," 28, 8:195; quoted in Crompton 99).

and was a celebrated lyric poet in her own time and after. Plato called Sappho "the tenth muse"; the Greeks held her in as high esteem as Homer and honored her with statues and vase paintings, and her hometown Mytilene was so proud of their native daughter that they emblazoned her image on their coins.[272] Sappho's verse has been celebrated for its intimacy, emotion, meter (appropriately called sapphic meter), and evocative language, but she's chiefly famous today for being openly lesbian—both a resident of the island of Lesbos and a lover of women. Most of her poetry was love poetry—to other women.

Of course, Sappho's lesbianism is one of the many details of Sappho's life that has been getting scholars hot and frothy with controversy for centuries. From her poetry and what scant details of her life exist, it seems likely that Sappho held a role as a kind of liberal arts headmistress or teacher of young women and girls, training them in the arts, music, dance, and poetry. Brides, bridegrooms, and weddings are mentioned in her poems, and some scholars have taken this to mean that Sappho's role was to train young women for marriage. They have gone so far as to surmise that her homoerotic poems are not homoerotic at all, but meant to praise a young, marriageable girl's beauty in a public way as to attract a suitor. To this, I'd say such scholars are trying mighty hard to manufacture a heteronormative reason for plainly and overtly homoerotic poetry.

If Sappho taught young women in the arts, then it's only natural that many of her students would finish their schooling and get married (to men) one day. This, however, has no bearing on Sappho's lesbianism. Even if Sappho's poems, which seem to have been meant for reciting or singing to music, were indeed performed in a public setting as part of rituals or marriage ceremonies, it is still Sappho's mind and tongue composing and performing these sexy sapphic odes. One of Sappho's most famous and most translated poems describes the embodied sensations of desire with visceral passion—and perhaps jealousy—as she watches her beloved talking with a man:

For when I see thee but a little, I have no utterance left, my tongue is broken down, and straightway a subtle fire has run under my skin, with my eyes I have no sight, my ears ring, sweat pours down, and a trembling seizes all my body; I am paler than grass, and seem in my madness little better than one dead. But I must dare all, since one so poor . . .[273]

The poem cuts off, the rest lost to time. For Sappho to be so talented in the discourse of desire that her poetry was lauded by the likes of Plato, Aristotle, Plutarch, and Ovid; translated and imitated two thousand years later by such Romantics as Percy Bysshe Shelley, Lord Byron, and Alfred Tennyson; and inspired lesbian poets and writers including H. D. (Hilda Doolittle), Amy Lowell, and Willa Cather,[274] I'd say Sappho is either *really good* at faking passion for women—or she's a lesbian. The latter seems the much simpler and more straightforward (or *queer*forward) option.

Is it so unconceivable that a woman who writes about desiring women actually . . . does?

Perhaps unsurprisingly, Sappho's patron goddess seems to have been Aphrodite, goddess of love, sex, and persuasion. Her famous poem number 1, sometimes referred to as a Hymn to Aphrodite, implores the goddess to spare her the agony of unrequited love: "Immortal Aphrodite of the broidered throne, daughter of Zeus, weaver of wiles, I pray thee break not my spirit with anguish and distress, O Queen. But come hither, if ever before thou didst hear my voice afar, and listen."[275] Aphrodite comes to Sappho and asks what new trouble causes her to summon the goddess and who she needs to persuade to fall in love with Sappho. Their exchange is worded with familiarity, as if Sappho has requested Aphrodite's aid in these matters before. Aphrodite speaks:

> What Beauty now wouldst thou draw to love thee? Who wrongs thee, Sappho? For even if she flies she shall soon follow, and if she rejects gifts shall yet give, and if she loves not shall soon love, however loth [reluctant].[276]

The fact that Sappho refers to herself by name and that the object of her affection is clearly feminine is unmistakably lesbian. Perhaps unsurprisingly, some translators of Sappho have attempted to erase the feminine beloved from the poem. The text I have quoted from is a literal prose translation by Henry Thornton Wharton, which I chose because he attempts to translate Sappho literally, rather than interpreting her ancient Greek into metered, sometimes rhyming (shudder), English verse. Wharton's text is also interesting because alongside his literal translation, he compiles eight verse translations by others, dated between 1711 and 1893. None of the eight verse translations use the feminine pronoun for Sappho's beloved. Seven use the masculine pronoun, and one takes pains to avoid gendering the beloved altogether. Wharton's literal translation alone uses the feminine *she*. Though he makes no comment on this, it does illuminate the difference in stark contrast. In the 20th and 21st centuries, matters have improved somewhat. Today, even translators and classicists who exert a lot of energy expounding on why they don't believe Sappho to be a lesbian usually acknowledge that her beloved in the Hymn to Aphrodite is a woman. They just follow it up with the usual, tired arguments about "not assuming authorial intent," or "maybe they were just good friends." It's apparently fine to assume heterosexuality, just not homosexuality. Heterosexual until proven homo.

Aside from being one of the most unmistakable references to same-sex female love in Sappho's remaining poems, the Hymn to Aphrodite is also remarkable for its resemblance to a spell. Sappho calls down the goddess and entreats her for aid in compelling or persuading another woman to love her, a domain that Aphrodite certainly oversaw, and Sappho does it using a mix of clerical hymn and magical summoning language.[277] Sappho does not *compel* the goddess to do her bidding, as later magical texts such as the Greek Magical Papyri do, but uses complimentary language and common epithets, symbols, and descriptions of the goddess to coax her to listen to Sappho's praise, not unlike *The Orphic Hymns*, which extoll the virtues and attributes of a deity at length and then end with a request. And as professor of ancient Greek literature J. C. B. Petropoulos shows, Aphrodite's response to Sappho in the poem bears resemblance to language found in the Greek Magical Papyri and curse tablets.

Obviously, compelling someone to fall in love or have sex with you via a spell or any other means is not consensual and would be sexual assault should it occur, and no one should attempt such a thing. But that Sappho seems to have written a homoerotic love spell around 600 B.C.E. is nonetheless illuminating as to her sexuality *and* her devotion, which may have incorporated magical elements. It's also worth pointing out that Sappho never asks for Aphrodite to compel her beloved—Aphrodite, goddess of persuasion, offers that all by herself. Sappho may hint at it, but only directly asks to be released from the agony of unrequited love:

> Come, I pray thee, now too, and release me from cruel cares; and all that my heart desires to accomplish, accomplish thou, and be thyself my ally.[278]

Further, as classicist Kristin Mathis notes in her analysis and translation, "There's another erotic relationship at play in the poem—the relationship between Sappho and Aphrodite."[279] Mathis points to the "tender, playful tone" that the two seem to have in their exchange, likening it to bedroom talk more than prayer. This is part of the magic of Sappho, says Mathis: "Her poems testify to a time when Love, Desire, and the Sacred were intertwined in an intimate embrace. When a Goddess could be in love with a woman, and vice-versa, and the two of them might set off in pursuit of a third girl—all in the name of Divine Love."[280]

What I find most tantalizing about Sappho's love poetry, however, is the gaps. In a world that insists on finite, quantifiable knowns, a world that will argue *ad nauseum* over the sexuality of a female poet who wrote erotic love poetry about women over 2,500 years ago, the fragmentary nature of most of Sappho's still-existing work is a tantalizing *fuck you* to the heteronormative patriarchal impulse that seeks to shove Sappho into a proper box and keep her there. Maybe Sappho loved women in real life, romantically or sexually or both, or maybe her homoeroticism was contained within the bounds of poetry only. That doesn't make her any less homoerotic, any less lesbian, in my regard. As most verifiable details of her life have faded into history, all that we have to go on—to savor—are her words and the ponderous gaps between them. Gaps that invite us to lean in, to listen, to imagine, and perhaps to fill them with our own delicious, agonizing, *bittersweet* (to use a word that Sappho coined) queer longing.

The Queer Love of Iphis and Ianthe

In *Metamorphoses*, Ovid tells the tale of a child named Iphis, a forbidden love, and a miraculous change. As the story goes, Iphis's father, Ligdus, decides that having a daughter would be too expensive, so he declares that if his wife Telethusa births a girl, he will put the babe to death. When Telethusa is heavily pregnant, the goddess Isis appears at the foot of her bed in a dream. Accompanied by an ensemble of Egyptian deities including Anubis, Horus, and Osiris, Isis instructs Telethusa to disobey her husband's orders and raise the child no matter its sex. So when Telethusa gives birth to a girl, she swaddles the child and pretends that it's a boy. Her husband, pleased to have a son, names the child Iphis—a conveniently unisex name that pleases Telethusa. Iphis is dressed and raised as a boy, with a "face such, that, whether you gave it to a girl or to a boy, either would be beautiful."[281] Eventually, Iphis is betrothed to Ianthe, a friend and schoolmate since childhood. Ovid tells us that the two were equally in love with each other: "Love . . . touches the inexperienced breasts of them both, and inflicts on each an equal wound; but *how* different are their hopes!" (emphasis original).[282] Ianthe dreams of marrying a man, and Iphis despairs that marriage is impossible due to her sex.

While one can argue that Ianthe's love for Iphis is heterosexual since she believes Iphis to be a (cisgender) man, Iphis's love for Ianthe is cast by Ovid in no uncertain terms as clearly lesbian. Ovid takes pains to emphasize Iphis's queer love with descriptions like "herself a maid, she burns with passion for a maid,"[283] but at the same time casts it as unusual, unnatural, and impossible. Still, despite his prejudice, Ovid describes Iphis and Ianthe's love and desire as mutual and consensual. He spares no space elaborating on how Iphis burns—flames or being inflamed are mentioned no fewer than four times—and writes: "No less does the other maid [Ianthe] burn, and she prays thee, Hymenæus [god of marriage], to come quickly."[284] Iphis and Ianthe's mutual love presents a stark contrast to the preponderance of unrequited loves, coercive marriages, and sexual assaults that otherwise populate the pages of *Metamorphoses*. And while Ovid calls Iphis's love "unnatural," he also paints Iphis in a clearly sympathetic light.

When the wedding day is upon them, Iphis and Telethusa are distraught over the impending discovery of Iphis's sex. Remembering the goddess's appearance to her once before, Telethusa takes Iphis to the temple of Isis and they pray together for the goddess's aid. Isis hears, the temple shakes, and the lunar horns on her icon glow. When mother and child leave the temple, Iphis walks "with longer strides than she had been wont; her fairness does not continue on her face; both her strength is increased, and her features are more stern; and shorter is the length of her scattered locks. There is more vigour, also, than she had *as* a female. *And* now thou art a male, who so lately wast a female" (emphasis original).[285] The goddess has changed Iphis's sex from female to male, and the next day he and his beloved Ianthe are happily married.

The story of Iphis and Ianthe is perhaps the clearest account in Greco-Roman mythology of female same-sex desire, but it also, to the modern reader, has obvious transgender themes, as well, complicating the tale as a story of clear-cut female homoeroticism. If we read Iphis and Ianthe as a sapphic love story, Iphis's transformation into a boy obliterates any happy lesbian ending by making the pair hetero in the end. While Iphis's same-sex female desire is undeniable in Ovid's poetry, in the end her love is made "acceptable" by her transformation into a boy, reinstating and reaffirming heterosexual love and marriage in the process. If, on the other hand, we read Iphis as a transgender man, no fewer problems arise. Iphis' transformation into a "real" (i.e., cis) boy undergirds transphobic gender-essentialist narratives that gender is defined and determined by sex only. Ovid even has a line about Iphis "fooling" himself, a line worthy of a transphobic Internet troll.

However, we can't expect ancient sources to live up to our modern standards, and Iphis's tale speaks to feelings that many modern-day queer and trans people still experience today. The sapphic pathos in Iphis's words could have been ripped straight from my (melodramatic) teenage diary: "What issue *of my love* awaits me, whom the anxieties unknown to any *before*, and *so* unnatural, of an unheard-of passion, have seized upon?" (emphasis original).[286] Iphis's despair that society will never approve of her love for Ianthe, will never let them be together openly, resonates with countless lesbians—and gay men—across history: "Lo, the longed-for time approaches, and the wedding-day is at hand, when Iänthe should be mine; and yet she will not fall to my lot. In the midst of water, I shall be athirst."[287] The trans longing is palpable when Iphis wonders, "But though the ingenuity of the whole world were to centre here, though Dædalus himself were to fly back again with his waxen wings, what could he do? Could he, by his skilful arts, make me from a maiden into a youth [a boy]?"[288] Iphis's anxiety about the wedding night resonates with the trans anxiety of disclosure, of weighing when or if to "come out" to potential sexual partners, and how. Then there's the delicious transmasculine gender euphoria of Iphis exiting the temple, his face courser, frame stronger, swagger in his step, as if the goddess Isis just endowed him with a divine super dose of T.

Depending on how one reads it, the story of Iphis and Ianthe can offer a tender account of same-sex female love or a divinely blessed transmasc transition. Since Isis instructs Telethusa to raise her child regardless of sex and then ultimately effects Iphis's transformation, we can consider Isis to be a guardian of transgender youths and a patron goddess of transition. Isis's mythology also has a potentially lesbian-coded aspect in her co-parenting of her son Horus with her sister-goddess Nephthys, both of whom were called Horus's mothers.* One of the most enduring parts of Isis's mythology is her mothering of Horus against stiff odds. From the moment she births her son in the marsh of the Nile Delta, surrounded by poisonous snakes and scorpions, Isis must protect Horus from natural dangers as well as from his uncle Set who wants him dead. All in all, Isis in her role as mother can be a powerful protector of queer and trans kids and their parents who strive in hostile environments to raise their children with all the love, safety, and freedom they deserve.

---

* Though Isis and Nephthys are sisters, sibling relationships never stopped any deities of the ancient world from pairing off. Isis and her consort Osiris were also siblings, and sibling marriage was common in the Egyptian royal line.

Artemis, Homoerotic Huntress and Guardian of Bodily Autonomy

Artemis is the Greek goddess of the hunt, of beasts and wilderness, and of virginity, childbirth, and the protection of young women and girls. She's often pictured with hunting dogs or a stag, her silver bow and quiver over her shoulder and a lunar crescent on her brow. She wears a tomboyish tunic that ends above the knee to accommodate running and hunting through the forests and over the mountains that are her domain. Her companions are female huntresses and nymphs who take vows of virginity like herself, never to sleep with a man or marry. Artemis and her female companions appear frequently in myth, skinny-dipping together in sylvan pools or racing through the forests after game, their bare legs and arms flashing through the trees.

While Artemis never explicitly takes a lover (of any gender), her myths hint that she and some of her companions may have been more than "very good friends." Take her favored companion Callisto. In *Metamorphoses*, Ovid tells the story of Callisto, a devotee of Diana (the Roman name for Artemis) and part of her band of huntresses, who did not care "to soften the wool by teasing, nor to vary her tresses in their arrangement,"[289] meaning she didn't care for typical women's tasks and/or to wear her hair in the usual feminine style—perhaps Hellenistic code that Callisto was butch. One day, Jove (aka Zeus) set his sights on the huntress while she lounged in a meadow, taking a break from the summer heat. He decides, as he too-often did, that he will seduce her, and whose form does he take to aid his seduction? Diana's. Jove metamorphoses into Diana and appears to Callisto, who sits up from the grass and greets her goddess warmly. Jove-as-Diana swoops in and "gives her kisses, not very moderate, nor such as would be given by a virgin."[290] indicating that this was no chaste kiss, but a passionate, lusty one. Far from thinking anything amiss, when their lips part, Callisto proceeds to tell her goddess about her day, as if such immodest and unvirginal kisses were an everyday occurrence. A mortal man, Leucippus, tried a similar tactic to woo Daphne, another huntress who was close to Artemis's heart. The 1st-century B.C.E. Greek poet Parthenius tells us that, "despairing of getting [Daphne] in any normal way, [Leucippus] dressed himself in women's clothing, made himself look like a girl, and went hunting with her. He managed to get close to her heart, and she always kept him around, embracing and hanging on him all the time."[291]

Although in both myths the seducers were men disguised as women, the female homoerotic implications are no less profound. That both Jove and Leucippus disguise themselves as women to seduce a huntress of Diana/Artemis suggests that they had reason to believe this tactic would succeed. Perhaps the band of women were known, or at least suspected, for sharing such "unvirginal" same-sex kisses as Ovid describes. Jen H. Oliver goes back to the original Latin of *Metamorphoses* to show that many of the words used in the Callisto episode are indicative of more than just the kind of love a devotee might feel toward their goddess, or the sort of favor a deity might bestow on their favorite.[292] For example, Ovid says that Callisto was "joined to the side of the goddess," and according to Oliver, "joined to the side" in Latin was used as a euphemism for sexual activity; indeed, Ovid uses it elsewhere to indicate sex.[293] Oliver also shows that Callisto's greeting to Diana (or who she believes to be Diana), calling the goddess "dearer to her than Jove," is a familiar lover's declaration, common to the point of cliché.[294] All in all, clues point to a sapphic relationship between Diana and Callisto that predated Jove's incognito kiss.

Then there's also Artemis's fierce protectiveness when it comes to all those nude baths with her nymphs and ladies, almost as if they're getting up to something that they don't want prying eyes to see. So while Artemis and her band of huntresses are never explicitly shown or said to share same-sex romantic love or engage in same-sex erotic acts, the implications are clear.

Artemis's emphatic virginity and that of her companions may seem an impediment to any lesbian lovemaking, but their vows of virginity seem to have been less about chastity than we'd think. In Callimachus's "Hymn to Artemis," a young Artemis sitting on her father Zeus's knee asks him to give her control over her own virginity, saying she wants to keep it forever. Her request is not couched in language of purity or piety, but of self-ownership and control. In a society where fathers arranged marriages for their daughters, wives were the property of their husbands, and women had no control over their own lives after marriage, Artemis's desire to control her own virginity is the desire to control her own body—and by extension, her life. Artemis's emphatic virginity is a declaration of independence and self-determination. The virginity of her companions is the same; if any of them were to marry or even to sleep with a man and conceive a child, her life would no longer be her own. She would no longer be able to run free through the wilderness, and Artemis would lose a dear companion to the "civilized" world of men.

Of course, the other potential reason for foreswearing sexual relationships with men is that Artemis and her huntresses were simply not interested in men, either because they were interested in women or asexual. Indeed, Artemis can also be interpreted as an asexual goddess, a theory supported by the attestation in the Homeric Hymn to Aphrodite that she was one of only three goddesses, along with fellow virgin goddesses Athena and Hestia, over which Aphrodite, the goddess of love and sex, had no influence.

Artemis is an inherently queer goddess because of the numerous ways that she disrupts and refuses the heteronormative, patriarchal world order. Her domains are paradoxical. She's called the "Mistress of Animals" who suckles wild beasts, but she's also the huntress that runs them down and slays them. She's emphatically a virgin but is also a goddess of childbirth. She's a protector of young girls but also a patroness of warriors, who sacrifice to her before battle. Artemis is protection and peril, as can be seen in the stories of her vengeance on those who trespass on her baths. She famously turned the hunter Actaeon into a deer for peeping on her bathing naked in the woods, after which he was chased down and ripped apart by his own hunting dogs. Her dual nature as nurturing and bloodthirsty, as virginal and savage, put her on the fringes of the familiar, and many of her sanctuaries were accordingly built on the farthest outskirts of the city, where civilization blended into the unconquered wild. This positioned her as a liminal border deity, so it's unsurprising that she became associated with and eventually absorbed attributes of the goddess of the crossroads, Hekate.

She also shares qualities with queer Dionysos: their wildness, the ecstasy of the hunt and the dance (Artemis leads dances when her twin brother Apollo plays his lyre), and their foreignness. Though

Artemis, like Dionysos, is a native Greek deity as well as one of the oldest, she was frequently treated as a goddess from elsewhere. In her study of ancient Greek cults, Larson attributes this to the otherness of Artemis's personality, which challenged cultural norms: "Like Dionysos, Artemis embodies much that stands in opposition to Greek cultural ideals: she is an untamed, powerful female, a deity of the wilds more than of the city, and her personality includes a savage element which must be suppressed in the making of a civilized society."[295]

Baring and Cashford posit that women prayed to virgin Artemis in childbirth because she was the Mistress of Animals, hence she could help women in labor ease into their animal side that instinctually knows how to give birth, and release the civilized side that shrinks from screaming, pain, and blood. Young women also prayed to Artemis before getting married. While others have proposed patriarchal rationale for why an avowed virgin who swore off marriage would oversee that institution, I wonder if marriageable girls and laboring women supplicated to Artemis in these times because, as a protector of women and girls, the goddess was wholly on their side and no one else's. As a virgin unbeholden to any man, Artemis was not swayed by patriarchal concerns. The perfect deity to pray to for guidance and protection during marriage and childbirth. Further, her placement as a threshold deity, on the borders of the civilized and the wild, positions her as a guardian for threshold moments in life.

Whether or not Diana/Artemis was "officially" a lesbian goddess, she was certainly read as homoerotic by readers of Greco-Roman myth through the centuries. Since Diana was secretly Jove in the Callisto episode, the kiss between Callisto and Diana was a safe subject for the artistic representation of female same-sex eroticism in heteronormative society. The sapphic moment appears in paintings such as François Boucher's 18th-century *Jupiter and Callisto*, which shows a luscious-bodied nude Callisto lounging in Diana's lap, their faces tilted toward each other as if about to kiss. In the 17th century, Karel Philips Spierincks painted the two embracing while Cupid aims an arrow at the pair. Others lean more erotic, such as Nicolas-René Jollain's *Diane et Callisto* (1770), where a nude Diana and Callisto lean toward each other, lips almost touching, hands caressing thighs and waists. Artemis/Diana's reputation for sapphic love is so firmly established that in the 20th century, Dianic Wiccans heartily embraced the goddess for what they saw as her feminist sensibilities as well as her lesbianism. Whether or not Diana/Artemis was definitively, beyond-a-shadow-of-a-doubt gay, she has been interpreted in terms of female homoerotic desire for centuries, and that's powerful.

Diana/Artemis is a goddess of female sovereignty. Her virginity didn't just mean foreswearing sex with men, it meant remaining the guardian of her own destiny. By never taking a male consort or getting married, Artemis and her huntresses controlled their own fates. She's a slayer of the male gaze, turning the men who dare to look upon her nakedness into deer, into stone, or in one instance, into a woman. In her attributes as a guardian of virgins as well as women in labor, in addition to her fierce protection of the privacy and autonomy of herself and her huntresses and nymphs, Artemis is a powerful goddess of bodily autonomy. She can be called on for aid and protection in the fight for the rights of women, people with uteruses, and transgender people to have complete control over their own body and life. Forswearing patriarchal society, racing through wilderness, skinny-dipping in woodland springs, dancing in moonlight, half-wild, Artemis and her huntresses lived by their own designs and forged their own destinies. As such, these powerful, self-determined women are more relevant today than ever.

Callisto, Bear-Mother, Sacred Survivor

Content warning: rape, sexual assault, PTSD.

I told you about the "unvirginal" kiss Callisto shared with Jove, who she thought to be her beloved goddess Diana, but I didn't tell you the whole story. It's a hard and infuriating story, and an all too common one in Greco-Roman mythology. After Jove-as-Diana lustily kisses Callisto, the woman starts to tell her beloved goddess about her hunting that day, but she never gets to finish her sentence. Jove drops his disguise and forces himself on Callisto while she ferociously fights back. But he's a god and she's a mortal, so even the mighty huntress can't fight him off. Jove rapes her.

Afterward, Callisto tells no one and hides the resulting pregnancy for as long as she can. She shows all the signs of PTSD, running from the real Diana when she sees her in the woods, afraid the goddess is Jove again in disguise. She becomes quiet and depressed. She no longer walks in her usual place at the goddess's side but hangs to the back of the troop instead, rarely lifting her eyes from the ground. She hates the woodland glade where it happened. Nine months later, Callisto, Diana, and her nymphs come upon a refreshing forest pool. Diana skims her toes in the water and declares it safe to disrobe and bathe together, as no one is nearby to see. When Callisto hesitates, the nymphs pull off her clothes, exposing her swollen belly. Diana, in shock and betrayal, banishes Callisto from her presence without giving Callisto a chance to explain.

Soon Callisto gives birth to a son, naming him Arcas. When Juno (Hera), the ever-vindictive wife of Jove, finds out her husband has sired yet another child with yet another woman, she jealously turns Callisto into a bear.* Her son Arcas grows up without her and becomes a hunter like his mother. Then one day, years later, he comes across a bear in the woods. Not knowing the bear is his mother, Arcas lifts his spear. Callisto recognizes her son and stares at him longingly, wanting to go to him, standing completely still while her son aims his spear for her heart. Before Arcas can strike, Jove intercedes, sweeping bear-mother and son into the heavens and immortalizing them as the constellations Ursa Major and Ursa Minor, the Great Bear and Little Bear.

There are numerous versions of the tale. In one, Hera turns Callisto into a bear before Artemis finds out about the pregnancy, and later, Artemis kills Callisto while hunting, not recognizing her. In others, Artemis turns Callisto into a bear, herself, or Zeus does it to hide her from Hera, and later Artemis slays her either knowingly or unknowingly. In some versions, Diana is active in condemning Callisto; in others, she's not. Instead of excusing Artemis's actions as motivated by betrayal or jealousy, we might instead let her be a mirror for the ways that we have blamed the victim and been swift to judge others in predicaments that we do not understand.

---

*   Interestingly, the bear is Artemis's theriomorphic form (her animal form), and in one of her cults, virgin girls dressed as bears, ran races, and danced (Baring & Cashford 326; Larson 108). In a way, by transforming Callisto into a bear, Juno makes her into the image of Artemis and, as a wild animal, puts her more firmly under Artemis's domain.

Undoubtedly, Callisto is treated horribly by Jove, Juno, and Diana herself. She is subject to an agonizing series of events, all of which happen to her against her will and none of which she deserved. Finishing Callisto's story certainly complicates Diana/Artemis' reputation as a protector of women and a goddess of bodily autonomy.

Callisto's myth is hard to stomach. But it's also important to read her story, as well as those of other survivors of sexual assault in Greco-Roman myth—Philomena, Daphne, Io, Leda, Europa, Caeneus, Medusa, Persephone, and too many more. The sheer preponderance of rapes and sexual assaults in Greco-Roman mythology has understandably led some to seek their gods elsewhere. At the same time, there's something to be said for a mythology that acknowledges the horrors and power abuses of the real world we all have to live in, where bad things happen to people who don't deserve them all the time. Why *shouldn't* we have sacred stories of survivors? Stories that, as hard as it is, tell us the stories of ourselves? Granted, it might be better to have sacred stories of survivors who aren't then turned into a tree (Daphne), a cow (Io), or a bear. It could be more empowering to read stories of survivors who go on to heal and thrive. Still, some of us may recognize ourselves in Callisto transformed, in her claws and teeth, in her "angry and threatening voice . . . full of terror," growling from her bear throat.[296] Everything is taken from Callisto: her beloved goddess, her place at Diana's side, her son, and even her body itself, not once but four times—rape, pregnancy, transformation into a bear, and transformation into a constellation. But as Ovid tells us, Callisto's mind remains her own. Even as a bear, her personhood, her identity, and her spirit can't be taken from her. Ever a Dianic huntress, Callisto belongs to herself and herself alone.

In her introduction to her translation of *Metamorphoses*, Stephanie McCarter observes that Ovid's inclusion of so many stories of rape suggests that he "felt such violence was worthy of critical interrogation, just as he shines a light on the negative repercussions of masculine heroics or divine power precisely in order to question, not celebrate, them."[297] She points out that these myths offer us opportunities to face, question, and combat such power abuses in our own world, as well as to do the thorny work of self-examination. "It is simply easier to talk about love rather than rape or to focus on ennobling values rather than try to grasp our own human failings," she writes.[298] But a spiritual life requires this grappling. Avoiding hard topics by escaping into a divine fantasy of love and light is called "spiritual bypassing." A term coined by psychotherapist John Welwood in the 1980s, spiritual bypassing is a tendency to bypass personal, emotional, psychological, and interpersonal issues using spiritual ideas and practices. A type of defense mechanism to avoid difficult emotions, spiritual bypassing ultimately does a disservice to ourselves and the interconnected world we live in by fostering escapism rather than supporting the hard work of accountability, healing, and change.

Sometimes we are unable to read stories like Callisto's because it may trigger trauma that is still too close and overpowering, or still ongoing, and that's okay. Sometimes, we need to shut off and escape for our health and well-being—as a practical recuperative skill to support our ongoing internal work, not on a permanent basis. But when we *are* capable of facing the brutal and unjust realities of the world—even though it will hurt, and stir up all kinds of grief, rage, and sorrow—doing so can be an act of devotion. To ourselves. And to everyone who has ever suffered, is suffering, or will suffer under the fist of abusive power.

Next time you're outside under a clear night sky, look up and find Ursa Major, the Great Bear, Callisto. With a growl in your throat and love in your heart, tell her that you haven't forgotten. Tell her you're fighting for her, for Philomena, and Leda and Europa and Medusa—for all of us. Tell her you're a huntress too.

Diana, Queen of the Witches

Many centuries after Artemis/Diana hunted the forests of the ancient Mediterranean, Diana became Queen of the Witches.

It seems the virgin huntress's name was never fully forgotten among the European peasantry, as it appears a number of times in reports and trial records of those accused of heresy or witchcraft in the Middle Ages. In *Witchcraft and the Gay Counterculture*, Arthur Evans collects a timeline that includes several examples of purported Diana-worship in Christian Europe, including multiple authors condemning the surviving practice of Diana-worship in Western Europe between 450 and 600 C.E., reports of a Christian missionary killed by the East Franks for trying to convert them away from Diana in 689, the indictment in 1370 of a woman in Milan for being a member of a "society of Diana," and increasingly frequent accounts from the 10th to 16th centuries of women gathering or flying out at night to worship the witch-goddess Diana.[299] Descriptions of a similar night-riding witch goddess who rules over animals, the natural world, spinning and weaving, sexuality (often homosexuality), and the realm of the dead also appeared under multiple different names, from Holda in Germany, to Hulla in Norway and Denmark, to Perchta in Switzerland and Austria, and Dame Habondia, Selga, Abundia, Satia, and others elsewhere.[300]

While many accounts can undoubtedly be chalked up to folklore and superstition rather than living worship practices—and "confessions" extracted under the Inquisition's torture tactics are dubious at best—it seems that Diana was a figure who still captured the imaginations of European peasants and loomed large in the anxieties of the Christian Church through the Middle Ages and into the Renaissance. Then, in 1890, Diana reappeared as the head of a supposed real-life underground witch-cult in folklorist Charles G. Leland's *Aradia: Gospel of the Witches*. In the mid-20th century, Gerald Gardner and Doreen Valiente took inspiration from Leland's Diana for the writing of some of the foundational liturgies of Wicca such as the Charge of the Goddess, which includes the famous line, "All acts of love and pleasure are my rituals."[301] Not long after, Diana exploded onto the scene as the patron goddess of women-centric Dianic Wicca that arose out of the second-wave feminist women's liberation movement of the 1970s in the U.S. The Dianic Wiccans embraced Diana not only as a feminist goddess, but also as a *lesbian* one.

But how did the virgin goddess of ancient Greece end up as a modern lesbian witch-goddess in California? Despite the appearance of Diana's name in medieval heresy trial records and now-discredited theories of a continuous pagan witch-cult in Europe, it is highly unlikely that any organized worship of Diana (or any other pagan deity) was practiced continuously from the ancient to the modern era. However, it's entirely possible that a faded echo of her survived in local legends, oral stories, and folklore, and that occasionally a freethinking person or two might have gazed up at the moon at night and whispered her name. Of all the Greek goddesses, Artemis's cults were the most numerous and widespread in antiquity, extending from modern-day Marseilles to Sicily, Greece, North Africa, and Asia Minor.[302] The Temple of Artemis in Ephesus was one of the seven ancient wonders of the world, and the strength of her worship there presented problems for the early Christian missionaries. The New Testament book of Acts tells that the Ephesians rioted when Paul of Tarsus attempted to convert them in the 1st century B.C.E., crying that Artemis, "who is worshiped throughout the province of Asia and the world, will be robbed of her divine majesty" (Acts 19:27). Under Romanized Europe, worship of Artemis extended all the way to the British Isles. It's not hard to imagine that such a powerful and pervasive goddess would be difficult to expunge completely, especially in the countryside and wilder edges of civilization that were always her domain.

The modern figure of Diana as Queen of the Witches owes a great debt to Leland's *Aradia*, which he claimed was the true gospel of an Italian Dianic witch-cult, obtained for him by his fortune-telling witch-contact Madallena. The authenticity of *Aradia* is uncertain; Leland claimed to have heard of the existence of a "Witch's Gospel" in 1886 and tasked Madallena to track it down for him. Eleven years later, Madallena finally supplied him with a manuscript in her own handwriting, the implication being that she copied it from a source that she was not able to take with her, recorded it from an oral history, or a combination of both. Due to the nature of the manuscript, the authenticity of the "Witch's Gospel" has been impossible to prove or disprove. The strongest skeptics suggest that Madallena was fake and Leland made it all up himself. Others speculate that he may have been duped by Madallena and that *she* made it all up herself. But there is the third possibility that Madallena delivered to Leland a manuscript that she believed to contain actual folk practices of witchcraft in Northern Italy. Maybe one day someone will crack the mystery. Until then, *Aradia* is a piece of modern mythology worth looking into, not only for its influence on the development of reconstructionist paganism and witchcraft in the 20th century, but for the bold and striking figure of Diana and her daughter Aradia writ in its pages.

In *Aradia*, Diana is a sexually liberated goddess of the oppressed; a creatrix of light and darkness, space and stars; the queen of fairies and goblins; and the mother of a female savior sent to earth to liberate any woman, man, or person who is ready to stand against the lords, landowners, bosses, priests, and abusers of power. *Aradia* includes a creation myth that tells us, "Diana was the first created before all creation; in her were all things," painting a picture of a goddess entirely whole and complete within herself.[303] The text then tells of how Diana, "the first darkness," divided herself into darkness and light, and the light was called Lucifer, "her brother and son, herself and her other half."[304] When she saw how beautiful was her other half—which was herself—she desired to be rejoined with it, to have it inside her, to swallow it up. We are told that this desire is the Dawn. But Lucifer (the light) flees from Diana (the dark) as the day does from the night, round and round the globe.

In another tale from *Aradia*, Diana has a child by Lucifer, a daughter named Aradia, for whom Leland's account is titled. We are told that it was a time of great inequality between rich and poor, with much slavery and other injustices, "in every palace tortures, in every castle prisoners."[305] When the enslaved people escaped, they fled into the countryside and became thieves to survive. Sometimes, they killed their kidnappers. In a twist on Artemis's band of huntresses roving the wilderness to escape marriage, the formerly enslaved "dwelt in the mountains and forests as robbers and assassins, all to avoid slavery."[306] In response to this, Diana charges her daughter Aradia to change from a spirit into a mortal and go to earth to aid them by teaching them the arts of witchcraft, including the arts of poisoning the lords, binding the oppressor's soul, and ruining the crops with hail and lightning. Aradia does so, and when she's done teaching the craft to the first generation of witches, she departs with these instructions to her pupils:

Whenever ye have need of anything,

Once in the month, and when the moon is full,

Ye shall assemble in some desert place,

Or in a forest all together join

To adore the potent spirit of your queen,

My mother, great *Diana*. . . .

And ye shall all be freed from slavery,

And so ye shall be free in everything;

And as the sign that ye are truly free,

Ye shall be naked in your rites, both men

And women also: this shall last until

The last of your oppressors shall be dead.[307]

The collection continues with other tales of Diana and Aradia, fragmentary instructions for holding a sabbat and invoking the goddess, cursing someone with bad luck, sending a goblin to torment your enemies, and spells for love, finding rare books for a good price, and growing a good vintage of wine.

Aradia strikes clear parallels with the figure of Jesus Christ. She's a divine (one might say "holy") spirit that takes mortal form in order to save the people of earth and deliver them from hell. Only in *Aradia*, hell is on earth, and she doesn't save the people with one fell swoop of divine martyrdom but by teaching the people how to save *themselves*. Instead of the Christ of official church doctrine, Aradia is arguably more like the real, historical Jesus, who was a spiritual teacher, spoke out against the abusive power of secular and religious authorities, ministered to the poor, sick, and socially outcast; hung out with sex workers, laborers, and lepers; and was known as a *magician*, a magic-worker. Granted, Jesus's magic-workings were more about healing the sick and feeding the hungry, not poisoning corrupt leaders and blighting their crops. And since Aradia is the daughter of Lucifer, many will be quicker to identify her with the *Antichrist* than Jesus. Indeed, Aradia is the inversion of many Christian narrative tropes. Instead of being the Son of God, she's the Daughter of a Goddess. Rather than being sent to earth as a sacrificial savior, she's sent to earth as a liberatory teacher. Instead of disappearing to heaven afterward, she provides step-by-step instructions for how to contact her for future aid. Instead of peaceful submission, she teaches her people how to fight back.*

While the tale of Diana and Aradia is obviously influenced by Christianity, it does bear some hints of the old, Hellenistic Diana/ Artemis. In several spells and rituals within its pages, the witch is instructed to ask Diana for a sign that she has heard them in the form of the croak of a frog, the song of a cricket, the hiss of a snake, or the like. Diana/Artemis of antiquity was the Mistress of Animals, the suckler of beasts. According to Baring and Cashford, "Artemis was called 'the sounding one,' *keladeine*, evolving out of the music of the wild, the spirit of the place, the language of animals, birds, fish, insects—the immanent presence of the whole of nature as a sacred reality."[308] *Aradia* also includes spells to compel a woman to sleep with you, which seems more up Aphrodite's alley than Diana's, what with her reputation for fiercely protecting the virginity of her female followers and unmarried girls. Then again, if you consider the fact that Leland describes the witches as almost exclusively female in the rest of the book, then the love spell may gain a sapphic valence—if a strongly problematic one for consent reasons—despite the spell-caster being referred to as "he" in the text. The Diana and Aradia of the Witch's Gospel are champions of the oppressed, and in antiquity, the sanctuaries of Artemis and Diana were known to provide asylum to fugitives and people who escaped from slavery. *Aradia* includes a strange tale about a goddess of thieves called "Laverna," a patroness of criminals, which may seem odd until one remembers the opening to the Witch's Gospel, where escaped enslaved people were forced to become thieves and murderers to survive oppression and resist reenslavement.

---

* Arguably, "peaceful submission" is not what Jesus taught. Rather, it was just how it was selectively cherry-picked afterward and portrayed by the institution of the Church that was more interested in getting people to follow doctrine without questioning it than in repeating Jesus's more radical teachings.

Though not overtly associated with sorcery in classical antiquity, Diana/Artemis was closely associated with witch-goddess Hekate and eventually accrued aspects of her in the Roman era. Hekate is the goddess of witchcraft, crossroads, and the restless spirits of the dead. In her iconography, she is accompanied by dogs and carries one or two torches to "light the way," symbols Diana/Artemis also appears with. Hekate appeared joined with Diana and Selene, goddess of the moon, under the epithet *Trivia* ("three-ways"), a three-part lunar goddess with Hekate representing the dark moon, Selene the full moon, and Artemis the new or waxing moon. It's no surprise, then, that Diana the Witch Queen of *Aradia* is a goddess of night, her sacred corn cakes baked in the shape of crescent moons, and her sacred rites performed in starry darkness. The consecration of the witches' sabbat bears elements of Christian communion—"I conjure thee, O Meal! / Who are indeed our body, since without thee / We could not live"—as well as the ancient Greek mystery religions that involved a ritual descent and return from darkness as a metaphor for the death and rebirth of the land—"thou who (at first as seed) / Before becoming flower went in the earth, / Where all deep secrets hide."[309] As in the Eleusinian Mysteries, the sacred plant is corn, and the witch-cakes are made of corn meal.

All in all, whether *Aradia: Gospel of the Witches* was an invention of Leland or Madallena or it represents a genuine folk collection of degraded and half-remembered pagan practices, the figure of Diana the Witch Queen does bear a resemblance to her ancient namesake. And while Diana/Artemis was not continuously worshipped from antiquity to today, she has undeniably reemerged.

Diana is the autonomous, self-determined lunar goddess of wilderness and wild things. She's a stubborn goddess with deep roots that patriarchal monotheism struggled for centuries to weed out. She's a vegetal goddess, so it's not so hard to imagine her waiting underground like a kernel of corn all this time, watered by the run-off of all the good things her people were forced to suppress under the rule of patriarchal monotheism—their sexuality, their intuition, their desire for freedom, their hope, their rage. The goddess took all of this into her seed-body and let it nourish her until she was full as the moon, and the time came to sprout again. Only this time, she rose up from the dark earth as virgin and whore, mother and father, god and devil, darkness and light. She's all the things we've been forced to repress and deny for too long, and she's blooming.

Diana Loves Trans Women: A Note on TERFs

While Dianic Wiccan covens are extremely lesbian-positive, some of them are also extremely TERF-y. TERF is an acronym for "trans-ex-clusionary radical feminist," and it describes a transphobic extreme of radical feminism that defines "women" by gender-essentialist terms. Such groups are "women"-only, intentionally excluding trans women. But I don't believe that's true to the spirit of Diana. Diana prized self-determination and bodily autonomy above all else, and trans people are just as deserving of the human right to self-determine and control their own body as anyone else. Diana was a protector of those most in danger from patriarchal society. In ancient Greece and Rome, that was unmarried women and girls but also people of all genders in need of asylum and enslaved people who had escaped their captors. At her largest temple, Artemis was served not only by virgins but also by eunuch priests.[310] I don't think Diana/Artemis's protectiveness was about creating a "no boys allowed" club, but about carving out a space free from the abusive and controlling dominion of patriarchy.

An even better word to use here than patriarchy is kyriarchy, a term introduced in 1992 by feminist theologian Elisabeth Schüssler Fiorenza to describe a social system built on interconnected systems of oppression including patriarchy, racism, sexism, ableism, homopho-bia, transphobia, classism, and more. Today, transgender people—especially trans women of color—are among those at the greatest risk of harm and death under kyriarchy. The same toxic society that creates rape culture and domestic abusers also manufactures the transphobia that results in discrimination and violence against trans people. So when TERFs cry "trans women aren't real women" and believe trans men are just "sellouts" trying to climb the patriarchal ladder, they are unwittingly parroting the same patriarchal vitriol that they claim to be so opposed to. Patriarchy isn't created just by males. Rather, it's a communal creation that people of all genders participate in, buy into, and perpetuate every single day. Patriarchy and kyriarchy can't be vanquished by excluding trans women from women's groups. In fact, doing so is only proof that the patriarchy is alive and well inside trans-exclusionary circles of women who only see other women for their body parts instead of their spirits.

If Artemis was still running through the woods and hills today—and she is—trans women would be running right alongside her, beloved among her huntresses, fierce and free. If Diana still gathers her witches on mountaintops—and she does—trans women are flying to meet her, dancing for the goddess of liberation, calling down the moon. Artemis is a goddess of protection, not of exclusion, and Diana the Witch Queen expands what protection can look like, including charms, talismans, and spells for getting what you need and fighting back. After all, the best protection isn't hiding in the woods or behind the closed doors of a sanctuary. The best protection is liberation.

QUEER DEVOTIONS

Queer Contemplations

- The Witch's Gospel of *Aradia* is a recent text compared to mythologies of the ancients or even the romances of the Middle Ages, and reconstructionist paganism is even newer. How does that make you feel about its spiritual value and authenticity? Does the age of a sacred text or tradition make it more valid? Remember that the Torah, the Bible, and the Quran were new once. (It's called the "New" Testament for a reason!) What gives value and validity to a spiritual practice, aside from age?

- The work of queering frequently requires us to follow the hints and speculate into the gaps left by the erasure of queer people and queer practices in history. When we can't find or modify old traditions, we have to make up new ones. Does that lessen the validity of forging a queer spiritual practice?

- Sappho's Hymn to Aphrodite compels a woman to love Sappho against her will. Aradia teaches the oppressed how to curse and compel people. How do you feel about such prayers and spells? Is there a time when so-called black magic is called for? What about when people are enslaved, abused, or persecuted, as they are in *Aradia*—do they have the right to defend themselves and resist oppression with the aid of their gods and spirits? You don't have to have definite answers to these questions, but it's important to think about because we tend to excuse violence and compulsion when it's those in power doing it, but denounce it when it comes from the least powerful. Why is that?

Ritual: Reclaiming Bodily Autonomy

For this ritual, all you'll need is your favorite body oil or moisturizer. It's great to do after you've just showered or bathed. You'll need to be as naked as Artemis and her nymphs in a woodland pool. Squeeze or pour your chosen moisturizer into your palm and imagine infusing the moisturizer with the divine light of fierce self-love and protection. Declare, "With this oil [or lotion, etc.] I claim my body and my power as my own. No other person can own, define, or control me, none can touch me without my consent. I am my own. I am protected. I am whole."

Apply the moisturizer to your entire body (all the areas that are safe to apply it), and as you massage it in, imagine reclaiming each inch of skin with fierce love and autonomy. As you go, imagine that the moisturizer leaves a protective barrier on your skin that deflects the gazes and intentions of anyone who wishes to harm or control you. When you're done, repeat, "I am my own. I am protected. I am whole. So it is." If you'd like, you can ask Artemis/Diana to watch over you as well.

If you're not a full-body moisturizer person, you can modify it for the shower as you wash your body, in which case I recommend using your bare hand for washing instead of a loofah or washcloth. Tactile skin contact is important here.

You can repeat this ritual whenever you feel the need, or you can perform it routinely after your shower.

Exercise: The Spirits of Marginal Places

There's something inherently queer about *margins*. The edges of the map, the borderlands between countries, the weeds that tangle and creep through the hedgerows and fences. These are places of possibility and decay, neither here nor there, where cultures meet and mix and civilizations clash, where the tidily ordered world breaks down into the chaotic order of nature, where anything can happen, emerge, disappear, bloom.

Seek out an interstitial place, a place on the edge of here and there. It might be the edge of a meadow where the long grass, wildflowers, and sunshine blend into underbrush, blackberry bushes, and loamy leaf-rot in the shadows of trees. It might be the stubborn weeds that grow along the edges of your garden, lace themselves through chain-link fences, or force their way through sidewalk cracks. It might be the muddy river's edge or the undulating rush and retreat of the sea across sand. It might be the bus stop, or the train, or the place where the playground pebbles spill into the park grass.

Sit there awhile. Observe. Watch what happens, or doesn't. Listen with all your senses. What does this place feel like? Can you sense its spirit(s)? Say hello. Introduce yourself. Listen more. What does this place have to teach you, if anything? What does it need from you, if anything? When you feel like you're done, thank the place. Maybe leave it a little offering. (If you're in nature, leave something biodegradable—don't litter!) Say good-bye and leave.

Recommended Reading

For those interested to explore an inclusive witchcraft path, check out *All Acts of Love and Pleasure: Inclusive Wicca* by Yvonne Aburrow, *Queering Your Craft* by Cassandra Snow, and the *Queer Magic: Power Beyond Boundaries* anthology edited by Lee Harrington and Tai Fenix Kulystin, and of course the seminal *The Spiral Dance* by Starhawk. Get the most recent edition if you can, because Starhawk's additional notes added over the years are wonderful and important. For an animist witchcraft perspective, *Alive with Spirits* by Althaea Sebastiani is excellent.

CHAPTER 10

Resurrecting the Erotic Body

Toward a Living Queer Devotion

There's a meme I see making the rounds every now and then. It shows a painting of Jesus with one arm raised to display a wound on the side of his chest. Another man leans in close to peer at the injury, fingertips reaching almost to touch it, his face in a posture of disbelief or awe. It's the episode of "Doubting Thomas," where St. Thomas couldn't believe that Jesus had resurrected from death, so Jesus shows him the wounds he sustained on the cross as proof. The wound appears as a small scar just under the outer edge of Jesus's pectoral muscle. The meme's caption reads, "Jesus showing off his top surgery to the boys."[*]

I find this meme delightful, but let's take it seriously for a moment. What if we *can* see top surgery—or any kind of gender-affirmation surgery—in the figure of the resurrected Jesus Christ? When Jesus shows his side wound to the disciples in order to prove he has come back from death, it is not so dissimilar to a trans man or nonbinary person unwrapping their chest bandages for the first time. We can see ourselves in Thomas, in his heart-in-your-throat disbelief and desire, the nerves, the hope, the awe at beholding the revelation of their new chest, the stitched incisions still red and

---

[*] Separate from the meme, contemporary photographer Elisabeth Ohlson Wallin created an actual piece of art that depicts a trans Jesus showing his top surgery scars to the disciples, based on Caravaggio's *The Incredulity of Saint Thomas*.

swollen, the plastic drain tubes that some of us get sliding into a small slit in the skin on each side, almost exactly where the side wound of Christ is shown in art. St. Bernard of Clairvaux imagined drinking blood and milk from that side wound, not unlike the mixture of blood and yellow-clear fluid that collects in the clear plastic bulbs of the Jackson-Pratt drains after surgery, the sacred fluid of the body healing itself.

One of the most moving parts of my own top surgery experience was those (gnarly, gory) drains because they externalized my body's healing where I could see it. I watched the fluid changing over the weeks from dark red to pink to yellow to clear, even while I couldn't look at my chest itself, still wrapped tightly under bandages. Those drains were a visible miracle: the miracle of my body knitting itself back together in a new shape, the miracle of my body healing me of wounds deeper than surgical scars. The twice-daily procedure of emptying the drains into a small plastic measuring cup and recording the quantity and color of the fluid became a sacred ritual, a communion of sorts, the blood of my body, given for me. I didn't *drink* it, of course—I flushed it down the toilet. But before I poured it into the bowl, I would say a small prayer of thanks for my miraculous queer body and its healing. Then, when the shroud of bandages was finally removed and I saw myself for the first time, it was a resurrection. My spirit, for so long buried in the tomb of dysphoria and dissociation, flew back into my reborn body.

When Jesus shows his side wound to the disciples in order to prove he has come back from death, we might see in that a transgender image: the trans man proudly revealing his top surgery scars to his partner(s) or friends, the trans woman showing off her new breasts to the girls, the nonbinary person reveling in their body's changes under hormone replacement therapy, as if to say, "Behold, it is me, finally *me*, resurrected from myself, reborn."

Playing on the traditional titles "God the Father" and "Mary, Queen of Heaven," queer theologian Marcella Althaus-Reid poses a provocative question:

Why not God the faggot? Why not Mary the Queer of Heaven? The fact that nothing is known of Mary or God's sexual identity liberates them; nothing is fixed, except for gender roles, and these are already well contested inside and outside Christianity. . . . Jesus may be a faggot, or a transvestite, so little we know of him except what other people saw in him; sexual appearances are so deceiving.[311]

And why not? Think about it: are Jesus and Mary straight? How do you know? According to Catholic doctrine, they both died virgins. Is God straight? Does immaculately inseminating Mary count as heterosexual intercourse? If so, that would seem to defeat the whole "Virgin Mary" enterprise. To paraphrase Sojourner Truth, Jesus came from God and a woman, and a man had nothing to do with it.[312] Seems pretty queer to me.

In the protestant church I grew up in, Mary was barely in the picture. After she was done being divinely inseminated and giving birth in a stable, she was packed away till next Christmas along with the donkeys and cows and the rest of the nativity scene, her role fulfilled. Even the birth part was skipped over—all that blood and shitting and screaming was simply too unseemly, too bodily, too *real* for the pristine virgin mother. (Can one stay a virgin after pushing out the head of a human baby? Are we still counting virginity in the currency of intact hymen or does it all, as usual, depend on a dick?) Mary represented everything I was expected to be and didn't want to be, and I hated her for that. Quiet, obedient, sexless, breeding, only defined by her relationship to men, kneeling forever beside a manger or packed away in a closet. A vessel more than a person.

But Mary and Jesus were real, historical people who lived two thousand years ago. They had bodies, complete with fluids and orifices and needs and desires, whether they acted on those desires or not—a matter that is up for debate. Mary was an unmarried pregnant teenager, making her a sexual transgressor and social outcast. Jesus hung out with sex workers, sinners, lepers, the poor and marginalized people of society. Yet the Church would have us believe that Mary never had a sexual life, despite the companionship of Joseph, and that Jesus went to the cross a 33-year-old virgin. According to Althaus-Reid, Jesus "has been dressed theologically as a heterosexually oriented (celibate) man. Jesus with erased genitalia; Jesus minus erotic body."[313] And Mary's got it just as bad with her "stone-walled hymen," as Althaus-Reid puts it, continually denied of pleasure yet perpetually expected to open her body for others' use.[314]

A while back, I was listening to the podcast *Living in This Queer Body*. The host Asher Pandjiris asks all their guests the same question: "What's the first memory you have of learning what it meant to have a body?"[315] I knew my answer immediately. The first thing I remember learning about having a body was that my body was not my own. Some trans people feel like they were born into the wrong body, but that's not what I mean. Rather, for as long as I can remember, I knew that my body was not my own because it was, in a sense, public property. From birth, the world looked upon my body and decided what it meant, who I was, and who I would be. The possibilities for my life and personhood were rolled out like a red carpet to a gendered prison cell. My clothes, interests, activities, and even facets of my personality were predetermined based on society and my body. Later, adult men desired my body and took it like it already belonged to them. Eventually, my body would be expected to birth children, and if I declined, it would be such a *shame*. Just like my tattoos were "such a shame," as I have been informed by more than a few complete strangers. Just like it was such a shame when I removed my perfectly good breasts and wasted my God-given female beauty on being trans.

My body was not my own because society coopted it the moment I was born—*before* I was born, the moment my fetal genitals showed up on a grainy sonogram. Other people filled my body with all their meanings, interpretations, and expectations. Not a person, but a vessel. Cis-heteronormative society does this to all of us, of every sex, making us into immaculate Marys for conceiving and reproducing its compulsory roles. The only difference is that some of us are more comfortable in those roles, or more privileged in them, than others.

I did what many of us learn to do: I separated myself from my body. I learned my body was not myself. I pulled a half-resurrection, unhitching my soul but leaving my body somewhere in a dark tomb, hidden beneath a pristine shroud, where I didn't have to think about it. Didn't have to *feel* about it. Ironically, this is not so unlike what all those monks and nuns have done for more than a thousand years, declaiming the sinful pleasures of the flesh so the soul can purify itself for eventual reunion with God after death. Only my body kept on sinning while my soul was off thinking of other things, and not usually about God.

In studying the Gnostic Gospels, I came across a verse in the Gospel of Mary Magdalene that excited me. Peter asks Jesus, "What is the sin of the world?" and Jesus replies, "There is no such thing as sin; rather you yourselves are what produces sin" (Gospel of Mary 3:2–4).[316] I was electrified. *This changes everything*, I thought. If there's no such thing as sin except for what we ourselves produce, does that mean the body is not innately sinful? Does this obliterate the doctrine of "original sin," the idea that by eating the forbidden fruit in the Garden of Eden, Eve cursed humanity with the taint of sinful nature forever? Is "sin" then something we've "produced," we've made up, in order to *control* people, scare them straight, oppress them, extort them? Is *that* what the real sin has been all along?

According to Karen L. King, a foremost scholar on the Gospel of Mary Magdalene, not quite. In the context of the Gospel of Mary, King explains, sin is not "real" because it is a product of the body, which is of the material realm. Since the material realm is inherently impermanent and will disintegrate into nothingness in the end, sin too is temporary.[317] Only the spiritual realm is eternal, and that is where the soul resides. In a move that directly contradicts the later views of Christianity concerning the body, King writes, "the *Gospel of Mary* does not regard the body as one's *self*. Only the soul infused with the spirit [of God] carries the truth of what it really means to be a human being" (emphasis mine).[318] When humans become consumed with the false and temporary material world instead of the true and eternal spiritual one, King explains, the soul becomes "adulterated," or polluted, by the material realm. The soul becomes estranged from God, and that estrangement or distance from God is the condition of "sin."[319]

On the one hand, this gnostic view wherein the *body* is not the *self* creates room in Christian theology for transgender people by locating the *personhood* of a person in the spirit or soul instead of the essentialist body. Through this lens, the body does not essentially define the identity, purpose, role, or gender of a person—the soul does. Determining the selfhood of a person based on the genitals of the material body is then the "sinful" act. In contrast, living in accordance with the authentic truth of one's soul becomes an act of spiritual devotion to God. This is what M. W. Bychowski calls embodying the transgender image of God (see Chapter 4), which the "transvestite" saints bravely showed through their lived examples. Self as *soul* instead of self as body also displaces the primacy of heterosexuality as the only spiritually "correct" sexuality. If the body is a temporary illusion, then it doesn't really matter who we choose to have sex with. Body parts dissolve back into the dust from whence they came. The only eternal thing is love.

On the other hand, a doctrine of spiritual disconnection from the body can just as easily lend itself to anti-trans and anti-gay interpretations. If the body is impermanent and "sin" is becoming enthralled with the material world, then hormone replacement therapy and gender-affirming surgeries could be construed as "sinful" dependence on the material plane. If the body is meant to be transcended, then dissociation becomes holy. If the sensual passions of the body are what lead the eternal soul away from God and into the trap of materialism, then *all* sexuality, gay or straight, remains a deceptive lure into sin. And we're right back where we started.

What a tragically self-negating thing, this theology of dissociation. What a *life*-negating cosmology that enfleshes souls into bodies not to *live* but to "transcend" the living body until they die into eternal life. It makes me want to scream or weep, this self-abnegation, this condemnation of the lush and vibrant and beautifully sensuous living world. What a tragedy to waste a life waiting for the afterlife.

Then again, scripture contradicts itself a lot, and there was never one singular "right" way to interpret Jesus's teachings, at least not until the Church became an institution and put their trademark on salvation. The Gospel of Thomas isn't your average gospel—it presents a markedly different view on life and embodiment than the Gospel of Mary does, and both present their own meaningful departures from the institutional Gospels. Instead of a narrative, Thomas is a collection of the sayings of Jesus, free of context or interpretation, like one of those quote-a-day calendars. But taken together, the sayings start to add up to something. A sometimes puzzling something, but something more life-affirming, less ascetic, and quite a bit queerer than the sayings of Jesus portrayed elsewhere. Of the Gospel of Thomas, Hal Taussig writes, "The spiritual path of wisdom does not point toward the end of time and the judgment day, nor does it hold up death as a crucial moment in the life of the individual. Instead, the origins of life and the world are the real signs of God's purpose for human beings."[320]

One of the most striking examples of this life-oriented perspective appears near the end of the gospel. Jesus's followers ask him, "When will the realm come?" The "realm" they ask about is the "Kingdom of Heaven," usually considered to be the reunification of Heaven on Earth that will come after the apocalypse of Revelation. Jesus answers, "It will not come by looking for it. It will not be a matter of saying, 'Here it is!' or 'Look! There it is.' Rather, the realm of the Father is spread out upon the earth, but people don't see it" (Gospel of Thomas 113:1-3).[321] In other words, heaven isn't *to come*, but is already here. It's been here all along, "spread out upon the earth." In the Gospel of Thomas, the "realm of God" is not displaced to the afterlife or the end of the world, but is embedded in everyday life experiences.[322] Heaven is something to be *lived now*, not earned by banking away the currency of righteousness like some afterlife retirement fund. But if heaven is here, how do we see it?

There's a phrase that Jesus repeats numerous times in Thomas, variations on, "Whoever has ears to hear, hear!" (Thomas 24:2).[323] The first time I read it, it struck me as a particularly queer turn of phrase. On the one hand, maybe it's just Jesus-speak for "Listen up!" or "Pay attention!" But it's repeated often enough that it seems intentional. If it didn't hold meaning, one would think it would be edited out of the relatively tight and slim Gospel of Thomas, like cutting the *ums* and *likes* from podcast audio. I think the implication of "whoever has ears to hear, hear!" is not that anyone with ears should listen, or not *just* that. Instead, it seems to suggest a particular *way* of hearing, like tuning in to a certain frequency or listening with more than one's plain old ears. It's the Biblical equivalent of "if you know, you know." It's a clue to look past the words, pick up on the trace, the hints, the queer evidence, the marks where something's been erased, the tantalizing gaps in the poem.

My mom used to recite an E. E. Cummings poem when I was young. She'd say it so often that I memorized all the words before I ever saw it on a page. The poem, "i thank You God for most this amazing," is a kind of naturalistic prayer to the Earth or to Life, in which Cummings asks how anyone with senses could doubt the Divine when surrounded by such miraculous natural splendor.[324] Cummings ends the poem with a curious parenthetical statement about the ears of his ears and the eyes of his eyes awakening. Jesus said the Kingdom of Heaven is here, all around us, but we can't see it. How do we see it? By listening not only with the physical senses but with the awakened spiritual senses, not as an abnegation of the body but as a *unification* of the spirit *and* body, a marriage of the soul and the earth on which heaven is already spread for us, ready and waiting. We hear with the ears of our ears and see with the eyes of our eyes, open and awake.

I don't think the point is leaving the so-called sinful body behind, but about *sensing past* the materialist world that monopolizes our sight, hearing, thinking, and dreaming and diminishes it into a pin-prick of survival. The "material world" that some of the gnostic texts warn us about is not the green-spirited natural world that affirmed Cummings's faith in God. No, the world of "sin" is the patriarchal, colonialist, capitalist world that makes us so small and desperate that we'll crawl over each other for the meagerest crumb of power. All that the Christian doctrine of repressing the body gets us is a fast track to subjugation. A person who has been disconnected from their body is easier to force to work 60 hours a week. A person who has unlearned how to feel will accept poverty and oppression with greater docility. A person detached from the eros of their strongest emotions, longings, and desires is less likely to riot when their human rights or those of their neighbors are stripped away. By disconnecting us all from our feeling, sensing, yearning, raging, fucking, emotional, wise bodies, the institutions and powers of the status quo have made us ever easier to control. They've made us perfect puppets by scooping out our meaty, bloody, corporeal insides and leaving an empty, "spiritual" shell. They tell us our salvation depends on our oppression, and we kneel at the altar for our scrap of bread and wine.

In lesbian feminist, essayist, and poet Audre Lorde's landmark essay "Uses of the Erotic," she writes that the "word *erotic* comes from the Greek word *eros*, the personification of love in all its aspects—born of Chaos, and personifying creative power and harmony."[325] She's referencing Hesiod's account of creation from *Theogony*, wherein Eros is the implicit driving force behind all life on Earth. The same Eros that the Orphics believed hatched from the cosmic egg at the beginning of creation. The same Eros that attended Aphrodite as she first stepped from the seafoam onto land. Appropriately, Lorde writes of the erotic as an assertion of life force, as empowered creative energy, and as "the sensual—those physical, emotional, and psychic expressions of what is deepest and strongest and richest within each of us, being shared: the passions of love, in its deepest meanings."[326] But most importantly, Lorde emphasizes the essential role of the erotic in the liberation of Black women and lesbians because, as she writes, "as we begin to recognize our deepest feelings, we begin to give up, of necessity, being satisfied with suffering and self-negation."[327] By connecting to the erotic within ourselves and connecting to the shared erotic with others, whether sexual or not, we will come to know the fullness of our capacity for joy. And, Lorde writes, "that deep and irreplaceable knowledge of [our] capacity for joy comes to demand from all of [our] life that it be lived within the knowledge that such satisfaction is possible, and does not have to be called *marriage,* nor *god,* nor *an afterlife.*"[328]

I want an Erotic spirituality. I want a Jesus with a body and a Mary who has sex. There are hints that Jesus may have had a sexual relationship with Mary Magdalene—the Gnostic Gospel of Philip tells us that Jesus would often kiss her on the lips. There are also indications that Jesus's love for Lazarus exceeded the bounds of heteronormative friendship. According to the (canonical) Gospel of John, when Jesus learned of the death of Lazarus, he returned to the town of Bethany near Jerusalem despite the threat of death he faced there. Outside Lazarus's tomb, Jesus burst into tears and, wailing and "groaning inwardly," called him back from the dead. Lazarus rose, wrapped head-to-toe in his white burial shroud. "Set him free," Jesus cried, "and let him go" (John 11:44).[329] Althaus-Reid writes about a Bible study with a group of gay men who read the hints of queer longing between Jesus and his friend, who John tells us Jesus loved. Reading a queer story in the tale of Jesus and Lazarus may seem absurd to straight Christianity, but that's only because heterosexual people don't often have the experience of closeted living that some gay people do. Althaus-Reid observes, "Only a man whose life experience had been made up of ruptures from and departures of lovers, in the tension of keeping the heterosexual masked ball going, in his job and family, is able to see a dramatic love story between Jesus and his intimate friend."[330] Far from discounting a gay reading of Jesus and Lazarus, however, the minority viewpoint that gay men can bring to such Bible stories illuminates the scriptures in beautiful and necessary ways that would simply never occur to a heterosexual reader. It's listening with the eyes of your eyes, the ears of your ears.

In a similar vein, the story of Mary's unwed immaculate conception can be read through a modern lens as a parallel of unconventional family structures, as Mary the lesbian conceiving through in vitro fertilization or Mary the single woman deciding to start a family by herself. Indeed, the Biblical Mary and her cousin and close friend Elizabeth, who is pregnant at the same time as Mary and has an unlikely pregnancy of her own as an older woman, have been interpreted in this light by theologians and laypeople alike.

Queer theologian Patrick S. Cheng gives the example of contemporary lesbian icons that emphasize Mary's motherhood *sans* male, such as photographer Elisabeth Ohlson's image of Mary and Elizabeth sitting on a bed, holding each other as lovers, while the angel Gabriel delivers them a test tube of semen.[331]* Cheng observes that "Mary deconstructs the heterosexist theologies of male-female complementariness that views the husband-wife marital bond as 'natural' or heavenly ordained."[332] While the supposed virginity of Mary can be and is used against women to enforce an inhumanly high bar of purity and selflessness, at the same time her "immaculate"

---

*   The popularity of this interpretation of the Immaculate Conception may be why the Vatican, in the same decree on the doctrine of "Infinity Dignity" that deprives said dignity to transgender people (see Chapter 4), declared that children conceived by "artificial" means are a grave affront to human dignity, because a "child is always a gift and never the basis of a commercial contract." Apparently, the Pope has forgotten that children were the basis of the commercial contract of marriage for centuries under Church leadership.

conception decentralizes the heterosexual hegemony so often upheld as the hieros gamos, or "sacred marriage," wherein a god and goddess, a man and woman, or the masculine and feminine principles converge in literal or metaphorical intercourse to renew the fertility of the land and/or perpetuate the cycle of life as symbolized by sexual reproduction. By asexually conceiving Jesus without a male partner, Mary complicates the sacred marriage trope. With a little help from God, who, as we've seen in Chapter 4, is not a man but is the singular-plural androgynous queer Everything, Mary grows life all by herself. Perhaps she's like the feminine power spoken of in the gnostic Revelation of Adam discovered at Nag Hammadi, who "came to a high mountain and relaxed there, so that she desired herself alone to become androgynous. She fulfilled her desire, and became pregnant from [her desire]."[333] Or maybe Mary is the imposing speaker of the queerly numinous "The Thunder, Perfect Mind," found with the Nag Hammadi discovery:

> I am the first and the last
>
> I am she who is honored and she who is mocked
>
> I am the whore and the holy woman
>
> I am the wife and the virgin
>
> I am he the mother and the daughter. . . .
>
> I am she whose wedding is extravagant and I didn't have a husband. . . .
>
> I am the bride and the bridegroom. . . .
>
> I am she, the lord.[334]

Imagining Jesus and Mary as queer may seem radically transgressive, but such readings and treatments of Mary and Jesus are not new, either in theology or in the real, lived devotions of actual people. The visionary and polymath abbess St. Hildegard of Bingen wrote and composed hymns to Mary that praised and lingered upon the Virgin's female body with homoerotic devotion. (And we've already seen all the things "virgin" can mean.) Althaus-Reid writes about Santa Librada, the "popular ambiguous divine cross-dresser of the poor" who appears as a crucified Virgin Mary or is maybe Jesus in Virgin Mary drag, and is worshipped in Argentina as a saint who protects the poor from the police.[335] In 2019, the icon of the "Rainbow Mary" of Czestochowa, Poland, became famous when three Polish LGBTQ+ activists were arrested for pasting posters of the Madonna of Czestochowa with rainbow halos behind her and the baby Jesus's heads in protest of a church's homophobic and transphobic display. In response to their arrest, hundreds of protesters carried the vibrant icon in the 10,000 Rainbow Marys march in Warsaw. In Haiti, the Madonna of Czestochowa's iconic scarred visage belongs to the Voudo lwa Erzuli Dantor, a patron of lesbians, unwed mothers, victims of domestic violence, and businesswomen.[336] Outside of Naples, Italy, the Madonna of Montevergine is celebrated as the patron saint of LGBTQIA2S+ Catholics because of a miracle she performed to save the lives of a gay male couple experiencing homophobic violence in the 13th century. Today, the Madonna of Montevergine is celebrated on Candlemas (February 2) with a Pride-like procession that attracts queer Italians and femminielli, a traditional gender-blurring people who have been socially accepted in the Neapolitan region for centuries, and features tambourines, singing and dancing, colorful and glamorous costumes, and, of course, plenty of queer devotion.[337]

One of the greatest tricks Christianity ever pulled was making the erotic bodies of Jesus and Mary *disappear*. When Mary's body is shown in art, it's a single breast nursing baby Jesus or sometimes her holy womb glowing transparently through her dress. When Jesus's body is shown, it's voyeuristically draped with a loincloth at the moment of his excruciating death, nailed to the cross. Their bodies are only revealed when they serve the purpose assigned to them by the Church: Mary as mother, Jesus as sacrifice. Then, as their pièce de résistance, the Church disappeared their bodies entirely. When Mary and post-resurrection Jesus finally die (or unresurrect, in Jesus's case, I guess), they ascend into Heaven and take their bodies with them in a magical disappearing act called the Assumption. Any trace of the living, breathing, bleeding humans they were is—*poof*—gone from the earth, evaporated back into the divine clouds they both supposedly came from. The violence of Christian doctrine against the human body is so extreme that they literally erased the bodies of Mary and Jesus from the earth.

I want a reverse Assumption. Instead of evaporating them body and soul into eternity, let's let Mary and Jesus fall back to earth like rain on the most humid summer day, the air itself wet with them, making all the stems and leaves turgid from drinking them up. Let's return Mary and Jesus to the earth itself so they can become dirt, so they fly in the belly of a bird, feed the fruiting phallus of mushrooms, ring the heartwood of a tree, rise proud as a cornstalk and be eaten by a goddess or a child and get stuck in their teeth. Let's give Mary her body back to do with as she sees fit, to fuck with it, touch herself, dance, run, to birth five more kids conceived in a decidedly *maculate* fashion or from a test tube with her wife, to throw off her blue robes and worship her own divine god-birthing cunt in the mirror. Let's give Jesus his body back so he can give his body unto Lazarus and Mary Magdalene in a Eucharist of bready bodies and wine-soaked kisses and mutual desire, so he can cruise the docks fishing for men, so he can experience passion not only on the cross but also in the divine ecstasy of orgasmic life.

What if, instead of his words to Mary Magdalene outside the tomb—*Noli me tangere* ("Don't touch me")—Jesus sang at the top of his lungs in a packed *Rocky Horror Picture Show* showing, in full Frank-N-Furter leather drag, "Touch-A, Touch-A, Touch Me." What if, when Mary said yes to the angel Gabriel to conceive the son of God, she was also saying yes to herself, yes to her pleasure, yes to her Erotic creative life force, yes to the ownership of her own body and all the divine things it can do.

I'm not interested in saviors. I *am* interested in the brave and thoughtful and corporeal human man who made such an impression that people are still dissecting, contemplating, arguing, and being inspired by his words two thousand years later. I'm interested in the Mary who was so in love or in lust that she acted on the erotic tug of bodily connection despite the repressive society she lived in, for better or worse. I'm interested in the man who loved Lazarus so much that he screamed outside his tomb and moved heaven and hell to bring his friend or lover back from death. I'm interested in the unwed teen mom who raised a radical. I'm interested in the man who said, "If you bring forth what is within you, what you bring forth will save you. If you do not bring forth what is within you, what you do not bring forth will destroy you."[338] I'm interested in the man who said, "You must awaken while in this body, for everything exists in it: Resurrect in this life."[339]

Theologians will say I've got it backward. They'll say the divinity of Mary and Jesus necessitates their freedom from the "original sin" of sexuality. They'll say I'm missing the whole point of Christianity, which is that the body is a temporary and sinful illusion, and the soul is the only real and eternal thing. But I've never been a good Christian, and I've done the dissociation trick.

I spent the better part of 36 years perfecting the art of leaving the body and its needs, pains, and desires behind. And I got to know my soul so well up there in that ether that I grew to love my soul, and I loved it so much that I decided it deserved to live in a body after all. So I pulled my own small act of divine creation, my own immaculately maculate conception, my own queer resurrection, and I gave my soul a body to live in. A stitched and scarred and beautifully formed body, a collaboration between me and the Divine.

Growing up, I was always told that the body is a temple. Now, finally, my body feels like a temple that my soul can call home. A temple to life, or the erotic, or love, which are the closest synonyms I've found for God. A temple for a living, breathing queer devotion. If that's not heaven on earth, I don't know what is.

QUEER DEVOTIONS

Queer Contemplations

- Is the body a temple? Does the body have to meet some standard of purity or perfection to be a temple? Try thinking of your body as a temple, right now, exactly how it is. How does that feel?

- Can a sexual body also be a spiritual body? Why or why not?

- How did you feel reading about Jesus and Mary as sexual beings? Did you feel resistance to considering them as gay, trans, and queer? If you did, where did that come from? The predominant culture, your upbringing, your family?

- Heterosexual love and sex have long been enshrined in various spiritualities and religions, from the "sacred marriage" to the "miracle of life." What can *queer* love reveal about the nature of Divine love? How is queer sex a reflection of the divine?

- How does Audre Lorde's concept of the erotic as deep emotional feeling and interpersonal connection expand possibilities for what Divine love is and how it is experienced? Remember: Erotic comes from Eros, and Eros means Love.

Activity: Unlearning Sin

Do something that you might have previously defined as "sinful." Eat chocolate cake. Masturbate. When you feel like you should push yourself to do something productive, do something you enjoy instead. Wear something you deem scandalous—but that you feel hot in. Do something that feels deliciously good. How is pleasure a spiritual experience? How is sensuality a language of the Divine? Do you feel closer to the Divine when you're in pain or in pleasure, and why? How can you make pleasure a devotion? Or make pain a devotion, if it's pleasurable to you?

Reflection: The End Is the Beginning

Now that you're at the end of the book, I want to ask you the same questions I did at the beginning.

What does queerness mean to you?
How is your queerness a reflection of the Divine?
What does devotion mean to you?
What are you devoted to?

Spend some time journaling your answers. Then, review your original answers from the Queer Contemplations at the end of the Introduction. What has changed since you read the first words of this book? Has your relationship to your gender or sexuality shifted or grown? How about your connection to the Divine? What has transformed inside (or outside) you?

If you have noticed things growing and changing, that's wonderful. But if you haven't, that's okay too. If anything, you have learned, and that's a gift. Cultivating a connection to the Divine of your understanding takes time, and so does building a devotional practice—and as you might recall from Chapter 1, stepping into spiritual waters often stirs up fears and challenges. Transformations aren't always fast, and they are seldom painless. Don't force it. There are no rules and no time limits on your spiritual journey—and, unfortunately, no maps. Wherever you're at on your path is exactly where you need to be. Remember what Dionysos taught us: Sometimes we have to get a little lost to find our way.

Un-Conclusion

I struggled to write a conclusion for this book because, frankly, it's not concluded. I can't put an endcap on a book called *Queer Devotion* because there is no end. There is no amount of words that I or anyone else could write that would be sufficient to draw *conclusions* about the Divine. There is no number of volumes that would be adequate to contain all the queer divinities, spirits, saints, beliefs, and devotions in the world. And there is no conclusion to the spiritual journey of queer devotion. As we live and learn, have new experiences, and make new connections, our relationship to the Divine will change. Mine has already changed since I put the last period on this book. There are seasons when our spirituality, faith, or devotion feels stable, settled, and warm, and there are seasons when everything we thought we knew is thrown into Chaos to be devoured and rebirthed, anew. Queer devotion is ever-evolving, adaptable, resilient, Erotic, always sprouting new green shoots and leaves.

In these pages, I hope you've learned that the Divine is not a singular, fixed and unchanging being or set of beings, but something much wilder and stranger. Something constantly creating Themself and co-creating with us, continually birthing, adapting, dying, being reborn. This is one of the reasons I'm fascinated with mythology, folklore, and the history of belief (if you didn't notice). Such a beautiful and immense variety and diversity of deities and stories exist that it is impossible to claim that any one religion, any one culture, or any one time period had it exactly right. If we look to Greek myth, for instance, most Greek gods and goddesses have more than one origin myth and stories that are told differently, sometimes contradicting each other depending on who's telling them. In the first several hundred years after Jesus's death, numerous and diverse forms of Christianity existed, and none of them any more or less valid than another. This highlights the constructed nature of sacred stories and the subjective nature of belief, and it offers a precedent and potential for telling stories differently yet again, this time queerer, gayer, transer. In ancient Greece, Egypt, and Mesopotamia just as in medieval Scandinavia, France, and the British Isles—and no doubt in numerous other places far and wide—the Divine was never just one thing. They were a multiplicity. Even individual deities were not singular, inert, or fixed. They changed, morphed, moved.

What if we adopted a similar approach to spiritual belief? What if we rewilded our gods, queered their stories, or penned new ones entirely? What if we allowed ourselves to engage in a more creative, intuitive, experiential personal practice? What if we dreamed our way into new streams of the Divine? This is the space of mysticism, the space where deities reveal themselves and are born into our human awareness. This is the practice of gnosis, the personal experiential knowledge of the divine. And this is what I hope you carry forward from this book. The myths, stories, and sacred texts offer us a brilliant starting place, but they do not hold all the answers, and they alone do not bestow a spiritual relationship with the Divine. That takes a lived practice of devotion. It's my dearest wish that this book has provided some inspiration to start.

We queers are sometimes called "godless" by those whose religious beliefs condemn us, but that only shows how little they truly know of us—and of the Divine. We are a people that is god*ful*. We are a people of Abrahamic gods and pagan deities, of ancient pantheons and modern goddess-worship, of occult spirits, ancestors, and the divinity of the natural world. Some of us worship in churches and temples, others in covens or moonlit rituals, others in bedrooms and backseats, gay bars and sex clubs, in the forest's canopied cathedral of green, or in the sacrament of brunch filled with the laughter of friends. Though organized religion largely still bars its gilded doors to us (or in some cases, begrudgingly cracks them open), we know the Divine lives everywhere, not only within institutional walls. The Divine lives in *us*. In the good, sweet miracle of our trans flesh and gay bones and living queer spirit.

So we'll keep telling our stories. We'll keep carrying our love into the world. Because we've always been here, and we've always been queer, and we've always been divine. Hallelujah. *Euai!* Hail Holy Queer.

Appendix 1

A Queered Rosary

Writing your own prayers can be an especially powerful and personal way to connect with the Divine. The labor it takes to craft a prayer can be an act of devotion in itself. For those who were raised in institutional religion or who still belong to an organized faith today, rewriting institutional prayers can be another way to forge a more intimate relationship with the Divine and to bring more queerness into the prayers. As I mention at the end of Chapter 4, this can be a powerful way to start healing negative associations with prayer caused by being compelled to pray words you didn't believe. Rewriting and *queering* our prayers can be a devotional act of reclamation, of asserting our sacred space and our rightful belonging in the divine cosmic order.

I was raised protestant, not Catholic, but my ancestors were Catholic on my paternal side (my grandpa was an altar boy), and my queer rosary practice has simultaneously been a way to reclaim prayers of my youth (the Lord's Prayer in particular), express my idiosyncratic brand of syncretic pagan-Christian(ish) mysticism, and connect with my ancestors. (Though some are certainly rolling in their graves.) My queered rosary prayers and practice have been influenced by Jonah Welch, whose own queer rosary practice I encountered on Instagram (@jonahwelch) at the same time as I was feeling into this practice, and by Clark Strand and Perdita Finn, whose book *The Way of the Rose* provided extra insight, history, inspiration, and companionship in my rosary journey.

For my rosary, I've remodeled the Lord's Prayer (The Our Father) in dedication to Dionysos, the genderqueer and ever-transforming Liberator who I mentioned in Chapter 3 has more than a few similarities with Jesus, and who I perceive in the figure of Jesus. The Hail

Mary and Hail Holy Queen are refashioned for the Queens of Heaven (Mary, Aphrodite-Venus, Astarte, Ishtar, and Inanna; see Chapter 2). The Glory Be and the prayers overall have been adjusted with nonbinary, non-gender-essentialist language, for the most part. I've kept the word *womb* because, as we've seen with Zeus and baby Dionysos, wombs can belong to people of any gender. Likewise, as innumerable drag queens have shown us, anyone can be a queen. As for the name Mary, it already has a longstanding place in queer slang as an affectionate, often playful address among gay men ("Look at you, Mary!").

How to Pray the Rosary

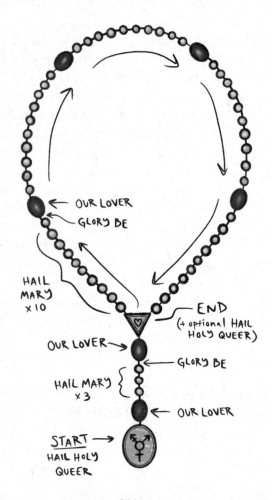

The rosary is a sequence of prayers that is usually prayed with the aid of prayer beads, also called a rosary. Owning a rosary isn't a requirement, but it does help keep track of which prayer you're supposed to say next. Standard rosaries are composed of 59 beads in two sizes, with the smaller beads representing Hail Marys and the larger ones representing Our Fathers. Holding the beads in your hands and starting where the crucifix hangs (you can find rosaries with other symbols, too), you will make a full circuit of the beads, moving your fingers along each one as you recite the corresponding prayers. The main part of the rosary is divided into five "decades" of 10 smaller Hail Mary beads, with one larger Our Father bead between each decade. At the end of each decade of Hail Marys, you will say the Glory Be. Then you'll move on to the big Our Father bead that starts the next decade, repeating the process till you reach the end. The Catholic rosary officially begins with the Apostle's Creed, a list of assertions of belief that was created, in part, to codify Catholic belief and alienate Gnostic belief, but I omit that and replace it with a queered Hail Holy Queen instead. A queer rewrite of the Apostle's Creed could be an excellent devotional activity for anyone interested in articulating their personal spiritual beliefs in prayer form.

Praying a full rosary can take a little while, but that makes it an excellent contemplative and meditative practice. As you get used to the prayers, you'll get into a rhythm that does wonders for clearing the head and centering the heart. It can even help shift consciousness and access trance states. I love that the beads include a tactile, somatic element that involves the body, not only the mind. This has been especially useful for me as someone for whom dissociation has long been a default state, as it is for many trans people and trauma survivors. Touching and moving the beads provides a physical anchor that gently tugs me back into my body while I pray.

Contemplation is actually a big part of the point of the rosary. In the Catholic tradition, practitioners will contemplate what are called "the Mysteries," important events in the life of Christ, with one "mystery" for each 10-bead decade of the rosary. Many people have adapted the rosary for various spiritual (and magical) purposes, substituting their own mysteries for contemplation instead. Remember the "Queer Mysteries" you came up with at the end of Chapter 1? This would be a great way to integrate those into your queer devotional practice. The five virtues of the pentangle that you created in Chapter 6 would also be superb here. I recommend getting familiar with the prayers and the pattern of the rosary before adding the contemplation layer, but once you feel comfortable, try contemplating one of your queer mysteries or pentangle virtues as you flow through the rhythmic Hail Marys.

The point isn't to solve the mystery, or even to think that hard about it, but to let your mind rest on the mystery and your heart feel the mystery. No judgments. No expectations. Just see what happens. Sometimes I don't contemplate anything at all. I just pray. And that's okay too.

The Hail Holy Queer (Hail Holy Queen)

Recite at the beginning and the end of the rosary.

Hail Holy Queer, Birther of stars!

Hail, our life, our desire, and our hope.

To Thee do we call, liberated children of Eve.

To Thee do we send up our songs,

Dancing and weeping through this veil of tears.

Turn then, most gracious advocate,

Thine eyes of mercy toward us,

And all through these our joys and trials,

Show unto us the blessed heart of Thy truth: Love.

O beautiful, O radiant, O queer Queen of Heaven! Amen.

The Our Lover (The Our Father or Lord's Prayer)

Recite at each large bead.

Our Lover, Who art with us,

Liber be Thy name,

Thy kingdom, here; Thy will be queer,

On Earth as it is in the Heavens.

Give us this day our wine and bread,

And sweeten each bitter heart toward us,

As we come together in loving liberation;

And lead us not into obedience

But deliver us through ecstasy.

For Thine is the dance, and the vine,

And the life, forever. Amen.

The Hail Mary

Recite at each small bead.

Hail Mary, full of grace, the World is with Thee.

Blessed art Thou among us, and blessed is the fruit of Thy womb.*

Holy Queer, Mother** of All, be with us now

And at the hour of our death. Amen.

The Glory Be

Recite at the end of each "decade," or series of 10, Hail Marys, before you recite the Our Lover (Our Father).

Glory be to the Lover, and to the Parent, and to the Child,

As it was in the beginning, is now, and ever shall be,

World without end. Amen.

---

*   If *womb* is uncomfortable for you, try "Blessed is the fruit of Thy creation" or "Thy heart."

**   I've kept *Mother* here because it feels important to me in relation to Mary in particular, but one could easily substitute *Parent*, *Creator*, or even *Nurturer*.

Appendix 2

A Queer Self-Initiation Ritual

Craft your own queer initiation ritual. This is especially powerful when beginning a new stage in your journey, such as coming out, starting HRT, applying to change your legal name or gender marker, starting consensual polyamory, or even the act of exploring your gender or sexuality. No matter how far you are down your queer path, you can always choose to recommit yourself to your own sacred queerness.[340] You might choose to adapt a version of the Queer Mystery initiation you wrote at the end of Chapter 1, or you might choose something entirely different. Your ritual can be as elaborate or simple as feels right to you.

The ritual below is a suggestion based on a simple but powerful ritual that I performed many years ago, near the start of my nonbinary trans journey. At the time, I thought of it as a spell—and it was—but in hindsight, it was also an initiation. It marked a transformation (the death of my former identity and birth of a new one), formalized a commitment (to myself and my queerness), and resulted in the revelation of new understanding (of my gender).

For this ritual, you'll need a pen, a marker (with a wider tip than the pen), and two pieces of paper—a scratch piece of paper for drafting, and a note card–size or smaller piece of paper for the actual ritual. It's helpful to be at your altar or in a place that feels special and safe. Some optional items: a candle, incense, and/or an offering bowl or cup. If there's a color of candle or scent of incense that reminds you of your gender or sexuality, those would be great additions.

1. Prepare yourself and your space. It can feel cleansing, both spiritually and physically, to take a bath or shower beforehand. You can also don clothing, makeup, or accessories that feel affirming to your gender—or just make you feel hot. Prepare your space in a way that feels comfortable, welcoming, or special. Light your candle and incense, if using. If you're of the magical persuasion, set your space, call the circle, or do whatever procedures you need to create sacred space.

2. Select a symbol that represents your gender or sexuality, the stage of transition you're entering, or your commitment to your queer self. (You can research this beforehand, if you wish.) You might choose a symbol with queer significance, such as the lambda, the interlocking male (Mars) symbols or interlocking female (Venus) symbols, the transgender symbol that combines the symbols for Mars and Venus, or the Mercury glyph that can represent nonbinary people or intersex people. You might choose a symbol that holds personal meaning to you or create one using sigil techniques. Use the scratch piece of paper to draft your symbol, if you need.

3. Using the scratch paper, write a pledge to yourself, a declaration of queerness or transness, or a statement to affirm your truth. Word it in present tense. It doesn't need to be long, and for this ritual it's best to keep it short—just a few lines will do. Prioritize clarity and simplicity. Your statement can say anything you want. The most important thing is for it to feel affirmative for you. It will be most powerful if you write it yourself, but here are a few examples, and you may edit and use them if they feel true:

   - *I claim my queerness with devotion and love. I am open to my queer journey and the change that comes. I am courageous and strong, beautiful and dynamic. Queer is sacred, and I am Queer.*

Or

- *I claim my nonbinary nature with devotion and love. I open myself to the changes of HRT with curiosity and wonder. I commit myself to myself, to the exploration of my gender and the discovery of my Truth, come what may. Nonbinary is sacred, and I am nonbinary.*

4. Now you're ready for the ritual proper. First, take the smaller piece of paper or cardstock that has not been written on yet. Draw your symbol in the center of the paper with the bold marker. It's okay for it to take up a lot of room. Look upon the symbol for a few moments and imagine filling it with self-love and intention so it glows on the page in your mind's eye.

5. Next, using the pen and beginning in the upper left corner (or whatever direction is natural in your language), start writing your statement. You will be using a technique called "cross-writing," where you write *across* your previous writing—hence, *cross-writing*—creating a gridlike, latticed effect. I prefer to write small and in cursive for this purpose, but you can do whatever feels good to you. Don't worry about neat handwriting—the statement will be illegible by the end of the ritual. Repeat your statement as many times as you need to fill up the page. You will be writing *over* the symbol you drew, not around it.

6. When you reach the bottom, turn the paper 90 degrees to the left so what used to be the right edge of the paper is now the top of the paper. Resume writing the statement once more, beginning at the new top of the paper and repeating as many times as needed to fill the page to the bottom.

7. When you reach the bottom edge of the page, turn the paper *another* 90 degrees to the left, and resume writing once more from the new top of the page until you reach the bottom. At this point, you will be writing directly over the original lines you wrote, but upside down. Repeat the turn-and-write operation one more time, until you've written your statement from all four directions of the page. You should end up with a cross-hatched effect, the paper covered with your writing in a dense and powerful knot or mesh. As you write, pour all the love, emotion, and commitment into it that you can. Envision yourself happy, liberated, and loved.

8. When you're done, place your dominant hand on the cross-written paper and your nondominant hand on your heart, or on another part of your body that feels appropriate, and read your statement aloud. Cross-writing makes things rather illegible, so you'll need to read it from the scratch paper if you don't have it memorized. Read with feeling, pride, and conviction. Repeat your statement as many times as you feel you need, and if you feel so moved, scream it. When you're finished, declare, "So it is."

9. Optional: If you are working with deities, spirits, or Ancestors, this can be a good time to call on them for guidance and support in your queer journey. You can script something out or you can just talk to them (aka pray). It's also polite to give them an offering—something as simple as water will do, or you can fancy it up if you like. See the altar-building activity at the end of Chapter 2 for some examples.

10. At this point, you can choose to burn the paper (in a firesafe bowl) and envision your commitment being lifted to the Divine on the smoke. Alternately, you can set the paper on your altar, set it under a glass candle and re-affirm your statement every time you light the candle until it's burned down, or carry the paper with you like a talisman or reminder.

11. If you set the space formally, release it. The ritual is complete.

Acknowledgments

Writing this book was, like all books, a labor of love. And it was also an act of devotion. Devotion to the queer deities, saints, and figures of myth and legend; to queerness itself, and most of all to queer people. Thank you to all the beautiful queer and trans folks who have inspired me and kept me going from up close and afar.

This work is indebted to the theological, mythological, theoretical, and/or creative work of José Esteban Muñoz, Audre Lorde, adrienne maree brown, Alok Vaid-Menon, Marcella Althaus-Reid, Starhawk, Arthur Evans, Judy Grahn, Jordy Rosenberg, and Sophie Strand. Thank you also to the wonderful people I've learned from in workshops, especially Eli Lawliet and Zel Amanzi.

None of my work would exist without my partner, best friend, and love of my life, Aaron. Thank you so much for your unconditional support and love, for the endless plates of cheese and crackers, and for your fearless bravery in being my first reader for every chapter. Your presence in my life singlehandedly made me believe in the Divine.

Thank you to so many friends who I've been in conversation with on this work in ways small and large, including Stephanie Adams-Santos, Joseph O'Hern, Erik Arneson, Kelsey, Iris, Rebecca, and Clare Edge (and you, too, Patrick). Thank you also to my token straight friends Sarah, Hannah, and Warren (and Harriet) for keeping me sane with dogs (including honorary dog Raz), drinks, and discussions of romantasy novels and/or niche European history.

The deepest of thanks to my parents, Dean and Donna, for all your love and guidance through this life, for believing in me no matter what weird things I do next, and for pretending you didn't know I was reading fantasy novels in the audiovisual booth during church.

Thank you to my wonderful agent, Kelly Van Sant, who is truly a divine gift to me from on high. Thank you to my equally wonderful editor, Anna Cooperberg. I'm so fortunate to get to work with you. Big thanks also to all the people who have touched my books at Hay

House, especially Pip, who worked a miracle by getting me on TikTok. (Sorry it only lasted a couple months.)

Humongous thanks to events coordinator Ava and Seagrape Apothecary in Portland, Oregon, for planting the seed of this book by inviting me to teach a class on queer devotion in 2023. When I sent Ava my epic PDF handout for class, they said, "This is a novel! You should write a book about this!" And you know what? I did.

Finally, thank you to my Lady, Queen of Heaven, Mother of Stars, for surprising the hell out of me in that thrift store, coming home with me, and changing my life. Hail Holy Queer.

Bibliography

Aburrow, Yvonne. *All Acts of Love and Pleasure: Inclusive Wicca*. London: Avalonia, 2014.

Adler, Margot. *Drawing Down the Moon: Witches, Druids, Goddess-Worshippers, and Other Pagans in America*. Revised and updated edition. New York: Penguin Books, 1986.

Althaus-Reid, Marcella. *Indecent Theology: Theological Perversions in Sex, Gender and Politics*. London: Routledge, 2000.

Althaus-Reid, Marcella. *The Queer God*. London: Routledge, 2003.

Athanassakis, Apostolos N. and Benjamin M. Wolkow, trans. *The Orphic Hymns*. Baltimore: Johns Hopkins University Press, 2013.

Athanassakis, Apostolos N., trans. *The Homeric Hymns*. 3rd edition. Baltimore: Johns Hopkins University Press, 2020.

Baring, Anne and Jules Cashford. *The Myth of the Goddess: Evolution of an Image*. London: Penguin Books, 1991.

Barret, W. P., ed., trans. *The Trial of Jeanne D'Arc: Translated into English from the Original Latin and French Documents*. Translated from French by Coley Taylor and Ruth H. Kerr. Gotham House, Inc., 1932; Internet History Sourcebooks Project, September 1999. Accessed April 30, 2024. https://sourcebooks.fordham.edu/basis/joanofarc-trial.asp.

Barstow, Anne Llewellyn. "Joan of Arc and Female Mysticism." *Journal of Feminist Studies in Religion* 1, no. 2 (1985): 29–42. http://www.jstor.org/stable/25002016.

Bellows, Henry Adams, trans. The *Poetic Edda*. New York: The American Scandinavian Society, 1923; Project Gutenberg, May 4, 2024. https://www.gutenberg.org/ebooks/73533.

Besserman, Lawrence. "The Idea of the Green Knight." *ELH* 53, no. 2 (1986): 219–39. https://doi.org/10.2307/2873255.

Boyd, David L. "Sodomy, Misogyny, and Displacement: Occluding Queer Desire in 'Sir Gawain and the Green Knight.'" *Arthuriana* 8, no. 2 (1998): 77–113. http://www.jstor.org/stable/27869340.

Brennan, Joseph. "'You Could Shame the Great Arthur Himself': A Queer Reading of Lancelot from BBC's 'Merlin' with Respect to the Character in Malory, White, and Bradley." *Arthuriana* 25, no. 2 (2015): 20–43. http://www.jstor.org/stable/24643469.

Burrus, Virginia. *The Sex Lives of Saints: An Erotics of Ancient Hagiography.* Philadelphia: University of Pennsylvania Press, 2004.

Butler, Judith. *Gender Trouble: Feminism and the Subversion of Identity.* New York: Routledge, 1990.

Bychowski, M. W. "The Authentic Lives of Transgender Saints: *Imago Dei* and Imitatio Christi in the Life of St Marinos the Monk." In *Trans and Genderqueer Subjects in Medieval Hagiography*, edited by Alicia Spencer-Hall and Blake Gutt, 245–66. Amsterdam: Amsterdam University Press, 2021.

Bynum, Caroline Walker. "Jesus as Mother and Abbot as Mother: Some Themes in Twelfth-Century Cistercian Writing." *The Harvard Theological Review* 70, no. 3/4 (1977): 257–84. http://www.jstor.org/stable/1509631.

Chandler, Jed. "Eunuchs of the Grail." In C*astration and Culture in the Middle Ages*, edited by Larissa Tracy, 229–54. Boydell & Brewer, 2013. http://www.jstor.org/stable/10.7722/j.ctt2tt1pr.18.

Cheng, Patrick S. *Radical Love: An Introduction to Queer Theology.* New York: Seabury Books, 2011.

Clover, Carol J. "Maiden Warriors and Other Sons." *The Journal of English and Germanic Philology* 85, no. 1 (1986): 35–49. http://www.jstor.org/stable/27709600.

Clover, Carol J. "Regardless of Sex: Men, Women, and Power in Early Northern Europe." *Speculum* 68, no. 2 (1993): 363–87. https://doi.org/10.2307/2864557.

Colwill, Lee. "The Queerly Departed: Narratives of Veneration in the Burials of Late Iron Age Scandinavia." In *Trans and Genderqueer Subjects in Medieval Hagiography*, edited by Alicia Spencer-Hall and Blake Gutt, 177–98. Amsterdam University Press, 2021.

Crompton, Louis. *Homosexuality and Civilization.* Cambridge: The Belknap Press of Harvard University Press, 2003.

Cummings, E. E. *Selected Poems.* United Kingdom: Liveright, 1994.

Dalley, Stephanie, trans. *Myths from Mesopotamia: Creation, the Flood, Gilgamesh, and Others.* Revised edition. Oxford, UK: Oxford University Press, 1989.

Davidson, H. R. Ellis. *Gods and Myths of Northern Europe.* London: Penguin Books, 1990.

DeVun, Leah. *The Shape of Sex: Nonbinary Gender from Genesis to the Renaissance.* New York: Columbia University Press, 2021.

Dinshaw, Carolyn. "A Kiss Is Just a Kiss: Heterosexuality and Its Consolations in Sir Gawain and the Green Knight." *Diacritics* 24, no. 2/3 (1994): 205–26. https://doi.org/10.2307/465173.

Dinshaw, Carolyn. "Chaucer's Queer Touches / A Queer Touches Chaucer." *Exemplaria* 7 (1995): 75-92.

Dinshaw, Carolyn. *Getting Medieval: Sexualities and Communities, Pre- and Postmodern.* Durham, NC: Duke University Press, 1999.

Donnelly, James S. "The Whiteboy Movement, 1761-5." *Irish Historical Studies* 21, no. 81 (1978): 20–54. http://www.jstor.org/stable/30005376.

DuBois, Thomas Andrew. *Nordic Religions in the Viking Age*. Philadelphia: University of Pennsylvania Press, 1999.

Eschenbach, Wolfram von. *Parzival: A Knightly Epic*. 2 vols. Translated by Jessie L. Weston. New York: G. E. Stechert & Co., 1912.

Euripides. *The Bacchae of Euripides*. 2nd edition. Translated by Gilbert Murray. London: George Allen, 1906.

Euripides. *The Bacchae*. Translated by Paul Woodruff. Indianapolis: Hackett Publishing Company, 1998.

Evans, Arthur. *Witchcraft and the Gay Counterculture: A Radical View of Western Civilization and Some of the People it Has Tried to Destroy*. Boston: Fag Rag Books, 1978; clandestiny: feral death coven, 2013.

Evelyn-White, Hugh G., trans. *Hesiod, Homer, and the Homerica*. United Kingdom: W. Heinemann, 1914.

Fausto-Sterling, Anne. *Sexing the Body: Gender Politics and the Construction of Sexuality*. Updated edition. New York: Basic Books, 2000, 2020.

Federici, Silvia. *Caliban and the Witch: Women, the Body, and Primitive Accumulation*. 2nd ed. Brooklyn: Autonomedia, 2014.

Feinberg, Leslie. *Transgender Warriors: Making History from Joan of Arc to Dennis Rodman*. Boston: Beacon Press, 1996.

Francis. "Declaration of the Dicastery for the Doctrine of the Faith '*Dignitas Infinita*' on Human Dignity." Vatican.va. April 8, 2024. https://press.vatican.va/content/salastampa/en/bollettino/pubblico/2024/04/08/240408c.html.

Frankki, James. "Cross-Dressing in the Poetic Edda: Mic Muno Æsir Argan Kalla." *Scandinavian Studies* 84, no. 4 (2012): 425–37. http://www.jstor.org/stable/41955688.

Goldhurst, William. "The Green and the Gold: The Major Theme of Gawain and the Green Knight." *College English* 20, no. 2 (1958): 61–65. https://doi.org/10.2307/372161.

Gornichec, Genevieve. *The Witch's Heart*. New York: Ace, 2021.

Grahn, Judy. *Another Mother Tongue: Gay Words, Gay Worlds*. Updated and expanded ed. Boston: Beacon Press, 1990.

Harper, George McLean. "The Legend of the Holy Grail." *PMLA* 8, no. 1 (1893): 77–140. https://doi.org/10.2307/456334.

Harrington, Lee and Tai Fenix Kulystin. *Queer Magic: Power Beyond Boundaries*. Anchorage, AK: Mystic Productions, 2018.

Hesiod. *Theogony, Works and Days, Shield*. 3rd edition. Translated by Apostolos N. Athanassakis. Baltimore, MD: Johns Hopkins University Press, 2022.

Heyem, Kit. *Before We Were Trans: A New History of Gender.* New York: Seal Press, 2022.

Hine, Phil. *Queerying Occultures.* Tempe, AZ: The Original Falcon Press, 2022.

Hinton, Thomas. "New Beginnings and False Dawns: A Reappraisal of the 'Elucidation' Prologue to the 'Conte del Graal' Cycle." *Medium Ævum* 80, no. 1 (2011): 41–55. https://doi.org/10.2307/43632464.

Hirschfeld, Magnus. "Selections from *The Transvestites: The Erotic Drive to Cross-Dress.*" In *The Transgender Studies Reader,* edited by Susan Stryker and Stephen Whittle, 28–39. New York: Routledge, 2006.

Hughes, Bettany. *Venus and Aphrodite: A Biography of Desire.* New York: Basic Books, 2020.

Johnston, Sarah Iles, ed. *Ancient Religions.* Cambridge: The Belknap Press of Harvard University Press, 2007.

Jones, Dan. *Queer Heroes of Myth and Legend: A Celebration of Gay Gods, Sapphic Saints & Queerness Through the Ages.* London: Radar, 2023.

Jones, Gwyn and Thomas Jones, trans. *The Mabinogion.* London: J. M. Dent & Sons, Ltd., 1949.

Kibler, William W., trans. *Elucidation.* The Camelot Project. Rochester, NY: University of Rochester, 2007. https://d.lib.rochester.edu/camelot/text/elucidation. Accessed 23 May 2024.

King, Karen L. *The Gospel of Mary of Magdala: Jesus and the First Woman Apostle.* Santa Rosa, CA: Polebridge Press, 2003.

Kivilo, Maarit. "Sappho." In *Early Greek Poets' Lives: The Shaping of the Tradition,* 322:167–200. Brill, 2010. http://www.jstor.org/stable/10.1163/j.ctv4cbgkd.11.

Lacy, Norris J. "The Elucidation: Introduction." The Camelot Project. Rochester, NY: University of Rochester, 2007. https://d.lib.rochester.edu/camelot/text/elucidation-introduction. Accessed 23 May 2024.

Laqueur, Thomas. *Making Sex: Body and Gender from the Greeks to Freud.* Cambridge: Harvard University Press, 1990.

Larrington, Carolyne, trans. *The Poetic Edda.* Revised edition. Oxford, UK: Oxford University Press, 2014.

Larson, Jennifer. *Ancient Greek Cults: A Guide.* New York,: Routledge, 2007.

Leighton, J. M. "Christian and Pagan Symbolism and Ritual in 'Sir Gawain and the Green Knight.'" *Theoria: A Journal of Social and Political Theory,* no. 43 (1974): 49–62. http://www.jstor.org/stable/41801571.

Leland, Charles G. *Aradia: Gospel of the Witches.* Custer, WA: Phoenix Publishing, Inc, 1990. First published 1890.

Leloup, Jean-Yves. *The Gospel of Philip: Jesus, Mary Magdalene, and the Gnosis of Sacred Union.* Translated by Joseph Rowe. Rochester, VT: Inner Traditions, 2003.

Loomis, Roger Sherman. *Celtic Myth and Arthurian Romance*. London: Constable, 1993.

Lorde, Audre. "Uses of the Erotic." *The Selected Works of Audres Lorde*. Edited by Roxane Gay, 29–37. New York: W. W. Norton & Company, 2000.

Lowery, David, dir. *The Green Knight*. A24, 2021.

Maddox, Kelly-Ann. *Rebel Witch: Carve the Craft that's Yours Alone*. London: Watkins, 2021.

Magdalene, Misha. *Outside the Charmed Circle: Exploring Gender and Sexuality in Magical Practice*. Woodbury, MN: Llewellyn Publications, 2020.

Mathis, Kristin. "My Translation of Sappho's Hymn to Aphrodite." Mysteria Mundi. January 27, 2023. https://mysteriamundi.substack.com/p/my-translation-of-sapphos-hymn-to.

McKinnell, John. "Myth as Therapy: The Usefulness of 'þRYMSKVIÐA.'" *Medium Ævum* 69, no. 1 (2000): 1–20. https://doi.org/10.2307/43631487.

Meyer, Marvin, ed. *The Nag Hammadi Scriptures: The Revised and Updated Translation of Sacred Gnostic Texts*. New York: HarperOne, 2007.

Muñoz, José Esteban. *Cruising Utopia: The Then and There of Queer Futurity*. 10th anniversary edition. New York: New York University Press, 2009.

Murray, Douglas T., ed. *Jeanne D'Arc: Maid of Orleans, Deliverer of France: Being the Story of Her Life, Her Achievements, and Her Death, as Attested on Oath and Set Forth in the Original Documents*. London: William Heinemann, 1902; Project Gutenberg, June 25, 2018. https://www.gutenberg.org/ebooks/57389.

Nietzsche, Friedrich. *Beyond Good and Evil*. Translated by Helen Zimmern. In *The Complete Works of Friedrich Nietzsche*, vol. 5, edited by Oscar Levy. Edinburgh: T. N. Foulis, 1909.

Oleszkiewicz-Perabla, Małgorzata. *The Black Madonna in Latin America and Europe*. Albuquerque, NM: University of New Mexico Press, 2007.

Oliver, Jen H. "'OSCULA IUNGIT NEC MODERATA SATIS NEC SIC A VIRGINE DANDA': Ovid's Callisto Episode, Female Homoeroticism, and the Study of Ancient Sexuality." *The American Journal of Philology* 136, no. 2 (2015): 281–312. http://www.jstor.org/stable/24562759.

Ovid. *Metamorphoses*. Translated by Stephanie McCarter. New York: Penguin Books, 2022.

Ovid. *The Metamorphoses of Ovid*. Volume 1. Translated by Henry T. Riley. London: George Bell & Sons, 1893; Project Gutenberg, June 8, 2007. https://www.gutenberg.org/ebooks/21765.

Ovid. *The Metamorphoses of Ovid*. Volume 2. Translated by Henry T. Riley. London: George Bell & Sons, 1893; Project Gutenberg, July 16, 2008. https://www.gutenberg.org/ebooks/26073.

Pagels, Elaine. *The Gnostic Gospels*. New York: Vintage Books, 1979.

Petropoulos, J. C. B. "Sappho the Sorceress: Another Look at Fr. 1 (LP)." *Zeitschrift Für Papyrologie Und Epigraphik* 97 (1993): 43–56. http://www.jstor.org/stable/20171905.

Rayor, Diane J. and André Lardinois. *Sappho: A New Translation of the Complete Works.* Cambridge, UK: Cambridge University Press, 2023.

Roberts, Anna. "Queer Fisher King: Castration as a Site of Queer Representation ('Perceval, Stabat Mater, The City of God')." *Arthuriana* 11, no. 3 (2001): 49–88. http://www.jstor.org/stable/27869652.

Roscoe, Will. "Priests of the Goddess: Gender Transgression in Ancient Religion." *History of Religions* 35, no. 3 (1996): 195–230. http://www.jstor.org/stable/1062813.

Sappho. *The Poems of Sappho.* Translated by Edwin Marion Cox. London: Williams and Norgate, 1924.

Schnurbein, Stefanie von. "The Function of Loki in Snorri Sturluson's 'Edda.'" *History of Religions* 40, no. 2 (2000): 109–24. http://www.jstor.org/stable/3176617.

Segal, Charles. "Eros and Incantation: Sappho and Oral Poetry." *Arethusa* 7, no. 2 (1974): 139–60. http://www.jstor.org/stable/26307420.

Self, Kathleen M. "The Valkyrie's Gender: Old Norse Shield-Maidens and Valkyries as a Third Gender." *Feminist Formations* 26, no. 1 (2014): 143–72. http://www.jstor.org/stable/43860730.

Serpentine, Ariana. *Sacred Gender: Create Trans & Nonbinary Spiritual Connections.* Woodbury, MN: Llewellyn Publications, 2022.

Sexon, Sophie. "Gender-Querying Christ's Wounds: A Non-Binary Interpretation of Christ's Body in Late Medieval Imagery." In *Trans and Genderqueer Subjects in Medieval Hagiography*, edited by Alicia Spencer-Hall and Blake Gutt, 133-154. Amsterdam: Amsterdam University Press, 2021.

Raffel, Burton, trans. *Sir Gawain and the Green Knight.* New York: Signet Classics, 1970.

Starhawk. *The Spiral Dance: A Rebirth of the Ancient Religion of the Great Goddess.* 20th anniversary edition. New York: HarperOne, 1999.

Strand, Clark. *Waking Up to the Dark: The Black Madonna's Gospel for an Age of Extinction and Collapse.* Rhinebeck, NY: Monkfish Book Publishing Company, 2022.

Strand, Sophie. *The Flowering Wand: Rewilding the Sacred Masculine.* Rochester, VT: Inner Traditions, 2022.

Strand, Sophie. "No Savior: Cracks in Joan of Arc's Armor." Make Me Good Soil. October 8, 2024. https://sophiestrand.substack.com/p/no-savior-933.

Stryker, Susan. *Transgender History: The Roots of Today's Revolution.* Revised edition. New York: Seal Press, 2017.

Sturluson, Snorri. "Ynglinga Saga." In *The Heimskringla; or, Chronicle of the Kings of Norway,* volume 1, translated by Samuel Laing, 216-261. London: Longman, Brown, Green and Longmans, 1844.

Sturluson, Snorri. *The Prose Edda.* Translated by Jesse L. Byock. London: Penguin Books, 2005.

Taussig, Hal, ed. *A New New Testament: A Bible for the 21st Century Combining Traditional and Newly Discovered Texts.* New York: HarperOne, 2013.

Taylor, Sonya Renee. *The Body is Not an Apology: The Power of Radical Self-Love.* 2nd edition. Oakland, CA: Berrett-Koehler Publishers, 2021.

Troyes, Chrétien de. "The Story of the Grail (Percival)." In *Arthurian Romances,* translated by William W. Kibler, 391–494. London: Penguin Books, 1991.

Trzaskoma, Stephen M., R. Scott Smith and Stephen Brunet, eds. *Anthology of Classical Myth: Primary Sources in Translation.* 2nd edition. Indianapolis: Hackett Publishing Company, Inc., 2016.

Xiang, Zairong. *Queer Ancient Ways: A Decolonial Exploration.* Earth, Milky Way: Punctum Books, 2018.

Wanner, Kevin J. "Cunning Intelligence in Norse Myth: Loki, Óðinn, and the Limits of Sovereignty." *History of Religions* 48, no. 3 (2009): 211–46. https://doi.org/10.1086/598231.

Wanner, Kevin J. "God on the Margins: Dislocation and Transience in the Myths of Óðinn." *History of Religions* 46, no. 4 (2007): 316–50. https://doi.org/10.1086/518812.

Wharton, Henry Thornton. *Sappho: Memoir, Text, Selected Renderings, and a Literal Translation.* 5th edition. London: J. Lane, 1908.

Wilcox, Melissa M. *Queer Religiosities: An Introduction to Queer and Transgender Studies in Religion.* Lanham, MD: Rowman & Littlefield, 2021.

Wolkstein, Diane and Samuel Noah Kramer. *Inanna: Queen of Heaven and Earth.* New York: Harper & Row, Publishers, Inc., 1983.

Zeikowitz, Richard E. "Befriending the Medieval Queer: A Pedagogy for Literature Classes." *College English* 65, no. 1 (2002): 67–80. https://doi.org/10.2307/3250731.

Endnotes

1. Ariana Serpentine, *Sacred Gender: Create Trans & Nonbinary Spiritual Connections* (Woodbury, MN: Llewellyn Publications, 2022), 3.

2. José Esteban Muñoz, *Cruising Utopia: The Then and There of Queer Futurity,* 10th anniversary ed. (New York: New York University Press, 2009), 65.

3. Ibid.

4. Ibid.

5. Anne Baring and Jules Cashford, *The Myth of the Goddess: Evolution of an Image* (London: Arkana, 1993), 381.

6. Paul Woodruff, Introduction to *The Bacchae* by Euripides (Indianapolis, IN: Hackett Publishing Company, 1998), xlii.

7. Baring and Cashford, 382.

8. Starhawk, *The Spiral Dance: A Rebirth of the Ancient Religion of the Great Goddess,* 20th anniversary ed. (New York: HarperOne, 1999), 188.

9. Judy Grahn, *Another Mother Tongue: Gay Words, Gay Worlds*, updated and expanded ed. (Boston: Beacon Press, 1984, 1990), 3.

10. Ibid., 29.

11. Baring and Cashford, 413.

12. Apostolos N. Athanassakis and Benjamin M. Wolkow, trans. *The Orphic Hymns* (Baltimore: Johns Hopkins University Press, 2013), 140.

13. Jennifer Larson, *Ancient Greek Cults: A Guide* (New York: Routledge, 2007), 126.

14. Athanassakis and Wolkow, 125.

15. Ibid.

16. Phil Hine, *Queerying Occultures* (Tempe, AZ: The Original Falcon Press, 2022), 79.

17. Ibid., 16.

18. Ibid., 16–7.

19. Serpentine, 155–6.

20. Yvonne Aburrow, *All Acts of Love and Pleasure: Inclusive Wicca* (London: Avalonia, 2014), 136.

21. Ibid, 137.

22. Hesiod, *Hesiod, The Homeric Hymns, and Homerica*, trans. Hugh G. Evelyn-White (United Kingdom: W. Heinemann, 1914), 91.

23. Ibid, 93.

24. Ibid.

25. *The Cypria*, fragment 6, transmitted in Athenaeus, 15.682 D–F, in *Hesiod, Homer, and the Homerica*, trans. Evelyn-White, 499.

26. Bettany Hughes, *Venus and Aphrodite: A Biography of Desire* (New York: Basic Books, 2020), 6.

27. Baring and Cashford, 352.

28. Hesiod, trans. Evelyn-White, 91.

29. Friedrich Nietzsche, *Beyond Good and Evil*, trans. Helen Zimmern, in *The Complete Works of Friedrich Nietzsche*, vol. 5, ed. Oscar Levy (Edinburgh: T. N. Foulis, 1909), 98.

30. Henry Thornton Wharton, *Sappho: Memoir, Text, Selected Renderings, and a Literal Translation*, 5th ed. (London: J. Lane, 1908), 96.

31. John 3:16, The Bible, King James Version.

32. Baring and Cashford, 353.

33. Diane Wolkstein and Samuel Noah Kramer, *Inanna: Queen of Heaven and Earth* (New York: Harper & Row Publishers, 1983), 99.

34. Ibid., 171.

35. Hesiod, trans. Evelyn-White, 411.

36. Serpentine, 76.

37. Baring and Cashford, 408.

38. Will Roscoe, "Priests of the Goddess: Gender Transgression in Ancient Religion," *History of Religions* 35, no. 3 (1996): 195–230, 213–215. http://www.jstor.org/stable/1062813.

39. Ibid., 203.

40. Ibid.

41. Larson, 115.

42. Ibid., 117.

43. Hughes, 53–5.

44. Ibid., 6–9, 55.

45. Athanassakis and Wolkow, trans., *The Orphic Hymns*, 45.

46. Hesiod, *Theogony, Works and Days, Shield*, 3rd ed., trans. Apostolos N. Athanassakis (Baltimore, MD: Johns Hopkins University Press, 2022), 41n.

47. Athanassakis and Wolkow, *Orphic Hymns*, 157.

48. Euripides, *The Bacchae*, trans. Paul Woodruff (Indianapolis: Hackett Publishing Company, 1998), 22.

49. Apollodorus, *"Library,"* in *Anthology of Classical Myth: Primary Sources in Translation*, 2nd ed., trans. Stephen M. Trzaskoma, R. Scott Smith and Stephen Brunet (Indianapolis: Hackett Publishing Company, Inc., 2016), 47.

50. Ibid., 48.

51. Statius, "Achilleid," in *Anthology of Classical Myth*, 355.

52. Larson, 129.

53. Athanassakis and Wolkow, *Orphic Hymns*, 126.

54. Ibid., 162.

55. Ovid, *The Metamorphoses of Ovid*, vol. 2, trans. Henry T. Riley (London: George Bell & Sons, 1893), 464.

56. Ibid.

57. Apostolos N. Athanassakis, trans., *The Homeric Hymns*, 3rd ed. (Baltimore: Johns Hopkins University Press, 2020), 97–98.

58. Woodruff, xv.

59. Euripides, trans. Woodruff, 19.

60. Larson, 132.

61. Ibid.

62. Euripides, *The Bacchae of Euripides*, 2nd ed., trans. Gilbert Murray (London: George Allen, 1906), 8.

63. Ibid., 27.

64. Euripides, trans. Woodruff, 18.

65. Ibid., 20.

66. Muñoz, 22.

67. Euripides, trans. Murray, 32.

68. Ibid., 56.

69. Ibid., 55.

70. Euripides, trans. Woodruff, 40.

71. Ibid., 35.

72. Larson, 141.

73. Athanassakis and Wolkow, *Orphic Hymns*, 126.

74. Larson, 141.

75. Ibid., 142.

76. Ibid.

77. Plutarch, *Crassus*, 9.3, quoted in Sophie Strand, *The Flowering Wand: Rewilding the Sacred Masculine* (Rochester, VT: Inner Traditions, 2022), 169.

78. Sophie Strand, *The Flowering Wand: Rewilding the Sacred Masculine* (Rochester, VT: Inner Traditions, 2022), 65.

79. John Scheid, "Religions in Contact," in *Ancient Religions*, 115.

80. Sarah Iles Johnston, ed., *Ancient Religions* (Cambridge: The Belknap Press of Harvard University Press, 2007), 101.

81. Ibid, 101–2.

82. Strand, 64.

83. Ovid, *The Metamorphoses of Ovid,* vol. 1, trans. Henry T. Riley (London: George Bell & Sons, 1893), 108–9.

84. Francis, "Declaration of the Dicastery for the Doctrine of the Faith '*Dignitas Infinita*' on Human Dignity," Vatican.va, April 8, 2024, paragraph 1, https://press.vatican.va/content/salastampa/en/bollettino/ pubblico/2024/04/08/240408c.html.

85. Francis, paragraph 15.

86. Zairong Xiang, *Queer Ancient Ways: A Decolonial Exploration* (Earth, Milky Way: Punctum Books, 2018), 83.

87. Ibid, 84.

88. Elaine Pagels, *The Gnostic Gospels* (New York: Vintage Books, 1979), 56.

89. Ibid, 50.

90. Leah DeVun, *The Shape of Sex: Nonbinary Gender from Genesis to the Renaissance* (New York: Columbia University Press, 2021), *passim.*

91. Ibid, 178–84.

92. Ibid, 19; Pagels, 56.

93. DeVun, 21.

94. Ibid.

95. Hal Taussig, ed., *A New New Testament: A Bible for the 21st Century Combining Traditional and Newly Discovered Texts* (New York: HarperOne, 2013), xxv.

96. Taussig, 503.

97. Ibid., 485.

98. Pagels, xxiii.

99. Ibid., 41.

100. Marvin Meyer, ed., *The Nag Hammadi Scriptures: The Revised and Updated Translation of Sacred Gnostic Texts* (New York: HarperOne, 2007), 6–7; Taussig, 505.

101. Pagels, xix.

102. Ibid., xxii.

103. Ibid., 51.

104. Ibid., 49.

105. Ibid.

106. Ibid., 50.

107. Ibid.

108. Meyer, 108.

109. Ibid., 110.

110. DeVun, 167.

111. Ibid., 170.

112. Ibid.

113. Ibid., 175.

114. Ibid.

115. Ibid., 185.

116. *The Book of the Holy Trinity,* quoted in DeVun, 185.

117. Ibid.

118. Ibid., 186.

119. Caroline Walker Bynum, "Jesus as Mother and Abbot as Mother: Some Themes in Twelfth-Century Cistercian Writing," *The Harvard Theological Review* 70, no. 3/4 (1977): 257–84, http://www.jstor.org/stable/1509631.

120. Bernard of Clairvaux, quoted in Bynum, 262.

121. Sophie Sexon, "Gender-Querying Christ's Wounds: A Non-Binary Interpretation of Christ's Body in Late Medieval Imagery," In *Trans and Genderqueer Subjects in Medieval Hagiography,* edited by Alicia Spencer-Hall and Blake Gutt, 133–154 (Amsterdam: Amsterdam University Press, 2021), 133–154.

122. Sexon, 140.

123. Ibid., 141.

124. Bynum, 267.

125. Aelred of Rievaulx, quoted in Bynum, 267.

126. Ibid., 273.

127. DeVun, 188–9.

128. Ibid., 25–6.

129. Ibid., 29.

130. Ibid., 5.

131. Ibid., 207.

132. Francis, paragraph 60.

133. M. W. Bychowski, "The Authentic Lives of Transgender Saints: Imago Dei and Imitatio Christi in the Life of St Marinos the Monk," In *Trans and Genderqueer Subjects in Medieval Hagiography,* eds. Alicia Spencer-Hall and Blake Gutt, 245–66 (Amsterdam: Amsterdam University Press, 2021), 252.

134. Bychowski, 255.

135. Ibid, 252.

136. Isazela Amanzi and Eli Lawliet, "Accessing Transcestral Wisdom," live online class, Oct. 24, 2023.

137. Sophie Strand, "No Savior: Cracks in Joan of Arc's Armor," Make Me Good Soil, October 8, 2024, https://sophiestrand.substack.com/p/no-savior-933.

138. Arthur Evans, *Witchcraft and the Gay Counterculture: A Radical View of Western Civilization and Some of the People it Has Tried to Destroy* (Boston: Fag Rag Books, 1978; clandestiny: feral death coven, 2013), 19; Leslie Feinberg, *Trangender Warriors: Making History from Joan of Arc to Dennis Rodman* (Boston, MA: Beacon Press, 1996), 34-5.

139. Strand, "No Savior."

140. Douglas T. Murray, ed., *Jeanne D'Arc: Maid of Orleans, Deliverer of France: Being the Story of Her Life, Her Achievements, and Her Death, as Attested on Oath and Set Forth in the Original Documents* (London: William Heinemann, 1902; Project Gutenberg, June 25, 2018), x, https://www.gutenberg.org/ebooks/57389.

141. Strand, "No Savior."

142. Ibid.

143. Evans, 19.

144. Murray, 21n.

145. Ibid., 20–1.

146. Ibid., 10.

147. Ibid.

148. Anne Llewellyn Barstow, "Joan of Arc and Female Mysticism," *Journal of Feminist Studies in Religion* 1, no. 2 (1985): 29–42, 32. http://www.jstor.org/stable/25002016.

149. Murray, 294.

150. W. P. Barret, ed, trans., *The Trial of Jeanne D'Arc: Translated into English from the Original Latin and French Documents*, trans. from French by Coley Taylor and Ruth H. Kerr (Gotham House, Inc., 1932; Internet History Sourcebooks Project, September 1999), accessed April 30, 2024, https://sourcebooks.fordham.edu/basis/joanofarc-trial.asp, 331–2.

151. Murray, 97, 243n.

152. Ibid., 136.

153. Ibid., 16.

154. Ibid., 18.

155. Ibid., 114.

156. Ibid., 348.

157. Evans, 18; Feinberg, 33.

158. *A Parisian Journal*, 40; quoted in Barstow, 36.

159. Ibid., 42.

160. Ibid., 40.

161. Ibid.

162. Evans, 19.

163. Murray, 346.

164. Ibid.

165. Feinberg, 34.

166. Strand, "No Savior."

167. Feinberg, 77.

168. Ibid.

169. Ibid., 75.

170. Ibid., 80.

171. Natalie Zemon Davis, "Women on Top: Symbolic Sexual Inversion and Political Disorder in Early Modern Europe," *The Reversible World: Symbolic Inversion in Art and Society*, ed. Barbara A. Babcock (Ithaca, NY: Cornell University Press, 1978), 178; quoted in Feinberg 79.

172. Feinberg, 78–9.

173. James S. Donnelly, "The Whiteboy Movement, 1761–5," *Irish Historical Studies* 21, no. 81 (1978): 23, 26, 27–8. http://www.jstor.org/stable/30005376.

174. Fenbeirg, 79.

175. Rictor Norton, "The History of the Word 'Gay' and Other Queerwords," Gay History and Literature, 2015, https://rictornorton.co.uk/though23.htm. First published in *Gay Times*, no. 321 (June 2005): 30, 32.

176. Ibid.

177. Louis Crompton, *Homosexuality and Civilization* (Cambridge: The Belknap Press of Harvard University Press, 2003), 190.

178. Harper Douglas, "Etymology of faggot," Online Etymology Dictionary, accessed October 6, 2024, https://www.etymonline.com/word/faggot.

179. Norton, "History of the Word 'Gay.'"

180. Silvia Federici, *Caliban and the Witch: Women, the Body, and Primitive Accumulation,* 2nd ed. (Brooklyn: Autonomedia, 2014), 197.

181. Evans, 25.

182. Ibid.

183. Ibid.

184. Strand, "No Savior."

185. Murray, 86.

186. Kelly-Ann Maddox, *Rebel Witch: Carve the Craft that's Yours Alone* (London: Watkins, 2021), 238.

187. *Sir Gawain and the Green Knight*, trans. Jessie L Weston (London: Davit Nutt, 1898; Project Gutenberg, August 18, 2021), 5, https://www.gutenberg.org/ebooks/66084.

188. *Sir Gawain*, 6.

189. Ibid., 5.

190. Ibid., 7.

191. Ibid., 8.

192. Ibid.

193. Ibid., 51.

194. Ibid., 59.

195. Ibid., 69–70.

196. Ibid., 88.

197. David L. Boyd, "Sodomy, Misogyny, and Displacement: Occluding Queer Desire in 'Sir Gawain and the Green Knight,'" *Arthuriana* 8, no. 2 (1998): 77–113, http://www.jstor.org/stable/27869340; Carolyn Dinshaw; "A Kiss Is Just a Kiss: Heterosexuality and Its Consolations in Sir Gawain and the Green Knight," *Diacritics* 24, no. 2/3 (1994): 205–26, https://doi .org/10.2307/465173.

198. Lawrence Besserman, "The Idea of the Green Knight," *ELH* 53, no. 2 (1986): 219–39, https://doi.org/10.2307/2873255.

199. *Sir Gawain*, 85.

200. Ibid.

201. David Lowery, director, *The Green Knight* (A24, 2021), 1:25:46–1:28:00.

202. Chrétien de Troyes, "The Story of the Grail (Percival)," in *Arthurian Romances*, trans. William W. Kibler, 391–494 (London: Penguin Books, 1991), 384.

203. Anna Roberts, "Queer Fisher King: Castration as a Site of Queer Representation ('Perceval, Stabat Mater, The City of God')," *Arthuriana* 11, no. 3 (2001): 49–88, http://www.jstor.org/stable/27869652, 50.

204. Wolfram von Eschenbach, *Parzival: A Knightly Epic*, 2 vols., trans. Jessie L. Weston (New York: G. E. Stechert & Co., 1912), 138.

205. Loomis offers a partial list. Roger Sherman Loomis, *Celtic Myth and Arthurian Romance* (London: Constable, 1993), 183–4.

206. Roberts, 62.

207. Ibid., 82.

208. Ibid., 69.

209. Ibid., 68–9.

210. Wolfram, vol. 1, 277.

211. Chrétien, 424.

212. Thomas Hinton, "New Beginnings and False Dawns: A Reappraisal of the 'Elucidation' Prologue to the 'Conte del Graal' Cycle," *Medium Ævum* 80, no. 1 (2011): 49, 50, https://doi.org/10.2307/43632464.

213. Norris J. Lacy, "The Elucidation: Introduction," The Camelot Project (Rochester, NY: University of Rochester, 2007), accessed May 23, 2024, https://d.lib.rochester.edu/camelot/text/elucidation-introduction.

214. Roger Sherman Loomis, *Celtic Myth and Arthurian Romance* (London: Constable, 1993), 237.

215. Loomis, 180.

216. Ibid., 182–3, 185.

217. *Elucidation,* trans. William W. Kibler, The Camelot Project (Rochester, NY: University of Rochester, 2007), line 32, accessed May 23, 2024, https://d. lib.rochester.edu/Camelot/text/elucidation.

218. Chrétien, 421.

219. Misha Magdalene, *Outside the Charmed Circle: Exploring Gender and Sexuality in Magical Practice* (Woodbury, MN: Llewellyn Publications, 2020), 255–6.

220. Carolyn Dinshaw, "Chaucer's Queer Touches / A Queer Touches Chaucer," *Exemplaria* 7 (1995): 76.

221. Elucidation, lines 189–193.

222. Strand, *Flowering Wand*, 105–6.

223. Hine, 182.

224. John McKinnell, "Myth as Therapy: The Usefulness of 'þRYMSKVIÐA,'" *Medium Ævum* 69, no. 1 (2000): 4, https://doi.org/10.2307/43631487.

225. Carolyne Larrington, trans., *The Poetic Edda*, rev. ed. (Oxford, UK: Oxford University Press, 2014), 96.

226. Snorri Sturluson, *The Prose Edda*, trans. Jesse L. Byock (London: Penguin Books, 2005), 52.

227. H. R. Ellis Davidson, *Gods and Myths of Northern Europe* (London: Penguin Books, 1990), 188.

228. Ibid, 181.

229. Stefanie von Schnurbein, "The Function of Loki in Snorri Sturluson's 'Edda,'" *History of Religions* 40, no. 2 (2000): 122, http://www.jstor.org/stable/3176617.

230. Sturluson, *Prose Edda,* 71–3.

231. Genevieve Gornichec, *The Witch's Heart* (New York: Ace, 2021), 30.

232. Davidson, 117, 121–22.

233. Thomas Andrew DuBois, *Nordic Religions in the Viking Age* (Philadelphia: University of Pennsylvania Press, 1999), 53.

234. Davidson, 147.

235. Kevin J. Wanner, "God on the Margins: Dislocation and Transience in the Myths of Óðinn," *History of Religions* 46, no. 4 (2007): 323, https://doi.org/10.1086/518812.

236. Ibid.

237. Ibid., 335n.

238. Snorri Sturluson, "Ynglinga Saga," in *The Heimskringla; or, Chronicle of the Kings of Norway,* vol. 1, trans. Samuel Laing, 216–61 (London: Longman, Brown, Green and Longmans, 1844), 222.

239. Davidson, 146–7.

240. Ibid., 142.

241. Sturluson, "Ynglinga Saga," 221.

242. Ibid., 222.

243. James Frankki, "Cross-Dressing in the Poetic Edda: Mic Muno Æsir Argan Kalla," *Scandinavian Studies* 84, no. 4 (2012): 429, http://www.jstor.org/stable/41955688; Larrington, 295.

244. Davidson, 96.

245. Lee Colwill, "The Queerly Departed: Narratives of Veneration in the Burials of Late Iron Age Scandinavia," in *Trans and Genderqueer Subjects in Medieval Hagiography*, ed. Alicia Spencer-Hall and Blake Gutt, (Amsterdam University Press, 2021), 177–98.

246. Ibid., 189.

247. Ibid., 183.

248. *The Poetic Edda,* trans. Henry Adams Bellows (New York: The American-Scandinavian Foundation, 1923; Project Gutenberg, May 4, 2024), 160, https://www.gutenberg.org/ebooks/73533.

249. Larrington, 85.

250. Kevin J. Wanner, "Cunning Intelligence in Norse Myth: Loki, Óðinn, and the Limits of Sovereignty," *History of Religions* 48, no. 3 (2009): 219, https://doi.org/10.1086/598231.

251. Carol J. Clover, "Regardless of Sex: Men, Women, and Power in Early Northern Europe," *Speculum* 68, no. 2 (1993): 375, https://doi.org/10.2307/2864557; Frankki, 428–9; Hine, 182–5.

252. Clover, "Regardless of Sex," 374; Frankki, 429.

253. Frankki, 428.

254. Folke Ström, ed., *Nið, Ergi and Old Norse Moral Attitudes* (London: U College, 1974), 10; quoted in Frankki, 429.

255. Davidson, 96.

256. Hine, 184.

257. Wanner, "Gods of the Margins," 328.

258. Ibid.

259. Ibid., 328, 329.

260. DuBois, 54.

261. Wanner, 345.

262. *The Poetic Edda,* trans. Bellows, 155.

263. Sturluson, *Prose Edda*, 77.

264. Wanner, 333.

265. "Binding the Wolf," A Beautiful Resistance, May 19, 2018, https://abeautifulresistance.org/site/2018/05/19/binding-the-wolf.

266. Siri Vincent Plouff, "Antiracist Heathen Resources," SiriVincentPlouff
.com, accessed May 13, 2024,https://www.sirivincentplouff.com/
antiracist-heathen-resources.

267. "Binding the Wolf."

268. Serpentine, 78–9.

269. Ibid., 79.

270. Crompton, 19; Jen H. Oliver, "'OSCULA IUNGIT NEC MODERATA SATIS
NEC SIC A VIRGINE DANDA': Ovid's Callisto Episode, Female Homoeroticism, and the Study of Ancient Sexuality," *The American Journal of Philology*
136, no. 2 (2015): 282, http://www.jstor.org/stable/24562759.

271. Oliver, 282.

272. Crompton, 18.

273. Sappho, trans. Wharton, 65.

274. Crompton, 20.

275. Sappho, trans. Wharton, 50.

276. Ibid.

277. Kristin Mathis, "My Translation of Sappho's Hymn to Aphrodite,"
Mysteria Mundi, January 27, 2023, https://mysteriamundi.substack
.com/p/my-translation-of-sapphos-hymn-to. Accessed 25 May, 2024;
J. C. B. Petropoulos, "Sappho the Sorceress: Another Look at Fr. 1 (LP),"
Zeitschrift Für Papyrologie Und Epigraphik 97 (1993): 43–56, http://www.
jstor.org/stable/20171905; Charles Segal, "Eros and Incantation: Sappho
and Oral Poetry," *Arethusa* 7, no. 2 (1974): 139–60, http://www.jstor.org/
stable/26307420.

278. Sappho, trans. Wharton, 65.

279. Mathis, "Sappho's Hymn."

280. Ibid.

281. Ovid, *The Metamorphoses,* vol. 2, 337.

282. Ibid.

283. Ibid.

284. Ibid., 338.

285. Ibid., 339.

286. Ibid., 337.

287. Ibid., 338.

288. Ibid., 337–8.

289. Ovid, *The Metamorphoses*, vol. 1, 75.

290. Ibid., 76.

291. Parthenius, *Sentimental Love Stories,* in *Anthology of Classical Myth*, 301–2.

292. Oliver, 289–90.

293. Oliver, 290.

294. Oliver, 295.

295. Larson, 104.

296. Ovid, *The Metamorphoses*, vol. 1, 78.

297. Stephanie McCarter, Introduction to *Metamorphoses* by Ovid (New York: Penguin Books, 2022), xxix.

298. Ibid., xxix.

299. Evans, 154–163, and *passim*.

300. Evans, 72.

301. Doreen Valiente, "Charge of the Goddess," quoted in Starhawk, 103.

302. Larson, 101.

303. Charles G. Leland, *Aradia, or the Gospel of the Witches* (London: David Nutt, 1899), 18.

304. Ibid., 18.

305. Ibid., 2.

306. Ibid.

307. Ibid, 6–7.

308. Baring and Cashford, 322.

309. Leland, 10.

310. Larson, 111.

311. Marcella Althaus-Reid, *Indecent Theology: Theological Perversions in Sex, Gender and Politics* (London: Routledge, 2000), 67–8.

312. Sojourner Truth, "Ain't I a Woman" Speech, Woman's Rights Convention (Akron, OH), May 29, 1851.

313. Althaus-Reid, 114.

314. Ibid., 71.

315. Asher Pandjiris, podcast host, *Living in This Queer Body*, https://www.livinginthisqueerbody.com/.

316. Karen L. King, *The Gospel of Mary of Magdala: Jesus and the First Woman Apostle* (Santa Rosa, CA: Polebridge Press, 2003), 13.

317. King, 49–50.

318. Ibid., 49.

319. Ibid., 50.

320. Taussig, 14.

321. Ibid., 23.

322. Ibid., 12.

323. Ibid., 17.

324. E. E. Cummings, *Selected Poems* (United Kingdom: Liveright, 1994), 167.

325. Audre Lorde, "Uses of the Erotic." *The Selected Works of Audres Lorde,* ed. Roxane Gay, 29–37 (New York: W. W. Norton & Company, 2000), 32.

326. Lorde, 32–3.

327. Ibid., 35.

328. Ibid., 33.

329. Taussig, 204.

330. Althaus-Reid, 129.

331. Patrick S. Cheng, *Radical Love: An Introduction to Queer Theology* (New York: Seabury Books, 2011), 90–1.

332. Cheng, 90.

333. Meyer, "The Revelation of Adam," in *Nag Hammadi Scriptures,* 353–4.

334. Taussig, 183.

335. Althaus-Reid, 80–1.

336. Kittredge Cherry, "Black Madonna of Czestochowa becomes lesbian defender Erzuli Dantor," Q Spirit, updated January 6, 2024, https://qspirit .net/black-madonna-lesbian-erzuli-dantor-czestochowa/.

337. Kittredge Cherry, "Madonna of Montevergine: Patron of LGBTQ People since Medieval Times," Q Spirit, updated May 27, 2024, https://qspirit.net/ madonna-montevergine-lgbtq/.

338. Gospel of Thomas 70:1.

339. *The Gospel of Philip*, trans. from Coptic by Jean-Yves Leloup, trans. to English by Joseph Rowe (Rochester, VT: Inner Traditions, 2003), 59.

340. Ariana Serpentine offers a beautiful gender self-initiation ritual in *Sacred Gender* that includes calling on trans Ancestors for guidance and support. I highly recommend her ritual and her entire book for trans, nonbinary, and gender-nonconforming individuals interested in exploring gender through magic and spirituality—and magic and spirituality through gender.

About the Author

Charlie Claire Burgess is a queer and trans-nonbinary writer, artist, tarot creator, and witch. They are the author of *Radical Tarot* and author-illustrator of the *Fifth Spirit Tarot* and *The Gay Marseille Tarot* decks. Charlie's short fiction and nonfiction have appeared in various literary journals and anthologies and have received a Pushcart Prize Special Mention and notable mentions in two *Best American* anthologies. They live in the Pacific Northwest with their partner, their one-eyed pug Apollo, and an extraordinary number of houseplants. Find them at **TheWordWitchTarot.com**.

Hay House Titles of Related Interest

We hope you enjoyed this Hay House book. If you'd like to receive our online catalog featuring additional information on Hay House books and products, or if you'd like to find out more about the Hay Foundation, please contact:

Hay House LLC, P.O. Box 5100, Carlsbad, CA 92018-5100
(760) 431-7695 or (800) 654-5126
www.hayhouse.com® • www.hayfoundation.org

———

Published in Australia by:
Hay House Australia Publishing Pty Ltd
18/36 Ralph St., Alexandria NSW 2015
Phone: +61 (02) 9669 4299
www.hayhouse.com.au

Published in the United Kingdom by:
Hay House UK Ltd
1st Floor, Crawford Corner,
91–93 Baker Street, London W1U 6QQ
Phone: +44 (0)20 3927 7290
www.hayhouse.co.uk

Published in India by:
Hay House Publishers (India) Pvt Ltd
Muskaan Complex, Plot No. 3,
B-2, Vasant Kunj, New Delhi 110 070
Phone: +91 11 41761620
www.hayhouse.co.in

———

Let Your Soul Grow

Experience life-changing transformation—one video at a time—with guidance from the world's leading experts.

www.healyourlifeplus.com